Peter Sestoft

Henrik I. Hansen

# C# Precisely

The MIT Press
Cambridge, Massachusetts
London, England

This book was set in Times by the authors using LATEX.

Printed and bound in the United States of America.

Library of Congress Cataloging-in-Publication Data

Sestoft, Peter.
    C# precisely / Peter Sestoft and Henrik I. Hansen.
      p.   cm.
    Includes bibliographic references and index.
    ISBN 0-262-69317-8 (pbk.: alk. paper)
    1. C# (Computer program language)  I. Hansen, Henrik I.  II. Title.
    QA76.73.C154S47    2004
    005.13′3—dc22

                                                            2004048288


10   9   8   7   6   5   4   3   2   1

# C# Precisely

# Contents

# Preface

This book describes the programming language C# (pronounced "c sharp"), version 2.0. It is a quick reference for the reader who has already learnt or is learning C# from a standard textbook and who wants to know the language in more detail. It should be particularly useful for readers who know the Java programming language and who want to learn C#.

C# is a class-based single-inheritance object-oriented programming language designed for the Common Language Runtime of Microsoft's .Net platform, a managed execution environment with a typesafe intermediate language and automatic memory management. Thus C# is similar to the Java programming language in many respects, but it is different in almost all details. In general, C# favors programmer convenience over language simplicity. It was designed by Anders Hejlsberg, Scott Wiltamuth and Peter Golde from Microsoft Corporation.

C# includes many useful features not found in Java: struct types, operator overloading, reference parameters, rectangular multi-dimensional arrays, user-definable conversions, properties and indexers (stylized methods) and delegates (methods as values), but omits Java's inner classes. See section 29 for a summary of the main differences.

C# may appear similar to C++, but its type safety is much better and its machine model is very different because of managed execution. In particular, there is no need to write destructors and finalizers, nor to aggressively copy objects or keep track of object ownership.

This book presents C# version 2.0 as used in Microsoft Visual Studio 2005, including generics, iterators, anonymous methods and partial type declarations, but excluding most of Microsoft's .Net Framework class libraries except threads, input-output, and generic collection classes. The book does not cover unsafe code, destructors, finalization, reflection, pre-processing directives (#define, #if, ...) or details of IEEE754 floating-point numbers.

General rules of the language are given on left-hand pages, and corresponding examples are shown on the facing right-hand page for easy reference. All examples are fragments of legal C# programs, available from <http://www.itu.dk/people/sestoft/csharpprecisely/>. For instance, you will find the code for example 17 in file Example17.cs.

**Acknowledgements:** Thanks to a stay at Microsoft Research in Cambridge, England, we could experiment with a very early version of Generic C#. Later, the .Net Framework Alpha Program provided an implementation of all the new C# 2.0 features, and Ecma International provided C# standards documents. Special thanks to Andrew Kennedy, Don Syme, Claudio Russo and Simon Peyton Jones for directly or indirectly making this possible. The Mono project developers provided another neat C# compiler and runtime environment, and rapid bug fixes. Thanks to Hans Dybkjær, Jørgen Steensgaard-Madsen, Jon Jagger and Niels Peter Svenningsen for comments and suggestions on draft manuscripts. It was a pleasure to work with Robert Prior, Valerie Geary and Deborah Cantor-Adams at The MIT Press. Thanks also to the Royal Veterinary and Agricultural University, Denmark and the IT University of Copenhagen, Denmark, for their support.

# Notational Conventions

| Symbol | Meaning |
| --- | --- |
| a | expression or value of array type |
| b | expression or value of boolean type |
| C | class |
| D | delegate type |
| e | expression |
| E | exception type or event name |
| f | field |
| i | expression or value of integer type |
| I | interface type |
| M | method |
| N | namespace |
| o | expression or value of object type |
| P | property name |
| s | expression of type string |
| S | struct type |
| *sig* | signature of method or constructor |
| t | type name or type expression (simple type or value type or reference type) |
| T, U | type parameters (generic types and methods) |
| u | expression or value of thread type |
| v | value of any type |
| x | variable or parameter or field or array element |

In this book, fragments of the C# grammar are presented using an informal notation, with non-terminal symbols such as *class-declaration* in italics, terminal symbols such as class in typewriter font, and metavariables such as C for class names and M for method names.

A complete and detailed grammar for C# can be found in the official language specification (see section 30). We do not include the complete grammar because it runs to more than 30 dense pages, and yet is too general: many well-formedness requirements must be expressed as additional side conditions on the grammar.

# C# Precisely

# 1    Compiling, Loading and Executing C# Programs

Running a C# program involves three stages: *compilation* (which first checks that the C# program is well-formed and then generates intermediate code, also called bytecode), *loading* (which loads and checks the bytecode and then generates machine code), and *execution* (which runs the machine code).

## 1.1    Source Files and Compilation

A C# *program* consists of one or more *source files* (with filename suffix .cs). A source file may contain one or more type declarations: classes, interfaces, struct types, enum types, and delegate types.

Before a C# program can be executed, it must be compiled and loaded. The C# compiler, such as Microsoft's csc or the Mono project's mcs, checks that the program conforms to the syntax for C# programs, that operators (such as +) are applied to the correct type of operands (such as 5 and x), and so on. If this is the case, the compiler generates a module or file containing intermediate code.

A *module* resulting from compilation may be an *executable* Prog.exe if it contains a static method Main() or Main(String[]) but not both, or a *library* Prog.dll, or a *raw module* Prog.netmodule.

An *assembly* consists of one or more modules, exactly one of which must be an executable (.exe) or a library (.dll). An assembly has a *manifest* with version number and other metadata, so it can be deployed on its own; a raw module cannot. A raw module can be added to an assembly as an *external module* using the /addmodule compile option when generating the assembly. The assembly can access both internal and public members (section 10.12) of the module. The module remains a separate file.

An assembly may be made to *refer* to another assembly by using the /reference compile option when generating the referring assembly. A reference to the .Net class library mscorlib.dll is included by default. The referring assembly can access only public members of the referred-to assembly.

| Compiler Option | Short Form | Meaning |
|---|---|---|
| /target:exe | /t:exe | Compile to an executable (.exe) file. The default |
| /target:library | /t:library | Compile to a library (.dll) file |
| /target:module | /t:module | Compile to a module (.netmodule) file |
| /reference:Lib.dll | /r:Lib.dll | Include reference to library Lib |
| /addmodule:M1.netmodule | | Include module M1.netmodule in assembly |
| /main:MyClass | /m:MyClass | Method Main in class MyClass is the entry point |
| /debug | | Add debugging information |
| /define:DEBUG | /d:DEBUG | Enable assertions (section 27) |

## 1.2    Execution

An executable file Prog.exe compiled from program Prog.cs can be (loaded and) executed by typing its name on the command line or by explicitly invoking the run-time system. This will execute the static method Main() or Main(String[] args) in Prog.cs, in the latter case binding the command line arguments *arg*1, *arg*2, ... to the array elements args[0], args[1], ...; see examples 1 and 2.

The /main compiler option can be used to specify the entry point: the class whose Main method must be executed after loading an executable.

**Example 1** Complete Program in File `Example1.cs`
Almost all programs need the `using System` directive (section 25.1) but we leave it out in later examples.

```
using System;
public class Sum {
  static void Main(String[] args) {
    int sum = 0;
    for (int i=0; i<args.Length; i++)
      sum += int.Parse(args[i]);
    Console.WriteLine("The sum is " + sum);
  }
}
```

**Example 2** Compiling and Running a Program from the Command Line
This example shows how to compile the file `Example1.cs` from the command line under Windows using Microsoft .Net (left) and under Linux or Windows using the Mono system (right). In both cases the program outputs the text: `The sum is 29.`

```
csc Example1.cs              mcs Example1.cs
Example1 7 9 13             mono Example1.exe 7 9 13
```

**Example 3** Compile an Executable with an External Module and Reference to a Library
We first compile file `Mod.cs` into a raw module `Mod.netmodule` and compile `Lib.cs` into a library `Lib.dll`. Then we compile the file `Prog.cs` and create an executable `Prog` in file `Prog.exe` that has external module `Mod` and refers to the library `Lib`. Finally, we run the executable `Prog.exe`:

```
csc /target:module Mod.cs
csc /target:library Lib.cs
csc /addmodule:Mod.netmodule /reference:Lib.dll Prog.cs
Prog
```

The resulting assembly consists of two files: the main file `Prog.exe`, and file `Mod.netmodule` that contains the external module. The assembly has a manifest with version number, other metadata, and references to two other assemblies: the library `Lib`, and `mscorlib` which is included by default.

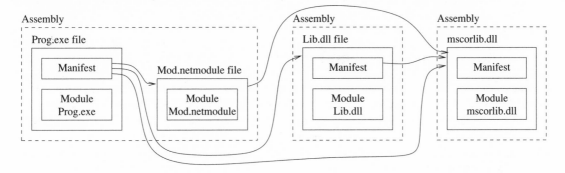

## 2    Names and Reserved Names

A legal *name* of a variable, parameter, method, field, indexer, property, class, struct, enum, delegate, interface or namespace starts with a letter or an underscore (_), and continues with zero or more letters or underscores or digits (0–9). Upper case letters and lower case letters are considered distinct. A legal name cannot be one of the following *keywords*, which are reserved names:

```
abstract as base bool break byte case catch char checked class const continue decimal
default delegate do double else enum event explicit extern false finally fixed float
for foreach goto if implicit in int interface internal is lock long namespace new
null object operator out override params private protected public readonly ref return
sbyte sealed short sizeof stackalloc static string struct switch this throw true try
typeof uint ulong unchecked unsafe ushort using virtual void volatile while
```

A keyword prefixed with the @ character can be used as a name, as in int @while = 17, where the @ character is not a part of the name proper. The pseudo-keywords add, alias, get, global, partial, remove, set, value, where and yield are reserved only in certain contexts.

## 3    C# Naming Conventions

The following naming conventions are often followed, although not enforced by the C# compiler:

- If a name is composed of several words, then each word (except possibly the first one) begins with an upper case letter. Examples: currentLayout, LayoutComponent.
- Names of local variables, parameters, and private or protected fields begin with a lower case letter. Examples: vehicle, currentVehicle. Avoid using lower case letter l or upper case O as names.
- Names of public or internal instance fields, static fields, and named constants begin with an upper case letter. Examples: Vehicle, MaxValue.
- Names of classes, methods, events, properties, and enum types begin with an upper case letter. Examples: Cube, ColorCube.
- Names of interfaces begin with the letter I followed by an upper case letter. Example: IEnumerable.
- A namespace name usually is a dot-separated sequence of names each of which begins with an upper case letter (System or System.Text or System.Text.RegularExpressions), but could also be a reverse domain name (dk.itu.c5 or ch.cern.mathlib).

## 4    Comments and Program Layout

A *comment* has no effect on the execution of the program, but is used to help humans understand the program. It may be inserted anywhere whitespace is permitted. There are two forms: one-line comments and delimited comments. Do not insert a delimited comment in the middle of a line as in example 5.

*Program layout* has no effect on the computer's execution of the program, but is used to help humans understand the structure of the program. For reasons of space we shall not always follow the recommended layout style in the rest of the book.

**Example 4** Using Keywords as Identifier Names
This feature is provided for interoperability with other programming languages, in which `class` or `public` may be a perfectly legal name for a field or method; it should not be used in ordinary C# programming. Note that for non-keywords such as `i`, the identifier `@i` is the same as `i`.

```
class School {
  const int @class = 2004;
  const bool @public = true;
  String @delegate = "J. Smith  ";
  public static int @double(int i) { return 2 * @i; }
}
...
School school = new School();
Console.WriteLine(school.@delegate.Trim() + " " + School.@class);
```

**Example 5** A One-line Comment, a Delimited Comment, and Abuse of a Delimited Comment

```
class Comment {
  // This is a one-line comment; it extends to the end of the line
  /* This is a delimited comment,
     extending over several lines.
   */
  int /* This delimited comment extends over part of a line */ x = 117;
}
```

**Example 6** Program Layout Style

```
class LayoutExample {                   // Class declaration
  int j;

  LayoutExample(int j) {
    this.j = j;                         // One-line body
  }

  int Sum(int b) {                      // Multi-line body
    if (j > 0) {                        // If statement
      return j + b;                     // Single statement
    } else if (j < 0) {                 // Nested if-else, block statement
      int res = -j + b;
      return res * 117;
    } else { // j == 0                  // Terminal else, block statement
      int sum = 0;
      for (int i=0; i<10; i++)          // For loop
        sum += (b - i) * (b - i);
      return sum;
    }
  }
}
```

# 5   Data and Types

A *type* is a set of data values and operations on them. Every variable, parameter, and field has a declared type, every method has a declared return type, and so on. The compiler will infer a type for every expression based on this information. This *compile-time type* determines which operations can be performed on the value of the expression.

Types are used in declarations of local variables; in declarations of classes, interfaces, struct types, and their members; in delegate types; in object and array creation expressions (sections 9 and 12.9); in type cast expressions (section 12.18); and in instance test expressions (section 12.11).

A type is either a value type (section 5.1) or a reference type (section 5.2).

## 5.1   Value Types and Simple Types

A *value type* is either a simple type (this section), a struct type (section 14), or an enum type (section 16). A variable of value type directly contains a value of that type, not just a reference to it. Assigning a value of value type to a variable or field or array element of value type makes a copy of the value.

A *simple type* is either `bool` or one of the numeric types. A *numeric* type is a signed or unsigned integer type, including the character type, or a floating-point type, or the fixed-point type `decimal` which is useful for exact calculations such as financial accounting. The tables opposite show the simple types, some example constants, value range, kind, and size (in bits). For escape sequences such as `\u0000` in character constants, see page 16. Integer constants may be written in decimal or hexadecimal notation:

| Notation | Base | Distinction | Example Integer Constants |
|---|---|---|---|
| Decimal | 10 | | `1234567890`, `0127`, `-127` |
| Hexadecimal | 16 | Leading `0x` | `0x12ABCDEF`, `0x7F`, `-0x7F` |

Two's complement representation is used for the signed integer types (`sbyte`, `short`, `int`, and `long`). The integer types are exact. The floating-point types are inexact and follow the IEEE754 floating point standard, with the number of significant digits indicated opposite.

For each simple type there is a predefined struct type (in the System namespace), also shown opposite. The simple type is an alias for the struct type and therefore has members:

- `int.Parse(String s)` of type `int` is the integer obtained by parsing s; see example 1. It throws ArgumentNullException if s is `null`, FormatException if s cannot be parsed as an integer, and OverflowException if the parsed number cannot be represented as an `int`. All simple types have similar `Parse` methods. The floating-point `Parse` methods are culture sensitive; see section 7.2.

- The smallest and greatest possible values of each numeric type are represented by constant fields `MinValue` and `MaxValue`, such as `int.MinValue` and `int.MaxValue`.

- The `float` and `double` types define several constants: `double.Epsilon` is the smallest number of type `double` greater than zero, `double.PositiveInfinity` and `double.NegativeInfinity` represent positive and negative infinity, and `double.NaN` is a `double` value that is not a number. These values are determined by the IEEE754 standard.

- The `decimal` type defines the constants `MinusOne`, `Zero`, and `One` of type `decimal` along with methods for computing with and converting numbers of type `decimal`.

**Example 7** Three Equivalent Declarations of an Integer Variable

```
using System;
...
int i1;
Int32 i2;
System.Int32 i3;
```

## Simple Types: Constants, Default Value, and Range

| Type | Example Constants | Default Value | Range (`MinValue...MaxValue`) |
|------|-------------------|---------------|-------------------------------|
| `bool` | `true` | `false` | `false,true` |
| `char` | `'A'`,`'\u0041'` | `'\u0000'` | `'\u0000'...'\uFFFF'` |
| `sbyte` | `-119` | `0` | $-128\ldots127$ |
| `byte` | `219` | `0` | $0\ldots255$ |
| `short` | `-30319` | `0` | $-32768\ldots32767$ |
| `ushort` | `60319` | `0` | $0\ldots65535$ |
| `int` | `-2111222319` | `0` | $-2147483648\ldots2147483647$ |
| `uint` | `4111222319` | `0` | $0\ldots4294967295$ |
| `long` | `-411122319L` | `0` | $-9223372036854775808\ldots9223372036854775807$ |
| `ulong` | `411122319UL` | `0` | $0\ldots18446744073709551615$ |
| `float` | `-1.99F, 3E8F` | `0.0` | $\pm10^{-44}\ldots\pm10^{38}$, 7 significant digits |
| `double` | `-1.99, 3E8` | `0.0` | $\pm10^{-323}\ldots\pm10^{308}$, 15–16 significant digits |
| `decimal` | `-1.99M` | `0.0` | $\pm10^{-28}\ldots\pm10^{28}$, 28–29 significant digits (*) |

(*) May be changed to range $\pm10^{-6143}\ldots\pm10^{6144}$ and 34 significant digits (IEEE754 decimal128).

## Simple Types: Kind, Size, and Struct Name

| Type Alias | Kind | Size | Struct Type |
|------------|------|------|-------------|
| `bool` | logical | 1 | System.Boolean |
| `char` | unsigned integer | 16 | System.Char |
| `sbyte` | integer | 8 | System.SByte |
| `byte` | unsigned integer | 8 | System.Byte |
| `short` | integer | 16 | System.Int16 |
| `ushort` | unsigned integer | 16 | System.UInt16 |
| `int` | integer | 32 | System.Int32 |
| `uint` | unsigned integer | 32 | System.UInt32 |
| `long` | integer | 64 | System.Int64 |
| `ulong` | unsigned integer | 64 | System.UInt64 |
| `float` | floating-point | 32 | System.Single |
| `double` | floating-point | 64 | System.Double |
| `decimal` | fixed-point | 128 | System.Decimal |

## 5.2   Reference Types

A *reference type* is a class, an interface, an array type, or a delegate type. A class is defined by a class declaration (section 10), an interface is defined by an interface declaration (section 15), and a delegate type is defined by a delegate declaration (section 17). Array types are discussed in section 9.

A variable of reference type either contains the special value null or a reference to an object or array or delegate which is allocated in the heap. The special value null does not refer to anything. The constant null, denoting the null value, can have any reference type. Assigning a reference value to a reference variable assigns only the reference and does not copy the object or array or delegate pointed to.

Types are organized in a type hierarchy as shown opposite, with class Object as the base class of all other types. The methods implemented by these top classes are inherited by their derived types.

**Class Object**   is the baseclass (superclass) of all classes. Let o1 and o2 be expressions of type Object:

- o1.Equals(o2) returns true if o1 and o2 are equal; otherwise false. By default, values of reference type are equal if created by the same execution of new; but (for example) class String overrides Equals to compare the string contents instead (section 7), and class ValueType overrides Equals so that two values of a struct type are equal if all their fields are equal.
- Object.ReferenceEquals(o1, o2) returns true if both o1 and o2 are null, or if both refer to the same object or array or delegate; otherwise false. False also if any of o1 or o2 has value type.
- Object.Equals(o1, o2) returns true if Object.ReferenceEquals(o1, o2) or o1.Equals(o2) does; otherwise false. This is inefficient for arguments of value type which get boxed and then compared using o1's Equals method.
- o1.GetType() returns the unique object of class Type that represents the run-time type of o1.
- o1.GetHashCode() returns a hash code for o1 as an int, useful when o1 is used as a key in a hashtable (section 24.7). Subclasses should override this method so that (1) if o1 and o2 are equal by Equals, then they have the same hash code; (2) modifications to o1 do not change its hash code; (3) the hash codes should be uniformly distributed; and (4) the method should be fast and must not throw exceptions. All simple types and class String have appropriate GetHashCode methods.
- o1.ToString() returns a human-readable culture sensitive representation of the object o1.

**Class String**   is a frequently used subclass of Object and is a reference type; see section 7.

**Class Array**   is a subclass of Object and the baseclass of all array types such as int[]; see section 9.

**Class ValueType**   is a subclass of Object and the baseclass of all value types, including the simple types, the struct types and the enum types. It is not itself a value type. If v1 and v2 have a struct type (that derives from ValueType) then v1.Equals(v2) uses reflection to compare the fields of v1 and v2 using Equals. This can be slow, so struct types should override Equals. Also, struct types that have modifiable fields should override GetHashCode; the default method may be unsuitable for such struct types.

**Class Enum**   is a subclass of ValueType and the baseclass of all enum types (section 16), but not itself an enum type. It implements enum-specific methods inherited by all enum types.

**Class Delegate**   is a subclass of Object and the baseclass of all delegate types (section 17), but is not itself a delegate type. It implements delegate-specific methods inherited by all delegate types.

**Example 8**  Methods Declared in Class Object

The methods declared in class Object are inherited by all types and therefore can be used on all values (unless the methods are hidden by a declaration in a subclass).

```
Object o1 = new Object(), o2 = new Object(), o3 = o1;
Console.WriteLine(o1.Equals(o3) + " " + o1.Equals(o2));      // True False
Console.WriteLine(o1.GetHashCode() == o3.GetHashCode());     // True
Console.WriteLine(o1.GetHashCode() == o2.GetHashCode());     // Usually False
Console.WriteLine(o1.GetHashCode() + " " + o2.GetHashCode()); // Usually distinct
Console.WriteLine(o1.GetType());                             // System.Object
String s1 = "abc", s2 = "ABC", s3 = s1 + "";
Console.WriteLine(s1.Equals(s3) + " " + s1.Equals(s2));      // True False
Console.WriteLine(s1.GetHashCode() == s3.GetHashCode());     // True
Console.WriteLine(s1.GetHashCode() == s2.GetHashCode());     // Usually False
Console.WriteLine(s1.GetHashCode() + " " + s2.GetHashCode()); // Usually distinct
Console.WriteLine(s1.GetType());                             // System.String
Console.WriteLine(117.GetHashCode());                       // 117
Console.WriteLine(5.GetType());                             // System.Int32
Console.WriteLine(5.0.GetType());                           // System.Double
int[] ia1 = { 7, 9, 13 }, ia2 = { 7, 9, 13 };
Console.WriteLine(ia1.GetType());                           // System.Int32[]
Console.WriteLine(ia1.Equals(ia2));                         // False
Console.WriteLine(Object.ReferenceEquals(ia1,ia2));        // False
Console.WriteLine(ia1.GetHashCode() == ia2.GetHashCode()); // Usually False
int[,] ia3 = new int[6,7];
Console.WriteLine(ia3.GetType());                          // System.Int32[,]
int[][] ia4 = new int[6][];
Console.WriteLine(ia4.GetType());                          // System.Int32[][]
```

## Top Layers of the Type Hierarchy

All these types are from the System namespace.

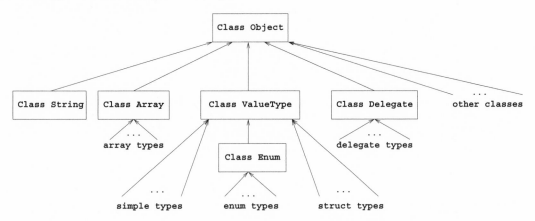

## 5.3   Conversion

For a given type ts there may exist an implicit or explicit *conversion* of a value of type ts into a value of another type tt. If there is an *implicit conversion* from type ts to type tt, then an expression of type ts can be used wherever an expression of type tt is expected. In particular, any value v of type ts may be bound to a variable or field or parameter x of type tt, for instance by the assignment x = v.

If there is an *explicit conversion* from ts to tt, then a cast expression (section 12.18) can be used to obtain a value of type tt from the value of type ts.

### 5.3.1   Standard Conversions between Simple Types

The standard conversions between simple types are shown in the table below. There are standard conversions between all the simple types except bool.

A conversion marked I is an implicit conversion (no cast required) and one marked E is an explicit conversion (cast required). More precisely, an implicit conversion marked I cannot lose precision, whereas one marked IL may lose precision; neither can throw an exception.

An explicit conversion marked ER rounds the source value and so may lose precision or produce an infinity, but throws no exception. An explicit conversion marked ET truncates the source value to the nearest integral number (rounds towards zero); in a checked context (section 12.3) it throws OverflowException if the result is too large, and in an unchecked context it produces an unspecified value in the target type. An explicit conversion marked ED rounds the source value, and throws OverflowException if the source value is too large or is a NaN.

Finally, an explicit conversion marked EB works on the bit pattern representing the source value. In a checked context (section 12.3) the conversion throws OverflowException if the source value is not representable in the target type. In an unchecked context, no exception is thrown. Instead, if the source type is larger than the target type (in bits, see page 7), the excess most significant bits are discarded from the source value. If the source type is smaller than the target type, the source value is padded (extended with most significant bits) to fit the target type, padding with the sign bit if the source type is signed, and padding with zeroes if it is unsigned.

| Source Type (ts) | Target Type (tt) | | | | | | | | | | | |
|---|---|---|---|---|---|---|---|---|---|---|---|---|
| | char | sbyte | byte | short | ushort | int | uint | long | ulong | float | double | decimal |
| char | I | EB | EB | EB | I | I | I | I | I | I | I | I |
| sbyte | EB | I | EB | I | EB | I | EB | I | EB | I | I | I |
| byte | EB | EB | I | I | I | I | I | I | I | I | I | I |
| short | EB | EB | EB | I | EB | I | EB | I | EB | I | I | I |
| ushort | EB | EB | EB | EB | I | I | I | I | I | I | I | I |
| int | EB | EB | EB | EB | EB | I | EB | I | EB | IL | I | I |
| uint | EB | EB | EB | EB | EB | EB | I | I | I | IL | I | I |
| long | EB | EB | EB | EB | EB | EB | EB | I | EB | IL | IL | I |
| ulong | EB | EB | EB | EB | EB | EB | EB | EB | I | IL | IL | I |
| float | ET | ET | ET | ET | ET | ET | ET | ET | ET | I | I | ED |
| double | ET | ET | ET | ET | ET | ET | ET | ET | ET | ER | I | ED |
| decimal | ET | ET | ET | ET | ET | ET | ET | ET | ET | ER | ER | I |

**Example 9** Conversions between Simple Types

```
double d = 2.9;
Console.WriteLine((int)d);                // ET double-->int; prints 2
Console.WriteLine((int)(-d));             // ET double-->int; prints -2
uint seconds = (uint)(24 * 60 * 60);      // EB int-->uint
double avgSecPerYear = 365.25 * seconds;  // I  uint-->double
float f = seconds;                        // IL uint-->float
long nationalDebt1 = 7030835252282;
double perSecond = 23148.14;
decimal perDay =                          // ED double-->decimal
  seconds * (decimal)perSecond;           // I  uint-->decimal
double nd2 = nationalDebt1 + (double)perDay;  // ER decimal-->double
long nd3 = (long)nd2;                     // ET double-->long
float nd4 = (float)nd2;                   // ER double-->float
```

**Summary of Standard Implicit Conversions between Simple Types**
If there is a thick-line path from a type ts up to a type tt then ts is implicitly convertible to tt. If there is any path from a type t up to a type u then t is *better than* u in overloading resolution (section 12.15.1).

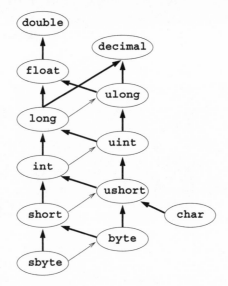

### 5.3.2   Standard Conversions between Reference Types or Type Parameters

If ts and tt are types, then a standard implicit conversion from ts to tt exists in these cases:

- ts is a reference type and tt is the class Object; or
- ts and tt are class types or interface types, and ts is derived from tt (section 10.4); or
- ts is a class type and tt is an interface implemented by ts or one of its base classes; or
- ts and tt are array types with the same number of dimensions, their element types are reference types, and there is an implicit conversion from the element type of ts to the element type of tt; or
- ts is an array type and tt is Array, or ts is a delegate type and tt is Delegate; or
- ts is t[] and tt is IList<t> or IList<u> with an implicit reference conversion from t to u; or
- ts is the type of the null expression and tt is a reference type or a nullable type (section 18); or
- ts is a type parameter (section 23.2) and tt a type bound for that parameter.

If ts and tt are types, then a standard explicit conversion from ts to tt exists in these cases:

- ts is the class Object and tt is a reference type; or
- ts and tt are class types, and tt is derived from ts; or
- ts is a non-sealed class type and tt is an interface, and ts does not implement tt; or
- ts is an interface and tt is a class type, and tt is not sealed or else tt implements ts; or
- ts and tt are interfaces and ts does not implement tt; or
- ts and tt are array types with the same number of dimensions, their element types are reference types, and there is an explicit conversion from the element type of ts to the element type of tt; or
- tt is an array type and ts is Array, or tt is a delegate type and ts is x'Delegate; or
- ts is IList<t> and tt is u[] and there is an implicit conversion from u[] to IList<t>; or
- tt is a type parameter (section 23.2) and ts a type bound for that parameter.

A standard implicit or explicit conversion from one reference type to another does not change the given reference value, nor does it produce a new one; only the compile-time type of the reference is affected.

### 5.3.3   Boxing and Unboxing Conversions

A *standard boxing conversion* is an implicit conversion from a value type ts to Object or to an interface type tt implemented by ts. A boxing conversion creates a copy of the value in the heap, including an indication of its type ts; see section 14.1. This permits values of simple types and struct types to be stored in non-generic collections. However, generic collections should usually be preferred for type safety and efficiency; see section 23.

An *unboxing conversion* is an explicit conversion (tt)v from a reference v of type Object or interface type ts to a value type tt that implements ts. An unboxing conversion first tests whether the type stored in the boxed object v is tt. If this is not so, or if v is null, it throws InvalidCastException; otherwise it copies the value out of v.

### 5.3.4   User-Defined Conversions

A class or struct type may declare implicit and explicit conversions for that type; see section 10.16.

**Example 10** Conversions between Reference Types
This example shows the cases of implicit and explicit reference conversion listed in section 5.3.2 opposite.
The explicit conversions are performed using type cast expressions (section 12.18).

```
interface I1 { }
interface I2 : I1 { }
interface J { }
class B : I2 { }
class C : B, J { }
delegate void D(String s);
...
Object b1 = new B();          // Implicit B-->Object
I2 b2 = new B();              // Implicit B-->I2
B c1 = new C();              // Implicit C-->B
I1 b3 = b2;                  // Implicit I2-->B
I1[] i2a1 = new I2[5];        // Implicit I2[]-->I1[]
Array inta1 = new int[5];     // Implicit int[]-->Array
Delegate d1 = new D(Print);   // Implicit D-->Delegate
C n = null;                  // Implicit null type-->C
B b4 = (B)b1;                // Explicit Object-->B
C c2 = (C)c1;                // Explicit B-->C
J b5 = (J)c1;                // Explicit C-->J
B b6 = (B)b2;                // Explicit I2-->B
I1 i2 = (I1)b2;              // Explicit I2-->I1
I2[] i2a2 = (I2[])i2a1;       // Explicit I1[]-->I2[]
int[] inta2 = (int[])inta1;   // Explicit Array-->int[]
D d2 = (D)d1;                // Explicit Delegate-->D
```

**Example 11** Boxing and Unboxing Conversions

```
interface I { void Print(); }
struct S : I {
  public int i;
  public S(int i) { this.i = i; }
  public void Print() { Console.WriteLine(i); }
}
...
int i = 7;
Object o = i;                 // Implicit boxing int-->Object
int j = 5 + (int)o;          // Explicit unboxing Object-->int
S s1 = new S(11);
I s2 = s1;                   // Implicit boxing S-->I
s1.i = 22;
s1.Print();                  // 22
s2.Print();                  // 11
S s3 = (S)s2;                // Explicit unboxing I-->S
s3.Print();                  // 11
```

# 6   Variables, Parameters, Fields, and Scope

A *variable* is declared inside a method body, constructor body, property body, indexer body, or another block statement (see section 13.2). The variable can be used only in that block statement, and only after it has been declared. A *parameter* is a special kind of variable: it is declared in the parameter list of a method, constructor, or indexer, and can be used only in that method or constructor or indexer. A *field* is declared inside a class or struct, but not inside a method or constructor or initializer block of the class.

A variable, parameter or field of *simple type* holds a *value* of that type, such as the boolean `false`, the integer 117, the floating-point number 1.7, or a value of struct type (section 14). A variable, parameter or field of *reference type* t either has value `null`, or holds a reference to an object or array or delegate.

## 6.1   Scope of Variables, Parameters and Members (Including Fields)

The *scope* of a name is that part of the program in which the name can be used unqualified. The scope of a variable extends from just after its declaration to the end of the inner-most enclosing block statement. The scope of a parameter of a method or constructor or operator or indexer is the entire function body.

The scope of a variable declared in the header of a `for` statement is the entire statement (header and body). The scope of the control variable in a `foreach` statement is the body only:

```
for (int x = ...; ...; ...) body
foreach (int x in ...) body
```

The scope of a variable or parameter x cannot contain a redeclaration of x. However, the scope of a class or struct member (such as a field x) may contain a declaration of a variable x that *shadows* the field, but only if the member has not been used in the same block prior to the declaration of the variable (see M3 and M4 in example 12). The scope of a member is the entire class, except where shadowed by a variable or parameter of the same name. The member can be used anywhere in the class, also textually before its declaration. If the member is `public` or `protected`, its scope includes subclasses, except where hidden by a subclass member of the same name. The scope of a static member also includes every nested class, except where shadowed by a member of the nested class, but it excludes subclasses of the nested class.

## 6.2   Default Values and Definite Assignment

For every type t there is a *default value*, which can be produced by the expression `default(t)`. For a simple type t the default value is shown on page 7. For a struct type t the default value is a struct whose fields have their default values. For a reference type t the default value is `null`. For an enum type the default value is that of its underlying representation type. For a nullable type t? the default value is `null`.

A field of an object or struct is automatically initialized with the default value for its type t.

Unlike a field, a variable or `out` parameter is not given an initial value. Instead the compiler requires that a variable is *definitely assigned* wherever its value is used. That is, regardless what conditional statements or loops have been executed between the declaration of a variable and a use of its value, the variable must have been assigned a value before its use.

Like a variable, an `out` parameter (section 10.7) must have been definitely assigned, in the function that declares it, whenever its value is used. On the other hand, a by-value parameter or `ref` parameter is always given a value when the function is called, and so is always definitely assigned.

**Example 12** Scope of Fields, Parameters, and Variables

This program declares five variables or fields all called x, and shows where each one is in scope. The field and the variables are labeled #1, ..., #5 for reference only.

```
class Scope {
  void M1(int x) {     // declaration of parameter x (#1); shadows x (#5)
    x = 7;             // x #1 in scope; legal, but no effect outside M1
  }                    //
  void M3() {          //
    int x;             // declaration of variable x (#2); shadows x (#5)
    x = 7;             // x #2 in scope
  }
  void M4() {          //
    x = 7;             // x #5 in scope
    // int x;          // would be ILLEGAL, giving a new meaning to x
  }
  void M5() {          //
    {                  //
      int x;           // declaration of variable x (#3); shadows x (#5)
      x = 7;           // x #3 in scope
    }                  //
    {                  //
      int x;           // declaration of variable x (#4); shadows x (#5)
      x = 7;           // x #4 in scope
    }                  //
  }
  public int x;        // declaration of field x (#5)
}
```

**Example 13** Definite Assignment

Variable x is definitely assigned at (#1) below because it gets assigned regardless which branch of the `if` statement is executed, but y is not, because it gets assigned in only one of the branches. Variable z is not definitely assigned at (#3) because it will be assigned only if the body of `for` loop gets executed (and the compiler does not take the value of variables in loop conditions into account when determining that).

```
int x, y, z;
if (args.Length == 0)
  x = y = 10;
else
  x = args.Length;
Console.WriteLine(x);          // x definitely assigned, y and z not (#1)
y = x;
for (int i=0; i<y; i++)        // x and y definitely assigned, z not (#2)
  z = i;
// Console.WriteLine(z);       // z still not definitely assigned!    (#3)
```

# 7   Strings

A *string* is an object of the predefined class String from namespace System. The keyword string is an alias for System.String. A string constant is a sequence of characters within double quotes, such as "New York", "B52", or the empty string "". Internally, a character is stored as a number using the Unicode character encoding, whose character codes 0–127 coincide with the ASCII character encoding. String constants and character constants may use character *escape codes*:

| Escape Code | Meaning |
|---|---|
| \a | alert (bell) |
| \b | backspace |
| \t | horizontal tab |
| \v | vertical tab |
| \n | new line |
| \f | form feed (page break) |
| \r | carriage return |
| \" | the double quote character |
| \' | the single quote character |
| \\ | the backslash character |
| \0 | the NUL character (ASCII or Unicode 0) |
| \x*d* | the character whose character code is the hexadecimal number *d* |
| \x*dd* | the character whose character code is the hexadecimal number *dd* |
| \x*ddd* | the character whose character code is the hexadecimal number *ddd* |
| \x*dddd* | the character whose character code is the hexadecimal number *dddd* |
| \u*dddd* | the character with four-digit hexadecimal Unicode encoding *dddd* |
| \U*dddddddd* | the character with eight-digit hexadecimal Unicode encoding *dddddddd* |

A character escape sequence represents a single character. Since the letter A has code 65 (decimal), which is written 41 in hexadecimal, the string constant "A\x41\u0041\U00000041" is the same as "AAAA". The \U*dddddddd* escape code can be used only in string constants, not in character constants.

A *verbatim string constant* is a string constant prefixed with the @ character. Any escape sequence in such a string denotes itself, just like ordinary characters, except that "" denotes the double quote character.

If s1 and s2 are expressions of type String, then:

- s1.ToString() simply returns s1 itself, and somewhat surprisingly, so does s1.Clone(), whereas String.Copy(s1) produces a new String object containing the same sequence of characters as s1.

- s1.Length of type int is the length of s1, that is, the number of characters in s1.

- s1[i] of type char is the character at position i in s1, counting from 0. If the index i is less than 0, or greater than or equal to s1.Length, then the exception IndexOutOfRangeException is thrown.

- s1.Equals(s2) of type bool is true if both s1 and s2 are non-null and contain the same sequence of characters. Uppercase and lowercase characters are considered distinct.

- s1 == s2 is true if both s1 and s2 are null, or if both are non-null and s1.Equals(s2); and the inequality s1 != s2 has the same meaning as !(s1 == s2). Hence s1 != "" is true when s1 is a non-empty string, but also when s1 is null.

**Example 14** Regular String Constants and Verbatim (@) String Constants

```
Console.WriteLine("\u0041BC");              // ABC
Console.WriteLine(@"\u0041BC");             // \u0041BC
Console.WriteLine("Say \"Hello\"!");        // Say "Hello"!
Console.WriteLine(@"Say ""Hello""!");       // Say "Hello"!
String s1 = @"Line 1
and Line 2";                                // Newline allowed only in verbatim string
String s2 = "Line 1\nand Line 2";           // s1 and s2 are equal
```

**Example 15** Equality of Strings
The comparison operator == applied to arguments of type String compares the contents of the strings: the character sequences. When applied to arguments of type Object, it compares the object references. Two strings that contain the same character sequences may be represented by a single String object (s1 and s2) if they are compile-time constants; otherwise they need not be (s2 and s4).

```
String s1 = "abc", s2 = "ab" + "c", s3 = null; // Compile-time constants
String s4 = args[0];                           // Value given at run-time
// Assume command line argument args[0] is "abc" so s4 is "abc":
Console.WriteLine(s1==s2);                      // True
Console.WriteLine((Object)s1==(Object)s2);      // Probably True
Console.WriteLine(s2==s4);                      // True
Console.WriteLine((Object)s2==(Object)s4);      // Probably False
Console.WriteLine("{0} {1} {2}", s3==s1, s3!=s1, s3==s3); // False True True
```

**Example 16** Counting the Number of e's in a String Using a String Indexer

```
static int eCount(String s) {
  int ecount = 0;
  for (int i=0; i<s.Length; i++)
    if (s[i] == 'e')
      ecount++;
  return ecount;
}
```

**Example 17** Concatenate All Command Line Arguments
When concatenating many strings, do not use += but a string builder, as shown in section 8 and example 28.

```
public static void Main(String[] args) {
  String res = "";                          // Inefficient
  for (int i=0; i<args.Length; i++)         // Inefficient
    res += args[i];                         // Inefficient
  Console.WriteLine(res);
}
```

**Example 18** The + Operator Is Left Associative

```
Console.WriteLine(10 + 25 + "A");  // Same as (10 + 25) + "A", that is "35A"
Console.WriteLine("A" + 10 + 25);  // Same as ("A" + 10) + 25, that is "A1025"
```

## 7.1   String Methods

Let s1, s2 and s3 be expressions of type String, let cs be an expression of type char[], and let v be an expression of any type, then:

- String.Compare(s1, s2) returns a negative integer, zero, or a positive integer, according as s1 precedes, equals, or follows s2 in the lexicographical ordering based on the Unicode character encoding and the culture of the current thread. The null reference precedes any non-null string.

- String.Compare(s1, s2, ignoreCase) works as above, but does not distinguish lowercase and uppercase if ignoreCase is true.

- s1.CompareTo(s2) has the same meaning as String.Compare(s1, s2) when s1 is not null.

- s1.ToUpper() and s1.ToLower() create a copy of s1 in uppercase and lowercase, respectively.

- s1 + s2 has the same meaning as String.Concat(s1, s2). It constructs the concatenation of s1 and s2: a new string consisting of the characters of s1 followed by the characters of s2.

- s1 + v and v + s1 are evaluated by converting v to a string with v.ToString() and then concatenating the two strings. If v or v.ToString() is null, the result of the concatenation is s1.

- s1.Substring(i, n) creates a new string consisting of the n characters from s1 with indices [i..(i+n-1)]. Throws ArgumentOutOfRangeException if i<0 or n<0 or i+n>s1.Length.

- s1.Split(cs) of type String[] is an array of the maximal (possibly empty) substrings of s1 that contain no characters from cs, in order from left to right. Here cs is either a single argument of type char[], or zero or more arguments of type char; see example 20. Namely, cs is a so-called parameter array; see section 12.15.3.

- s1.StartsWith(s2) and s1.EndsWith(s2), both of type bool, determine whether s1 starts, respectively ends, with the substring s2.

- s1.Remove(i, n) creates a new string from s1 by removing the n characters that have indices [i..(i+n-1)]. Throws ArgumentOutOfRangeException if i<0 or n<0 or i+n>s1.Length.

- s1.Replace(s2, s3) creates a new string from s1 by replacing all non-overlapping occurrences of the substring s2 with s3 from left to right. If each of s1 and s2 is a single character c1 and c2, it is much faster to use s1.Replace(c1, c2) with signature Replace(char, char).

- s1.Trim(cs) creates a new string from s1 by removing all occurrences of characters in char[] cs from the beginning and end of s1. To remove white space characters (including space, newline, tabulator, form feed, and vertical tab) from the beginning and end of s1, use s1.Trim(). If string s1 contains only ASCII characters, this is equivalent to s1.Trim(" \n\r\t\f\v".ToCharArray()).

- The effect of s1.TrimStart(cs) and s1.TrimEnd(cs) is the same as that of s1.Trim(cs), except that characters are only removed at the beginning or end, respectively, of s1.

- s1.ToCharArray() returns a new character array containing the characters of s1.

- More String methods are described in the .Net Framework class library; see section 30.

**Example 19** Determine Whether Strings Occur in Increasing Order

```
static bool Sorted(String[] a) {
  for (int i=1; i<a.Length; i++)
    if (a[i-1].CompareTo(a[i]) > 0)
      return false;
  return true;
}
```

**Example 20** Calculating a Readability Index
The readability index of a text can be calculated using the following formula, where *#sentences* is the number of sentences, *#words* the number of words, and *#longwords* the number of words longer than 6 letters:

$$Readability\ index = \frac{\#words}{\#sentences} + \frac{100 \times \#longwords}{\#words}$$

Using the Split method, a text given as a String can be crudely split into sentences (separated by full stops), and the sentences can be further split into words (separated by commas or white space).

```
static double Readability(String text) {
  int wordCount = 0, longWordsCount = 0;
  String[] sentences = text.Split(new char[] {'.'});          // Split into sentences
  foreach (String sentence in sentences) {
    String[] words = sentence.Split(' ', ',');                // Split into words
    // String[] words = sentence.Split(new char[] {' ', ','}); // Equivalent alternative
    wordCount += words.Length;
    foreach (String word in words) {
      if (word.Length > 6)
        longWordsCount++;
      else if (word.Length == 0)
        wordCount--;
    }
  }
  return (wordCount*1.0)/sentences.Length + (longWordsCount*100.0)/wordCount;
}
```

**Example 21** Using a Class That Overrides the ToString Method
Class Point in example 40 declares a ToString method which returns a string of the point coordinates. The operator (+) below implicitly calls the ToString method to convert the Point objects to strings:

```
Point p1 = new Point(10, 20), p2 = new Point(30, 40);
Console.WriteLine("p1 is " + p1);      // Prints: p1 is (10, 20)
Console.WriteLine("p2 is " + p2);      // Prints: p2 is (30, 40)
p2.Move(7, 7);
Console.WriteLine("p2 is " + p2);      // Prints: p2 is (37, 47)
```

## 7.2   String Formatting

When producing a string to the console, to an output stream, to a string builder, or similar, the output string may contain numeric values, dates and other values that require special formatting such as right or left justification, padding, and so on. The formatting can be specified using a *format specification*, which is a sequence of characters of one of these four forms

$$\{index, align\!:\!code\} \quad \{index, align\} \quad \{index\!:\!code\} \quad \{index\}$$

where *index* is a non-negative integer $0, 1, \ldots$ specifying which value is to be formatted, and *align* is an integer whose absolute value specifies the minimum number of characters in the resulting string. When *align* is positive then the string to be formatted is right-justified (padded on the left) if shorter than the minimum width, and when *align* is negative then the string to be formatted is left-justified (padded on the right) if shorter than the minimum width. The *code* is a formatting pattern (sections 7.2.1 and 7.2.2).

Let `fmt` be a string that contains one or more format specifications, and let `v0, v1, ..., vn` be values of any type. Then:

- `String.Format(fmt, v0, v1, ...)` of type String is `fmt` in which the format specifications with *index* $0, 1, \ldots$ are replaced by the formatted string representations of `v0, v1, ...`, according to the format specifications in `fmt`.

If the type of `vi` is DateTime or a numeric type (section 5.1), the format specification $\{i, align\!:\!code\}$ is replaced by the result of formatting `vi` using *code* as shown in sections 7.2.1 and 7.2.2 and the associated examples. Otherwise, the format specification is replaced with `vi.ToString()`. In both cases, the resulting string is aligned as specified by *align*.

The `String.Format` method throws a FormatException if the *index* of a format specification is less than 0 or greater than n, or if a formatting code in `fmt` is invalid.

The `String.Format` method is usually not called explicitly, but it is called implicitly from

- `Console.WriteLine(String fmt, Object v)` and its overloads (example 23), and from other similar output stream methods (section 22).

- `AppendFormat(String fmt, Object v)` and its overloads (section 8).

String formatting is *culture sensitive*: The actual characters used for decimal points, thousand separator, currency symbols and so on, and the actual date formatting patterns, weekday names, month names and so on depend on the `NumberFormat` and `DateTimeFormat` properties of the `CurrentCulture` property of the current thread; see example 27. The culture also affects the parsing of floating-point numbers. A culture is represented by an object of class CultureInfo, and the culture of the current thread is either determined externally by the operating environment or set explicitly in the source code. For instance, to use the predefined U.S. English culture:

```
Thread.CurrentThread.CurrentCulture = new CultureInfo("en-US");
```

**Example 22**  String Formatting Using the `String.Format` Method
The result s below is | ⎵⎵⎵⎵⎵3D326 | ⎵⎵⎵⎵250662 | 3D326 | 250662 |, where the symbol ⎵ denotes a
blank. The format specifiers are explained in section 7.2.1.

```
int i = 250662;
String s = String.Format("|{0,10:X}|{1,10}|{2:X}|{3}|", i, i, i, i);
```

**Example 23**  String Formatting Using the `Console.WriteLine` Method
This example rolls 1000 dice and counts frequencies; the frequencies are written to the console (as in
example 31), but string formatting is used instead of string concatenation.

```
Random rnd = new Random();          // Random number generator
int[] freq = new int[6];            // All initialized to 0
for (int i=0; i<1000; i++) {
  int die = rnd.Next(1, 7);         // Random integer in range 1..6
  freq[die-1] += 1;
}
for (int c=1; c<=6; c++)
  Console.WriteLine("{0} came up {1} times", c, freq[c-1]);
```

**Example 24**  String Alignment in Text Output
A 3 × 5 matrix represented by a two-dimensional array is filled with random numbers from 0 to 999. The
matrix is then printed with the numbers right-justified in each column.

```
Random rnd = new Random();          // Random number generator
int[,] m = new int[3,5];            // 3x5 matrix
for (int i=0; i<m.GetLength(0); i++)
  for (int j=0; j<m.GetLength(1); j++)
    m[i,j] = rnd.Next(1000);        // Random integer in range 0..999

for (int i=0; i<m.GetLength(0); i++)
  Console.WriteLine("{0,4} {1,4} {2,4} {3,4} {4,4}", m[i,0], m[i,1], m[i,2], m[i,3], m[i,4]);
```

The console output may look like this:

```
932   930   417    17    14
993   492   329   828    63
455   721   920    70   520
```

### 7.2.1 Number Formatting

The *code* part of a format specification for a value of numeric type may be a standard number formatting code, which has the form *c* or *cy* or *cyy* where *c* is a code character and *y* is a digit. The following standard number formatting codes are predefined for integers (I) or floating-point numbers (F) or both (IF):

| Code *c* | String Format | Precision Specifier *y* or *yy* | Type |
|---|---|---|---|
| D or d | Decimal number (possibly padded with zeroes) | Minimum number of digits | I |
| X or x | Hexadecimal (possibly padded with zeroes) | Minimum number of digits | I |
| G or g | General (default) | Max. number of significant digits | IF |
| N or n | Number with thousand separators | Number of fractional digits | IF |
| F or f | Fixed-point number | Number of fractional digits | IF |
| R or r | Lossless value-string-value conversion | (none) | F |
| E or e | Exponential notation | Number of fractional digits | IF |
| P or p | Percent (value multiplied by 100 %) | Number of fractional digits | IF |
| C or c | Currency amount | Number of fractional digits | IF |

The *code* part of a format specification for a value of a numeric type may also be a custom number formatting pattern, which is a combination of one or more of the following predefined custom number formatting codes:

$$0 \quad \# \quad . \quad , \quad \% \quad E0 \quad e0 \quad E+0 \quad e+0 \quad E-0 \quad e-0 \quad ; \quad \textit{'string'} \quad \textit{"string"}$$

See example 26 and the .Net Framework class library documentation for details.

### 7.2.2 DateTime Formatting

The *code* part of a format specification for an object of type DateTime may be one of the predefined standard DateTime formatting codes:

| Code Character | Format |
|---|---|
| F or f | Full date and time (with or without seconds) |
| G or g | General date and time (with or without seconds) |
| s | Sortable date and time in ISO8601 format |
| u | Universal sortable local date and time |
| U | Universal sortable date and time: F converted to UTC |
| R and r | RFC1123 standard full date and time |
| D or d | Full date (long or short format) |
| Y and y | Year and month |
| M and m | Month and date |
| T or t | Time (with or without seconds) |

The *code* part of a format specification for an object of type DateTime may also be a custom DateTime formatting pattern, which is a combination of one or more of the many predefined custom DateTime formatting codes. See the .Net Framework documentation for details.

**Example 25**  Some Standard Number Format Patterns and Their Effect
Formatting is culture sensitive. This table shows the formatting obtained in the en-US culture.

| Number | Format Specifications | | | | | | |
|---|---|---|---|---|---|---|---|
| | {0:D4} | {0,7} | {0:F0} | {0:F2} | {0,8:F3} | {0:E4} | {0,9:C} |
| 0 | 0000 | 0 | 0 | 0.00 | 0.000 | 0.0000E+000 | $0.00 |
| 1 | 0001 | 1 | 1 | 1.00 | 1.000 | 1.0000E+000 | $1.00 |
| 145 | 0145 | 145 | 145 | 145.00 | 145.000 | 1.4500E+002 | $145.00 |
| -1 | -0001 | -1 | -1 | -1.00 | -1.000 | -1.0000E+000 | ($1.00) |
| 2.5 | | 2.5 | 3 | 2.50 | 2.500 | 2.5000E+000 | $2.50 |
| -1.5 | | -1.5 | -2 | -1.50 | -1.500 | -1.5000E+000 | ($1.50) |
| 330.8 | | 330.8 | 331 | 330.80 | 330.800 | 3.3080E+002 | $330.80 |
| 1234.516 | | 1234.516 | 1235 | 1234.52 | 1234.516 | 1.2345E+003 | $1,234.52 |

**Example 26**  Custom Number Formatting

| Number | Format Specifications | | | | |
|---|---|---|---|---|---|
| | {0:000.0} | {0:###.#} | {0:##0.0} | {0:#0E+0} | {0:00##;'(neg)';'-'} |
| 1230.1 | 1230.1 | 1230.1 | 1230.1 | 12E+2 | 1230 |
| 17 | 017.0 | 17 | 17.0 | 17E+0 | 0017 |
| 0.15 | 000.2 | .2 | 0.2 | 15E-2 | - |
| 0 | 000.0 | | 0.0 | 00E+0 | - |
| -26 | -026.0 | -26 | -26.0 | -26E+0 | (neg) |

**Example 27**  Standard DateTime Formatting Codes and Their Effect
Here a DateTime value is shown in all standard formats using the en-US culture and the de-DE culture:

| Format | U.S. English | German |
|---|---|---|
| F | Monday, June 09, 2003 10:49:41 PM | Montag, 9. Juni 2003 22:49:41 |
| f | Monday, June 09, 2003 10:49 PM | Montag, 9. Juni 2003 22:49 |
| G | 6/9/2003 10:49:41 PM | 09.06.2003 22:49:41 |
| g | 6/9/2003 10:49 PM | 09.06.2003 22:49 |
| s | 2003-06-09T22:49:41 | 2003-06-09T22:49:41 |
| u | 2003-06-09 22:49:41Z | 2003-06-09 22:49:41Z |
| U | Monday, June 09, 2003 8:49:41 PM | Montag, 9. Juni 2003 20:49:41 |
| R | Mon, 09 Jun 2003 22:49:41 GMT | Mon, 09 Jun 2003 22:49:41 GMT |
| D | Monday, June 09, 2003 | Montag, 9. Juni 2003 |
| d | 6/9/2003 | 09.06.2003 |
| Y | June, 2003 | Juni 2003 |
| M | June 09 | 09 Juni |
| T | 10:49:41 PM | 22:49:41 |
| t | 10:49 PM | 22:49 |

# 8 String Builders

A string builder, which is an object of class System.Text.StringBuilder, is an extensible and modifiable string. Characters can be appended to a string builder without copying those characters already in the string builder; the string builder is automatically and efficiently extended as needed.

By contrast, a String object s1, once created, cannot be modified. Using s1 + s2 one can append s1 and s2, but that creates a new string object by copying all the characters from s1 and s2; there is no way to extend s1 itself by appending more characters to it. Thus to concatenate $n$ strings each of length $k$ by repeated string concatenation (+), we must copy $k + 2k + 3k + \cdots + nk = kn(n+1)/2$ characters, and the time required to do this is proportional to $n^2$, which grows rapidly as $n$ grows.

Using a string builder, the concatenation of $n$ strings each of length $k$ requires only time proportional to $n$, considerably faster than $n^2$ for large $n$. To gradually build a string, use a string builder, especially for repeated concatenation in a loop, as in examples 17 and 28. The expression s1 + $\cdots$ + sn is efficient; it actually means new StringBuilder().Append(s1). ... .Append(sn).ToString().

Let sb be a StringBuilder, s a String, and v an expression of any type, then

- new StringBuilder() creates a new empty string builder.

- sb.Append(v) appends the string representation of the value v to the string builder, converting v to a string by v.ToString(), see section 7. Extends sb as needed. Returns sb.

- sb.AppendFormat(String fmt, object v) appends the string String.Format(fmt, v) to the string builder. Extends sb as needed. Returns sb. For possible formatting specifiers fmt, see section 7.2.

- sb.Length of type int is the length of sb, that is, the number of characters currently in sb.

- sb[i] is character number i in the string builder, counting from zero. Thus sb[i] = c sets the character at index i to c. Throws IndexOutOfRangeException (when getting a character) or ArgumentOutOfRangeException (when setting a character) if i<0 or i>=sb.Length.

- sb.Remove(i, n) deletes the characters with index i..(i+n-1) from the string builder, reducing its length by n characters. Throws ArgumentOutOfRangeException if i<0 or n<0 or i+n>sb.Length. Returns sb.

- sb.Insert(i, v) inserts the string representation of v obtained by v.ToString()) into the string builder, starting at position i, extending sb as needed. Returns sb. Throws ArgumentOutOfRange-Exception if i<0 or i>sb.Length.

- sb.ToString() of type String is a new string containing the characters currently in sb.

Method Append is fast, but Remove and Insert may be slow when they need to move large parts of the string builder's contents, that is, when both i and i+n are much smaller than Length.

More StringBuilder methods are described in the .Net Framework class library; see section 30.

**Example 28** Efficiently Concatenate All Command Line Arguments
When there are many (more than 50) command line arguments, this is much faster than example 17.

```
using System;
using System.Text;              // StringBuilder

class StringBuilderConcatenate {
  public static void Main(String[] args) {
    StringBuilder res = new StringBuilder();
    for (int i=0; i<args.Length; i++)
      res.Append(args[i]);
    Console.WriteLine(res.ToString());
  }
}
```

**Example 29** Replacing Occurrences of a Character by a String
To replace occurrences of character c1 with the string s2 in string s, it is best to use a string builder for the result, since the size of the resulting string is not known in advance. This works well also when replacing a character c1 with another character c2, but in that case the length of the result is known in advance (it equals the length of s), and one can use a character array instead. Solving this problem by repeated string concatenation (using res += s2 where res has type String) would be very slow.

```
static String ReplaceCharString(String s, char c1, String s2) {
  StringBuilder res = new StringBuilder();
  for (int i=0; i<s.Length; i++)
    if (s[i] == c1)
      res.Append(s2);
    else
      res.Append(s[i]);
  return res.ToString();
}
```

**Example 30** An Inefficient Way to Replace Occurrences of a Character by a String
The problem from example 29 above can also be solved by destructively modifying a string builder with Remove and Insert. However, repeated use of Remove and Insert is very inefficient: for a string of 200,000 random characters this method is approximately 100 times slower than the above one.

```
static void ReplaceCharString(StringBuilder sb, char c1, String s2) {
  int i = 0;                              // Inefficient
  while (i < sb.Length) {                 // Inefficient
    if (sb[i] == c1) {                    // Inefficient
      sb.Remove(i, 1);                    // Inefficient
      sb.Insert(i, s2);                   // Inefficient
      i += s2.Length;                     // Inefficient
    } else                                // Inefficient
      i += 1;                             // Inefficient
  } }                                     // Inefficient
```

# 9   Arrays

An *array* is an indexed collection of zero or more variables, called *elements*. An array has a given *element type* t, which can be any type. The value of an expression of an array type such as t[] is either null or a reference to an array whose element type u is t or implicitly convertible to t. If t is a value type, u must equal t. Assignment of an array to a variable assigns only the reference; it does not copy the array, as illustrated by arr1 and arr2 in example 64.

The *rank* of an array is the number of index expressions required to access an element. Although an array of rank *n* is sometimes called an *n*-dimensional array, note that a Java-style 'multi-dimensional' array of type t[]...[] is actually an array of rank one, whose elements happen to be arrays; see section 9.2.2.

## 9.1   One-dimensional Arrays

In an array with rank one and *length* $\ell \geq 0$, the elements are indexed by the integers $0, 1, \ldots, \ell - 1$. A new array of length $\ell$ with element type t is created (allocated) using an *array creation expression*, which can take two forms. The first form of array creation expression is:

```
new t[ℓ]
```

where $\ell$ is an expression of type int. This creates a new array with rank one, also called a one-dimensional array, with $\ell$ elements, all initialized with the default value for type t (section 6.2). The size argument $\ell$ may be zero, but if it is negative then OverflowException is thrown.

The second form of array creation expression explicitly lists the elements of the new array:

```
new t[] { expression, ..., expression }
```

The type of each *expression* must be implicitly convertible to t. This array creation expression is evaluated by creating a distinct new array of rank one whose length equals the number of expressions. Then the expressions are evaluated from left to right and their values are converted to type t and stored in the array,

A local variable or field of array type may be initialized at declaration, by assigning null or an array to it. When an array creation expression is used to initialize an array variable at its declaration, the part "new t[]" may be left out, so these two declarations are equivalent:

```
t[] a = new t[] { expression, ..., expression };
t[] a = { expression, ..., expression };
```

Note that the declared variable a cannot occur in the *expressions*: it has not yet been initialized when the expressions are being evaluated. Also note that there are no array constants: a new distinct array is created every time an array creation expression is evaluated.

Let a be an array expression of type t[] whose value is an array of length $\ell$ with element type u. Then the *array access* expression a[i] denotes element number i of a, counting from 0; this expression has type t. The integer expression i is called the *array index*. If the value of i is less than 0 or greater than or equal to $\ell$, then an IndexOutOfRangeException is thrown.

When the element type u is a reference type, then every array element assignment a[i] = e checks that the value of e is null or is implicitly convertible to the element type u. If this is not the case, then an ArrayTypeMismatchException is thrown. This check is made before every array element assignment at run-time, but only for reference types. For value types, the type check is performed at compile-time.

**Example 31** Creating and Using One-dimensional Arrays
This example rolls a die one thousand times, then prints the frequencies of the outcomes.

```
Random rnd = new Random();              // Random number generator
int[] freq = new int[6];                // All elements initialized to 0
for (int i=0; i<1000; i++) {
  int die = rnd.Next(1, 7);             // Roll die
  freq[die-1] += 1;                     // Increment frequency
}
for (int c=1; c<=6; c++) Console.WriteLine(c + " came up " + freq[c-1] + " times");
```

**Example 32** Using an Initialized Array
Method `CheckDate` below checks whether a given date is legal in a non-leap year. The array should be created once, outside the method; otherwise a distinct new array is created for every call to the method.

```
static readonly int[] days = { 31, 28, 31, 30, 31, 30, 31, 31, 30, 31, 30, 31 };
static bool CheckDate(int mth, int day)
{ return (mth >= 1) && (mth <= 12) && (day >= 1) && (day <= days[mth-1]); }
```

**Example 33** Array Element Assignment Type Check at Run-Time
This program compiles OK, but at run-time `a[2]=p1` throws ArrayTypeMismatchException, since the class Point of the object bound to `p1` is not implicitly convertible to a's element type RedPoint:

```
Point[] a = new RedPoint[10];       // Length 10, element type RedPoint
Point p1 = new Point(42, 117);      // Compile-time type Point, class Point
RedPoint cp = new RedPoint(3,4);    // Compile-time type RedPoint, class RedPoint
Point p2 = cp;                      // Compile-time type Point, class RedPoint
a[0] = cp;                          // OK, RedPoint is subclass of RedPoint
a[1] = p2;                          // OK, RedPoint is subclass of RedPoint
a[2] = p1;                          // Run-time error: Point not subclass of RedPoint
```

**Example 34** Array Assignment Compatibility
In an assignment `a = e` where a and e have array type, e must be implicitly convertible to a as defined in section 5.3.2. Below, the assignment to `a1` is legal because String and Object are reference types and String is implicitly convertible to Object. The assignment to `a2` is obviously legal as the arrays have the same element type, and the array creation expression is legal because the integers 1 and 2 are implicitly convertible to Object by a boxing conversion. The assignments to `a3` and `a4` are illegal because int is not a reference type and so `int[]` is not implicitly convertible to `Object[]` or `double[]`.

```
Object[] a1 = new String[] { "a", "bc" };   // Legal:   array conversion
Object[] a2 = new Object[] { 1, 2 };        // Legal:   conversion of 1, 2
// Object[] a3 = new int[] { 1, 2 };        // Illegal: no array conversion
// double[] a4 = new int[] { 1, 2 };        // Illegal: no array conversion
```

## 9.2  Multi-dimensional Arrays

There are two ways to form multi-dimensional arrays: *rectangular arrays* and *jagged arrays*. Here is a rectangular 3-by-2 array and a "two-dimensional" jagged array; example 35 shows how to create them:

| | | | | | |
|---|---|---|---|---|---|
| 0.0 | 0.1 | | 0.0 | | |
| 1.0 | 1.1 | | 1.0 | 1.1 | |
| 2.0 | 2.1 | | 2.0 | 2.1 | 2.2 |

### 9.2.1  Rectangular Arrays

Rectangular (C-style) arrays have types of form `t[]`, `t[,]`, `t[,,]`, and so on, where `t` is not an array type. The array type `t[,...,]`, with $n-1$ commas, has rank $n$ and is also called an $n$-dimensional array type. When $n = 1$ this is just a one-dimensional array type `t[]` as in section 9.1. A variable of type `t[,...,]` is either `null` or holds a reference to an $n$-dimensional array; assignment of an array does not copy it.

A rectangular $n$-dimensional array may be created in one operation by an array creation expression:

    new t[ℓ₁,...,ℓₙ]

where $\ell_1,\ldots,\ell_n$ are expressions of type `int`, as for one-dimensional arrays. This creates an array with $\ell_1 \cdot \ell_2 \cdots \ell_n$ elements, all initialized with the default value for type `t` (section 6.2). Alternatively, an array creation expression for a rectangular $n$-dimensional array may have this form:

    new t[,...,] { ... { expression,...,expression }, { expression,...,expression }, ... }

where there are $n-1$ commas in `t[,...,]` and the nesting depth of curly braces is $n$. The expressions are evaluated from left to right and implicitly converted to type `t` as for one-dimensional arrays.

To access an element of an $n$-dimensional rectangular array a, use $n$ index expressions: `a[i₁,...,iₙ]`.

### 9.2.2  Arrays of Arrays (Jagged Arrays)

In general, an array type has form `t[K₁][K₂]...[Kₕ]` where each $K_i$ is a list of $k_i - 1$ commas, $k_i \geq 1$, and `t` is not an array type. This type describes $k_1$-dimensional rectangular arrays of $k_2$-dimensional rectangular arrays of ... $k_h$-dimensional arrays of element type `t`. For instance, `double[,][]` is the type of two-dimensional arrays of one-dimensional arrays of `double`.

A common special case is Java-style "$h$-dimensional" array types `t[]...[]` where $k_1 = \ldots = k_h = 1$. Thus a "two-dimensional" array of type `t[][]` is a one-dimensional array whose elements are arrays of type `t[]`. The element arrays may have different lengths, so the array may be non-rectangular or "jagged".

A jagged (Java-style) "$h$-dimensional" array `t[][]...[]`, with $h$ empty square brackets `[]`, must be created one dimension at a time:

    new t[ℓ₁][]...[]

This creates a one-dimensional array with $\ell_1$ elements, all initialized to `null`, and all of type `t[]...[]`, where there are $h-1$ empty square brackets `[]`. One may subsequently create arrays of type `t[]...[]` and assign them to the elements of the one-dimensional array.

To access an element of an $h$-dimensional jagged array a, use $h$ index expressions: `a[i₁][i₂]...[iₙ]`. Element access in a jagged array is likely to be less efficient than in a rectangular array.

**Example 35** Creating Multi-dimensional Arrays

This example shows two ways (r1, r2) to create the rectangular array shown opposite, and three ways (t1, t2, t3) to create the jagged array. One cannot create a jagged array in one operation (as in t4):

```
double[,] r1 = { { 0.0, 0.1 }, { 1.0, 1.1 }, { 2.0, 2.1 } };
double[,] r2 = new double[3,2];
for (int i=0; i<3; i++)
  for (int j=0; j<2; j++)
    r2[i,j] = i + 0.1 * j;

double[] row0 = { 0.0 }, row1 = { 1.0, 1.1 }, row2 = { 2.0, 2.1, 2.2 };
double[][] t1 = { row0, row1, row2 };
double[][] t2 = { new double[] {0.0},
                  new double[] {1.0, 1.1},
                  new double[] {2.0,2.1,2.2}};
double[][] t3 = new double[3][];          // Create first dimension array
for (int i=0; i<3; i++) {
  t3[i] = new double[i+1];                // Create second dimension arrays
  for (int j=0; j<=i; j++)
    t3[i][j] = i + 0.1 * j;
}
// double[][] t4 = new double[3][3];      // Illegal array creation
```

**Example 36** Using Multi-dimensional Arrays

To store the exchange rate between US dollars and Euros ($US per Euro) for every day in the years 2000–2009 we can use an array rate of type double[,][]: a two-dimensional rectangular array of one-dimensional arrays with element type double. The idea is that rate[$y,m$][$d$] holds the exchange rate for year $y + 2000$, month $m + 1$, day $d + 1$. We use an array of type double[,][] because each of the 10 years has 12 months (hence rectangular), but not all months have the same number of days (hence jagged).

```
double[,][] rate = new double[10,12][];
rate[0, 0] = new double[31];       // Jan 2000 has 31 days
rate[0, 1] = new double[29];       // Feb 2000 has 29 days
rate[0, 2] = new double[31];       // Mar 2000 has 31 days
rate[0, 3] = new double[30];       // Apr 2000 has 30 days
rate[1, 1] = new double[28];       // Feb 2001 has 28 days
...
rate[0, 1][27] = 0.9748;           // 28 Feb 2000
rate[0, 1][28] = 0.9723;           // 29 Feb 2000
rate[0, 2][ 0] = 0.9651;           //  1 Mar 2000
...
for (int y=0; y<rate.GetLength(0); y++)
  for (int m=0; m<rate.GetLength(1); m++)
    if (rate[y,m] != null)
      for (int d=0; d<rate[y,m].Length; d++)
        if (rate[y,m][d] != 0.0)
          Console.WriteLine("{0:D4}-{1:D2}-{2:D2}: {3:F4} $US/Euro",
                            y+2000, m+1, d+1, rate[y,m][d]);
```

## 9.3   Class Array

All array types are derived from class Array, and the members of an array type are those inherited from class Array. Let a be a reference of array type, o an object of any type, and i, i1, ..., in integers. Then:

- a.Length of type int is the length of a, that is, the total number of elements in a, if a is a one-dimensional or a rectangular multi-dimensional array, or the number of elements in the first dimension of a, if a is a jagged array.

- a.Rank of type int is the rank of a; see sections 9 and 9.2.2 .

- a.GetEnumerator() of type IEnumerator is an enumerator (section 24.2) for iterating through a. It is used by the foreach statement to iterate over an array; see section 13.6.2 and example 37.

- a.GetLength(i) of type int is the number of elements in dimension i; see examples 24 and 36.

- a.SetValue(o, i1,..,in) of type void performs the same assignment as a[i1,...,in] = o when a has rank n; and a.GetValue(i1,...,in) of type Object is the same as a[i1,...,in]. More precisely, if a[i1,...,in] has reference type, then GetValue returns the same reference; otherwise it returns a boxed copy of the value of a[i1,...,in].

- a.Equals(o) of type bool returns true if a and o refer to the same array object, otherwise false.

Class Array provides static utility methods, some of which are listed below. These methods can be used on the ordinary array types t[] which derive from class Array. The methods throw ArgumentNullException if the given array a is null, and throw RankException if a is not one-dimensional.

- static int BinarySearch(Array a, Object k) searches the one-dimensional array a for k using binary search. Returns an index i>=0 for which a[i].CompareTo(k) == 0, if any; otherwise returns i<0 such that ~i would be the proper position for k. The array a must be sorted, as by Sort(a), or else the result is undefined; and its elements must implement IComparable.

- static int BinarySearch(Array a, Object k, IComparer cmp) works as above, but compares array elements using the method cmp.Compare; see section 24.3. The array must be sorted, as by Sort(a, cmp), or else the result is undefined.

- static void Reverse(Array a) reverses the contents of one-dimensional array a.

- static void Reverse(Array a, int i, int n) reverses the contents of a[i..(i+n-1)].

- static void Sort(Array a) sorts the one-dimensional array a using quicksort, comparing array elements using their CompareTo method; see section 24.3. The array elements must implement IComparable. The sort is not stable: elements that are equal may be swapped.

- static void Sort(Array a, IComparer cmp) works as above, but compares array elements using the method cmp.Compare; see section 24.3.

- static void Sort(Array a, int i, int n) works as above but sorts a[i..(i+n-1)].

- static void Sort(Array a, int i, int n, IComparer cmp) sorts a[i..(i+n-1)] using cmp.Compare.

**Example 37** Array Length, Rank, Indexing, and Foreach
This example uses the rectangular array r2 and the jagged array t2 from example 35.

```
static void ArrayInfo(String name, Array a) {
  Console.Write("{0} has length={1} rank={2} [", name, a.Length, a.Rank);
  for (int i=0, stop=a.Rank; i<stop; i++)
    Console.Write(" {0}", a.GetLength(i));
  Console.WriteLine(" ]");
}
...
ArrayInfo("r2", r2);                                // length=6 rank=2 [ 3 2 ]
ArrayInfo("t2", t2);                                // length=3 rank=1 [ 3 ]
r2.SetValue(10.0, 1, 0);                            // Same as r2[1,0] = 10.0;
r2.SetValue(21.0, 2, 1);                            // Same as r2[2,1] = 21.0;
((double[])t2.GetValue(1)).SetValue(10.0, 0);       // Same as t2[1][0] = 10.0;
((double[])t2.GetValue(2)).SetValue(21.0, 1);       // Same as t2[2][1] = 21.0;
foreach (double d in r2)                            // 0 0.1 10 1.1 2.0 21
  Console.Write(d + " ");
```

**Example 38** Binary Search in an Array

```
static String[] a = { "Armonk", "Chicago", "London", "Paris", "Seattle" };
static void Search(String c) {
  int i = Array.BinarySearch(a, c);
  if (i >= 0)
    Console.WriteLine("{0} found in position {1}", c, i);
  else
    Console.WriteLine("{0} not found; belongs in position {1}", c, ~i);
}
...
Search("London");                  // found in position 2
Search("Aachen");                  // belongs in position 0
Search("Copenhagen");              // belongs in position 2
Search("Washington");              // belongs in position 5
```

**Example 39** Swapping Two Array Segments
Two array segments a[0..k] and a[k..m-1] can be swapped without using extra storage by reversing each segment individually and then reversing the whole array. This example swaps the blocks of US and European cities without changing the order of cities within each block:

```
String[] a = { "Armonk", "Chicago", "Seattle", "London", "Paris" };
Array.Reverse(a, 0, 3);
Array.Reverse(a, 3, 2);
Array.Reverse(a);
foreach (String s in a)
  Console.Write(s + " ");
```

# 10  Classes

## 10.1  Class Declarations and Class Bodies

A *class-declaration* of class C has the form

> *class-modifiers* class C *class-base-clause*
>     *class-body*

A declaration of class C introduces class C, which is a reference type. The *class-modifiers* may be at most one of abstract, sealed and static (section 10.2), and a class access modifier (section 10.12). Inside an enclosing class D it may also be new to hide another member C inherited from the base class of D.

The *class-base-clause* may be used to specify the base class or superclass of class C (section 10.4) and to specify the interfaces implemented by class C (section 15.2).

A class declaration may consist of one or more partial type declarations; see section 26.

The *class-body* may contain declarations of *data members* (constants and fields), *function members* (instance constructors, static constructor, methods, properties, indexers, user-defined overloaded operators, and events), and *nested types* (classes, struct types, interfaces, enum types, and delegate types):

> {
>     *constant-declarations*
>     *field-declarations*
>     *constructor-declarations*
>     *static-constructor-declaration*
>     *method-declarations*
>     *property-declarations*
>     *indexer-declarations*
>     *operator-declarations*
>     *event-declarations*
>     *type-declarations*
> }

The declarations in a *class-body* may appear in any order: A field, method, property, indexer or event may be declared static. Operators *must* be declared static, and type members are implicitly static. A non-static member is called an *instance member*.

There can be no two members with the same name, except that methods may have the same name if they have different signatures (method overloading, see section 10.7). The scope of a member is the entire class body, except where shadowed by a variable or parameter of a method or property or indexer, or by a member of a nested class. However, instance fields and the current object reference this cannot be used in initializer expressions of fields, whether static or not.

By *static code* we mean expressions and statements in initializers of fields and events, in static constructors, static methods, static properties, static indexers, and in operators. By *non-static code* we mean expressions and statements in instance constructors, instance methods, instance properties, instance indexers, and instance events. Non-static code is executed inside a *current object*, which can be referred to as this; see section 12.14. Static code cannot refer to instance members or to this, only to static members.

Most of what is said about class declarations in this section is true of struct type declarations also, with the modifications listed in section 14.

**Example 40** Class Declaration
The Point class is declared to have two instance fields x and y, one constructor, and two instance methods.
It is used in examples 21 and 64.

```
public class Point {
  protected internal int x, y;
  public Point(int x, int y) { this.x = x; this.y = y; }
  public void Move(int dx, int dy) { x += dx; y += dy; }
  public override String ToString() { return "(" + x + ", " + y + ")"; }
}
```

**Example 41** Class with Static and Instance Members
The APoint class declares a static field allpoints and two instance fields x and y. Thus each APoint
object has its own x and y fields, but all objects share the same allpoints field in the APoint class.

The constructor inserts the new object (this) in the ArrayList object allpoints. The instance method
GetIndex returns the point's index in the arraylist. The static method GetSize returns the number of
APoints created so far. Instead of the methods GetIndex and GetSize it would be natural to use an
instance property and a static property; see section 10.13 and example 59. The static method GetPoint
returns the i'th APoint in the arraylist. The class is used in example 81.

Beware that every APoint created will be reachable from allpoints. This prevents automatic recy-
cling (garbage collection) of APoint objects at run-time; objects should not be kept live in this way unless
there is a very good reason to do so.

```
public class APoint {
  private static ArrayList allpoints = new ArrayList();
  private int x, y;
  public APoint(int x, int y) {
    allpoints.Add(this); this.x = x; this.y = y;
  }
  public void Move(int dx, int dy) {
    x += dx; y += dy;
  }
  public override String ToString() {
    return "(" + x + ", " + y + ")";
  }
  public int GetIndex() {
    return allpoints.IndexOf(this);
  }
  public static int GetSize() {
    return allpoints.Count;
  }
  public static APoint GetPoint(int i) {
    return (APoint)allpoints[i];
  }
}
```

## 10.2   Class Modifiers `abstract, sealed, static`

If a class C is declared `abstract`, then it cannot be instantiated, but non-abstract subclasses of C can be instantiated. An abstract class may have constructors that can be called from constructors in subclasses, by means of `base(...)` calls, when instantiating non-abstract subclasses. An abstract class may declare abstract and non-abstract methods; but a non-abstract class cannot declare abstract methods.

If a class C is declared `sealed`, then one cannot declare subclasses of C, and hence cannot override or hide any methods declared in C. This is useful for preventing rogue subclasses from violating data representation invariants.

A class cannot be both `abstract` and `sealed`, since no objects of that class could ever be created. However, a class may be declared `static`, in which case it can have only static members, and no instances can be created from it. This is useful for declaring utility classes such as System.Math.

## 10.3   Member Access Modifiers `private, protected, internal, public`

A member (data, function, or type) is always accessible in the class in which it is declared, except where shadowed by a variable or parameter of a function member, or by a member of a nested class or struct.

The following *access modifiers* may be used to make the member accessible elsewhere. The following access modifiers are legal (in a class declaration C or a struct type declaration S):

| Member Access Modifier | Accessible Within | In |
|---|---|---|
| private or absent | This class or struct | CS |
| internal | This assembly | CS |
| protected | This class + its subclasses | C- |
| protected internal | This assembly + this class's subclasses | C- |
| public | Everywhere | CS |

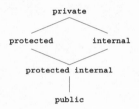

The modifiers `protected` and `protected internal` can be used on members of a class but not on members of a struct type (section 14) because it cannot have subtypes. All members of an interface (section 15) are implicitly public and only the `public` access modifier may, but need not, be used.

- If a member is declared `private` in a class C, it is accessible in C and its nested classes and struct types, but not in their subclasses outside C, nor in other classes.

  A member without an explicit access modifier is `private`.

- If a member in class C is declared `internal`, then it is accessible everywhere C is, but only within the same assembly (see section 1.1) as C.

- If a member in class C is declared `protected`, then it is accessible in subclasses of C.

- If a member in class C is declared `protected internal`, then it is accessible everywhere class C is, within the same assembly as C, and in subclasses of C. (This is similar to Java's notion of a protected member).

- If a member in class C is declared `public`, then it is accessible everywhere class C is, also in other assemblies.

**Example 42** Abstract Classes, Subclasses, and Overriding
The abstract class Vessel models the concept of a vessel for holding liquids: its field `contents` represents its actual contents, the abstract method `Capacity` computes its maximal capacity, and method `Fill` fills in more, but only up to its capacity; the excess will be lost. The abstract class has subclasses Tank (a rectangular vessel), Cube (a cubic vessel, subclass of Tank) and Barrel (a cylindric vessel). The subclasses implement the `Capacity` method, they inherit the `contents` field and the `Fill` method from the base class, and they override the `ToString` method (inherited from class Object) to format each vessel object:

```
public abstract class Vessel {
  private double contents;
  public abstract double Capacity();
  public void Fill(double amount) { contents = Math.Min(contents + amount, Capacity()); }
  public double Contents { get { return contents; } }
}
public class Tank : Vessel {
  protected readonly double length, width, height;
  public Tank(double length, double width, double height)
  { this.length = length; this.width = width; this.height = height; }
  public override double Capacity() { return length * width * height; }
  public override String ToString()
  { return "tank (" + length + ", " + width + ", " + height + ")"; }
}
public class Cube : Tank {
  public Cube(double side) : base(side, side, side) {}
  public override String ToString() { return "cube (" + length + ")"; }
}
public class Barrel : Vessel {
  private readonly double radius, height;
  public Barrel(double radius, double height) { this.radius = radius; this.height = height; }
  public override double Capacity() { return height * Math.PI * radius * radius; }
  public override String ToString() { return "barrel (" + radius + ", " + height + ")"; }
}
```

**Example 43** Member Access Modifiers
The member access modifiers in the vessel hierarchy in example 42 are justified as follows: (1) the `contents` field in Vessel is made private to prevent modification, (2) a public property `Contents` permits reading the field, and (3) the fields of Tank and Barrel are declared protected to permit access from subclasses.

Since the field `contents` in Vessel is private, it is not accessible in the subclasses (Tank, Barrel, ...), but the subclasses still inherit the field. Every vessel subclass object has room for storing the field, but can change and access it only by using the `Fill` method or the `Contents` property inherited from the abstract base class.

## 10.4    Subclass, Base Class, Inheritance and Hiding

The declaration of a class C may explicitly declare its *base class* B, using a *class-base-clause*:

```
: B
```

where B is a class. Then C is an *immediate subclass* of B, is said to be *derived* from B, and is a subclass also of any class of which B is a subclass. If class C does not explicitly declare its base class B, then the base class is Object. The *class-base-clause* is used also to list the interfaces implemented by C; see section 15.2.

Class C inherits all non-private members except constructors, and also private fields (although they are not accessible within class C), from B.

A class can have at most one immediate base class. The predefined class Object is a base class of all other classes; class Object itself has no base class. Hence the classes form a *class hierarchy* in which every class except Object is a descendant of its unique immediate base class (see section 5.2).

A constructor (section 10.9) in subclass C may be declared to explicitly call a particular constructor in the base class B, using this syntax:

*constructor-modifier* C(*formal-list*) : base(*actual-list*)
    *constructor-body*

If a constructor C(...) in subclass C does not explicitly call base(...) this way, then it implicitly calls the argumentless default constructor B() in base class B as its first action, as if by base(). In this case B must have a non-private argumentless constructor B(). Conversely, if there is no argumentless constructor B() in B, then a constructor C(...) in C must use base(...) to explicitly call another constructor in B.

A method declaration in C may *override* any non-sealed virtual method M inherited from B by declaring a method M with the exact same signature. An overridden B-method M can be referred to as base.M inside C's instance constructors and instance methods. The overriding method M in C:

- must be at least as accessible (section 10.3) as the overridden method in B;
- must have the same signature and return type as the overridden method in B.

However, the declaration of a class C cannot redeclare a field f inherited from B, only hide it and declare an additional field of the same name; see section 10.5. The hidden B-field can be referred to as base.f inside C's instance constructors and instance methods.

A declaration in C may *hide* members inherited from the base class B, as detailed below. Example 52 illustrates the difference between overriding and hiding for methods. The hiding member in C should have the modifier new; otherwise a compiler warning is given.

- The declaration of a method with signature M(*formal-list*) hides any inherited method with the same signature, and any inherited non-method member named M.

- The declaration of a field, property, event or type named M hides all inherited members named M, also methods.

- The declaration of an indexer this[*formal-list*] hides inherited indexers with the same signature.

**Example 44** Using the Vessel Hierarchy from Example 42

The call vs[i].Capacity() is legal because Capacity is declared in abstract class Vessel (example 42):

```
public static void Main(String[] args) {
  Vessel v1 = new Barrel(3, 10);
  Vessel v2 = new Tank(10, 20, 12);
  Vessel v3 = new Cube(4);
  Vessel[] vs = { v1, v2, v3 };
  v1.Fill(90); v1.Fill(10); v2.Fill(100); v3.Fill(80);
  double sum = 0;
  for (int i=0; i<vs.Length; i++)
    sum += vs[i].Capacity();
  Console.WriteLine("Total capacity is " + sum);
  sum = 0;
  for (int i=0; i<vs.Length; i++)
    sum += vs[i].Contents;
  Console.WriteLine("Total contents is " + sum);
  for (int i=0; i<vs.Length; i++)
    Console.WriteLine("vessel number " + i + ": " + vs[i]);
}
```

**Example 45** Accessing Base Class Constructor, Field, Methods, Property, and Indexer

Class C uses the base keyword to access instance members of its base class B: a constructor, a field, a property (section 10.13), an indexer (section 10.14), and non-virtual as well as virtual methods.

```
class B {
  public int f;
  public B(int f) { this.f = f; }
  public void M1()         { Console.Write("B.M1 "); }   // Non-virtual instance method
  public virtual void M2() { Console.Write("B.M2 "); }   // Virtual instance method
  public int FVal { get { return f; } }                  // Property
  public int this[int i] { get { return f+i; } }         // Indexer
}
class C : B {
  public new int f;
  public C(int f) : base(f/2) {
    this.f = f;
    Console.WriteLine("{0} {1} {2}", base.f, base.FVal, base[5]); // 11 11 16
    Console.WriteLine("{0} {1} {2}", f, FVal, this[5]);           // 22 22 27
  }
  public new void M1()     { base.M1(); Console.Write("C.M1 "); }
  public override void M2() { base.M2(); Console.Write("C.M2 "); }
  public new int FVal { get { return f; } }
  public new int this[int i] { get { return f+i; } }
}
...
C c = new C(22);
c.M1(); c.M2();                                         // B.M1 C.M1 B.M2 C.M2
```

## 10.5   Field Declarations in Classes

The purpose of a *field* is to hold a value inside an object (if non-static) or a class (if static). A field must be declared in a class declaration. A *field-declaration* has one of the forms:

> *field-modifiers type fieldname1, fieldname2, ... ;*
> *field-modifiers type fieldname1 = initializer1, ... ;*

The *field-modifiers* is a list of static, readonly, new and a member access modifier (section 10.3).

If a field f in class C is declared static, then f is associated with the class C and can be referred to independently of any objects of class C as C.f, or, in the declaration of C and C's subclasses, as f. If a field f in class C is not declared static, then f is an instance field associated with an object of class C, and every object has its own instance of the field. The field can be referred to as o.f where o is an expression of type C, or, in non-static code inside the declaration of C and C's subclasses, as f.

If a field f is declared readonly, then the field can be assigned only by its initializer expression and in constructors (possibly multiple times). It cannot be assigned elsewhere, nor be passed as an out or ref parameter. If f has reference type and points to an object or array, then that object's fields or that array's elements may still be modified. If f is a struct, then assignments to its fields f.x are allowed, but such assignments, and method calls f.M(), work on a temporary copy of f and have no effect on f.

A field *initializer* may be any expression, or an array initialization (section 9.1). No field initializer can refer to instance fields or to the current object reference this. A static field initializer can refer only to static members of C. Thus a field initializer is static code (section 10.1).

A field is given a *default initial value* depending on its type t. If t is a simple type, then the field is initialized to 0 (when t is in an integer type) or 0.0 (when t is float or double or decimal) or false (when t is bool) or a struct whose fields have their default initial values (when t is a struct type). If t is a reference type, the default initial value is null.

Static fields are initialized when the class is loaded. First all static fields are given their default initial values, then the static field initializers are executed, in order of appearance in the class declaration, and then the static constructor (section 10.10), if any, is executed.

Instance fields are initialized when an instance constructor is called, at which time all static fields have been initialized already; see section 10.9.

If a class C declares an instance field f, and C is a subclass of a class B that has an instance field f, then the declaration of f should have the new modifier. Every object of class C then has two fields both called f: one is the B-field f declared in the base class B, and one is the C-field f declared in C itself. What field is referred to by a field access o.f is determined by the type of o; see section 12.13.

## 10.6   Constant Declarations in Classes

A *constant* in a class is similar to a static readonly field, but its value is computed at compile-time:

> *const-modifier* const *type fieldname1 = initializer1, ... ;*

A constant is implicitly static. The *const-modifier* must be one of the member access modifiers (section 10.3). The *type* must be a simple type (section 5.1) or String or a reference type. The *initializer* expressions must be compile-time constant expressions; for reference types other than String the only possible value is null.

**Example 46** Field Declarations

The APoint class (example 41) declares a static field `allpoints` and two instance fields x and y.

Example 53 declares a static field ps of array type `double[]`. Its field initializer allocates a six-element array and binds it to ps, and then the static constructor (section 10.10) stores some numbers into the array.

The Barrel class in example 42 declares two instance fields `radius` and `height`. The fields are read-only, and therefore must be initialized in the constructor.

**Example 47** Multiple Fields with the Same Name

An object of class C below has two instance fields called nf: one declared in the base class B, and one declared in C itself. Similarly, an object of class D has three instance fields called nf. Class B and class C each have a static field called sf. Class D does not declare a static field sf, so in class D the name sf refers to the static field sf in the base class C. Examples 48 and 77 use these classes.

```
class B {                       // One instance field nf, one static field sf
  public int nf;
  public static int sf;
  public B(int i) { nf = i; sf = i+1; }
}
class C : B {                   // Two instance fields nf, one static field sf
  new public int nf;
  new public static int sf;
  public C(int i) : base(i+20) { nf = i; sf = i+2; }
}
class D : C {                   // Three instance fields nf
  new public int nf;
  public D(int i) : base(i+40) { nf = i; sf = i+4; }
}
```

**Example 48** Objects with Multiple Fields of the Same Name

This is the computer store at the end of the Main method in example 77, using the classes from example 47. The classes B and C each have a single static field sf; class D has none, but D.sf refers to sf in D's superclass C. The two objects of class C each have two instance fields nf (called B/nf and C/nf in the figure), and the class D object has three instance fields nf.

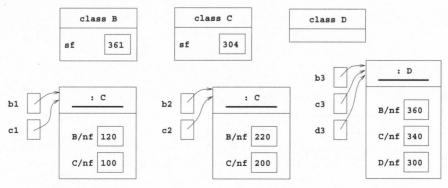

## 10.7   Method Declarations

A *method* must be declared inside a class (or struct, section 14). A *method-declaration* declaring method M has the form:

> *method-modifiers   returntype* M(*formal-list*)
>    *method-body*

The *formal-list* is a comma-separated list of zero or more *formal parameter declarations*, each of one of these forms:

> *parameter-modifier   type   parametername*
> params *type*[] *parametername*

The params form must appear last in a *formal-list* if at all; it can occur only once, and it cannot be used with the ref or out modifiers. A *parameter-modifier* may be out or ref or absent. A parameter that is neither an out parameter nor a ref parameter is a *by-value* parameter. The *type* is any type expression. The *parametername* is any name, but no two parameters in a *formal-list* can have the same name. The scope of a parameter is the *method-body*.

A by-value parameter is similar to a local variable, initialized with the value of a corresponding argument expression. An out parameter is similar to an uninitialized variable; and assignments to it immediately affects the corresponding argument variable. A ref parameter is similar to a variable initialized from the corresponding argument variable; and assignments to it immediately affects that argument variable. See section 12.15.2 for details on by-value, ref, and out parameter passing. Ref and out parameters can be used only with methods, constructors, delegates, and anonymous methods; not with properties, events, indexers, or operators.

The params modifier is used when declaring a method that can take a variable number of arguments. The formal params parameter in the method declaration must have array type; in a method call it gets bound to an array holding the values of zero or more arguments not bound to the preceding formal parameters. See also section 12.15.3. Parameter arrays cannot be used with anonymous methods.

The method name M together with the list $t_1, \ldots, t_n$ of declared parameter types in the *formal-list* determine the method *signature* $M(t_1, \ldots, t_n)$. The signature includes any ref and out modifiers, but not the params modifier (if any) and not the *returntype*.

A class may declare more than one method with the same name M, provided they have different signatures. This is called *overloading* of the method name. Overloaded methods may have different return types.

The *method-body* is a *block-statement* (section 13.2). In particular, the *method-body* may contain return statements. If the *returntype* is void, then the method does not return a value, and no return statement in the *method-body* can have an expression argument. If the *returntype* is not void, it must be a type and the method must return a value: it must not be possible for execution to reach the end of *method-body* without executing a return statement. Moreover, every return statement must have an expression argument whose type is implicitly convertible to the *returntype*.

The legal *method-modifiers* consist of a member access modifier as described in section 10.3 and a method kind modifier as described in section 10.8.

In a class whose *class-base-clause* includes interface I, the method name in a method declaration may be written I.M to explicitly state that it implements a method from interface I; in that case, there can be no *method-modifiers*. See section 15.3.

**Example 49** Method Name Overloading and Signatures
This class declares four overloaded methods M whose signatures are M(int) and M(bool) and M(int, double) and M(double, double). Some of the overloaded methods are static, others are instance methods. The overloaded methods may have different return types, as shown here. Example 82 explains the method calls.

It would be legal to declare an additional method with signature M(double, int), but then the method call M(10, 20) would become ambiguous and illegal. Namely, there is no best signature among M(double, double) and M(int, double) or M(double, int); see section 12.15.1.

```
public class Overloading {
  double M(int i) { return i; }
  bool M(bool b) { return !b; }
  static double M(int x, double y) { return x + y + 1; }
  static double M(double x, double y) { return x + y + 3; }

  public static void Main(String[] args) {
    Console.WriteLine(M(10, 20));          // Prints 31
    Console.WriteLine(M(10, 20.0));        // Prints 31
    Console.WriteLine(M(10.0, 20));        // Prints 33
    Console.WriteLine(M(10.0, 20.0));      // Prints 33
  }
}
```

**Example 50** Method Overriding
In the vessel hierarchy (example 42), the classes Tank and Barrel override the method ToString inherited from the universal base class Object, and class Cube overrides ToString inherited from class Tank.

**Example 51** Parameter Arrays and Overloading
This example declares three overloads of the Max method, including one with a parameter array (params). When the params-overload is called, the first argument will be bound to parameter x0 of Max, and all remaining arguments will be stored in a new array, bound to the parameter xr. Example 85 shows several calls to these methods. Example 132 demonstrates a parameter array in an indexer.

```
public static int Max(int a, double b) {
  return a > b ? a : (int) b;
}
public static int Max(int a, int b, int c) {
  a = a > b ? a : b;
  return a > c ? a : c;
}
public static int Max(int x0, params int[] xr) {
  foreach (int i in xr)
    if (i > x0)
      x0 = i;
  return x0;
}
```

## 10.8 Method Modifiers `static`, `new`, `virtual`, `override`, `sealed`, `abstract`

The *method-modifiers* are used in method declarations (section 10.7), property declarations (section 10.13), and indexer declarations (section 10.14). See also section 10.3 for member access modifiers. The following *method-modifiers* are legal (in classes `C`, structs `S`, or interfaces `I`):

| Method Modifier | Meaning for This Method | Allowable Base Class Method | In |
|---|---|---|---|
| `static` | static method | no method, or `private` | CS- |
| `new static` | static method; hide base | any method | CS- |
| (none) | non-virtual instance method | no method, or `private` | CS- |
| `new` | non-virtual instance method; hide | any method | CSI |
| `virtual` | virtual method | no method, or `private` | C-- |
| `override` | virtual; override base | `virtual`/`override`/`abstract` | CS- |
| `sealed override` | virtual; prevent further overriding | `virtual` or `abstract` | C-- |
| `new virtual` | virtual; hide base | any method | C-- |
| `abstract` | virtual and abstract: no body | no method, or `private` | C-- |
| `abstract override` | virtual and abstract; override base | `virtual` or `abstract` | C-- |
| `new abstract` | virtual and abstract; hide base | any method | C-- |

When a method's accessibility (section 10.3) is not explicitly specified, it defaults to `private`, which is not permitted for methods that are `abstract`, `virtual` or `override`. There are several kinds of methods:

- A *static method* is a method `M` (in a class or struct type `C`) that is declared `static`. Then `M` is associated with the *class* itself; it can be called without any object of class `C`. The method may be called as `C.M(...)` or, inside methods, constructors, field initializers, initializer blocks and nested classes and structs in `C`, simply as `M(...)`. A static method cannot use the current object reference `this` and can refer only to static members of the enclosing class.

- An *instance method* is a method `M` (in a class or struct type `C`) that is not declared `static`. Then every call to `M` is associated with an instance of class `C` or a subclass. Outside the class, the method must be called as `o.M(...)` where `o` is an object of class `C` or a subclass, or, inside instance methods and constructors `C`, simply as `M(...)` which has the same meaning as `this.M(...)`. An instance method can refer to all members of class `C`, static or not. There are two kinds of instance methods:

  - A *non-virtual instance method* is one not declared `virtual` or `override`. In a call `o.M(...)` to such a method, only the compile-time type of `o` determines which method is called; see section 12.15.5.

  - A *virtual instance method* is one declared `virtual` or `override`. In a call `o.M(...)` to such a method, the compile-time type of `o` and the run-time class of the object `o` together determine which method is called; see section 12.15.5. Only class types can have virtual instance methods; struct types (section 14) cannot. A `sealed` method cannot be overridden in subclasses. The combination `sealed virtual` is illegal; that would just mean non-virtual.

- A *abstract method* is a method `M` (in a class `C`) declared `abstract`. Then class `C` must be abstract too, and so cannot be instantiated. The declaration of an abstract method has no method body:

  `abstract` *method-modifiers returntype* `M`(*formal-list*)`;`

**Example 52** Method Inheritance, Hiding and Overriding

The abstract class A declares static method M1, non-virtual instance method M2, virtual method M3, and abstract virtual method M4. Class B overrides M4 and inherits the other ones. Class C hides the static M1 by a new static method M1 and hides non-virtual M2 by a new non-virtual M2, and overrides the virtual M3. Abstract class D hides non-virtual method M2 and virtual method M3 and overrides M3 by an abstract method. Class E overrides M2 and M4 with virtual methods. Calls to these methods are shown in example 87.

```
abstract class A {
  public static void M1() { Console.Write("A.M1 "); }
  public void M2() { Console.Write("A.M2 "); }
  public virtual void M3() { Console.Write("A.M3 "); }
  public abstract void M4();
}
class B : A { public override void M4() { Console.Write("B.M4 "); } }
class C : B {
  public new static void M1() { Console.Write("C.M1 "); }
  public new void M2() { Console.Write("C.M2 "); }
  public override void M3() { Console.Write("C.M3 "); }
}
abstract class D : C {
  public new abstract void M2();
  public new virtual void M3() { Console.Write("D.M3 "); }
  public abstract override void M4();
}
class E : D {
  public sealed override void M2() { Console.Write("E.M2 "); }
  public override void M3() { Console.Write("E.M3 "); }
  public override void M4() { Console.Write("E.M4 "); }
}
```

**Example 53** Static Field Initializers and the Static Constructor

The initializer of static field ps creates an array and binds it to ps. The static constructor (section 10.10) fills the array with an increasing sequence of pseudo-random numbers, then scales them so the last number is 1.0. This is useful for generating a random loaded die, and cannot be done using a static field initializer.

```
class InitializerExample {
  static double[] ps = new double[6];
  static readonly Random rnd = new Random();
  static InitializerExample() {        // Static constructor
    double sum = 0;
    for (int i=0; i<ps.Length; i++)    // Fill with increasing random numbers
      ps[i] = sum += rnd.NextDouble(); // Random number 0 <= x < 1
    for (int i=0; i<ps.Length; i++)    // Scale so last ps element is 1.0
      ps[i] /= sum;
  }
  ...
}
```

## 10.9   Constructor Declarations

The purpose of an instance constructor in class C is to initialize a new object (instance) of the class. A *constructor-declaration* in class C has the form:

> *constructor-modifier* C(*formal-list*)
>     *constructor-body*

The *constructor-modifier* is one of the member access modifiers (section 10.3), and the *formal-list* is as for a method (section 10.7). A constructor cannot be abstract or sealed. For the static constructor, see section 10.10. A constructor has no return type.

Instance constructors may be overloaded in the same way as methods: the *constructor signature* (a list of the parameter types in *formal-list*) is used to distinguish instance constructors in the same class. A constructor may call another overloaded constructor in the same class using the syntax:

> *constructor-modifier* C(*formal-list*) : this(*actual-list*)
>     *constructor-body*

but a constructor may not call itself, directly or indirectly. The argument expressions in *actual-list* are static code and so cannot use the current object reference this or any instance member of class C, but can use the parameters from *formal-list*.

The *constructor-body* is a *block-statement* (section 13.2) and so may contain statements as well as declarations of variables. The *constructor-body* may contain return statements, but no return statement can take an expression argument.

A class which does not explicitly declare a constructor, instead implicitly declares a public, argument-less *default constructor* whose only action is to call the base class constructor (section 10.4):

```
public C() : base() { }
```

When new creates a new object in the computer store (section 12.9), a constructor is called to initialize the fields of the object. First the initializers of the object's instance fields are executed once, in order of appearance in the class declaration. Then either another constructor this(...) in the same class or a base class constructor base(...) is called (explicitly or implicitly, see examples 55 and 88). Finally, the body of the constructor itself is executed. See example 56.

The call to a base class constructor will cause a call to a constructor in its base class, and execution of its instance field initializers, and so on, until reaching the constructor Object().

## 10.10   Static Field Initialization and the Static Constructor

A static field of an object or struct may be initialized by a static field initializer (section 10.5) or by a parameterless *static constructor*, declared as follows:

```
static C()
    block-statement
```

See example 53. All static field initializers are executed, in order of appearance in the class declaration, when the class is loaded. Then the body of the static constructor (if any) is executed. If the execution of a static field initializer or a static constructor throws an exception (section 19), then a TypeInitializationException is thrown instead, and the class is not loaded.

**Example 54** Constructor Overloading; Calling Another Constructor
We add a new constructor to the Point class (example 40), thus overloading its constructors. The old constructor has signature `Point(int, int)` and the new one `Point(Point)`. The new constructor makes a copy of the point p by calling the old constructor using the syntax : `this(p.x, p.y)`.

```
public class Point {
  protected internal int x, y;

  public Point(int x, int y)            // overloaded constructor
  { this.x = x; this.y = y; }

  public Point(Point p)                 // overloaded constructor
    : this(p.x, p.y) {}                 // calls the first constructor

  public void Move(int dx, int dy)
  { x += dx; y += dy; }

  public override String ToString()
  { return "(" + x + ", " + y + ")"; }
}
```

**Example 55** Calling a Baseclass Constructor
The constructor in the ColoredPoint subclass (example 130) calls its baseclass constructor using the syntax : `base(x, y)` in the header of the constructor declaration.

**Example 56** The Execution Order of Field Initializers and Constructor Bodies
Evaluating `new C()` will execute the instance field initializers in class C, execute the instance field initializers in base class B, execute the body of the `B()` constructor, execute the body of the `C(int)` constructor, and finally execute the body of the `C()` constructor. That is, it will print 1 2 3 4 5 6 7.

```
class B {
  public readonly int fb1 = Print(3);
  public B(int k) { Print(5); }
  public readonly int fb2 = Print(4);
  public static int Print(int i) { Console.Write(i + " "); return i; }
}

class C : B {
  public readonly int fc1 = Print(1);
  public C() : this(0) { Print(7); }
  public C(int k) : base(k) { Print(6); }
  public readonly int fc2 = Print(2);
}
```

## 10.11   Member Classes or Nested Classes

A nested class is a class declared inside another class or struct type declaration. The code of a nested class may refer to all static members, even private ones, of the enclosing class or struct type, but cannot refer to its instance members except through a reference to an instance of the enclosing class or struct type. In contrast to Java, C# has no notion of an *inner class*, whose instances would contain a reference to an instance of the enclosing class.

A member name used in a nested class C denotes a member from the innermost enclosing class that declares or inherits a member of that name. That is, if class C has base class B and is declared as a nested class in E, then name resolution in C prefers members declared in C or (non-private) members inherited from base class B over members of the enclosing class E; see example 80.

A nested class may have static members as well as instance members.

## 10.12   Class Access Modifiers

The *class-modifiers* (section 10.1) may include an access modifier to control the accessibility of the class.

For a class declared at top-level in a compilation unit or at top-level inside a namespace (section 25), the access modifier may be `public` or `internal` or absent (which means `internal`). A `public` top-level class is accessible in all assemblies; an `internal` top-level class is accessible only in the assembly (section 1.1) to which it belongs.

For a class declared inside a class or struct type, the access modifier may be one of the member access modifiers; see section 10.3.

**Example 57** An Enumerator As a Member Class

The member class SeqEnumerator, declared inside struct Seq from example 61, supports enumeration of the elements of a sequence using a `foreach` statement (section 13.6.2). The SeqEnumerator class must have a property `Current` to get the current sequence element and a method `MoveNext` to move to the next one. If it has also a method `Reset`, then it can implement interface IEnumerator (section 24.2), but this is not required for use in the `foreach` statement. In C# 2.0 an enumerator can be implemented more conveniently using the `yield` statement; see section 13.12 and example 123.

```
private class SeqEnumerator : IEnumerator {    // Static member class
  private readonly Seq seq;
  private int i;
  public SeqEnumerator(Seq seq) { this.seq = seq; Reset(); }
  public Object Current {
    get {
      if (0 <= i && i < seq.n)
        return seq.b + seq.k * i;
      else
        throw new InvalidOperationException();
    }
  }
  public bool MoveNext() {
    i++;
    return i < seq.n;
  }
  public void Reset() { i = -1; }
}
```

**Example 58** Nested Classes Can Access All Static Members of Enclosing Class

The nested class C.D can access all static members of the enclosing class C, even private ones, as well as non-private static members of the base class B of the enclosing class. The enclosing class C cannot access the private members of a nested class C.D.

```
class B {
  protected static int bx = 10;
  private static int bz = 10;
}
class C : B {
  private static int cx = 11;
  public class D {
    private static int dx = bx + cx;  // Can access protected bx and private cx
    // public static int dz = bz + 2; // Cannot access private bz in base class
  }
  static void m() {
    // int z = D.dx;                   // Cannot access private dx in nested class
  }
}
```

## 10.13  Property Declarations

A *property* is used to get or set a value, using notations `C.P` and `o.P` and `C.P=e` and `o.P=e` similar to those for accessing or assigning a static or instance field; see section 12.16. Properties typically provide controlled access to private fields. A property may be *read-only* or *write-only* or *read-write*, according as it defines only a get-accessor or only a set-accessor or both. A declaration of the property `P` has the form

```
method-modifiers t P {
   get get-body
   set set-body
}
```

The get-accessor or set-accessor, but not both, may be left out. The type `t` cannot be `void`. The *method-modifiers* are as in section 10.7. A *get-body* is a *block-statement* which must return a value of type `t`. A *set-body* is a *block-statement* that cannot return a value. It is executed when an assignment `P=e` is performed, and can use the variable `value` of type `t` which initially holds the value of `e`.

The get-accessor of a property `P` of type `t` is a method `t get_P()`, the set-accessor is a method `void set_P(t value)`, and the accessors follow the restrictions imposed on such methods. For instance, the *get-body* and *set-body* of an `abstract` property must consist of a semicolon (`;`) only. A class can declare any number of properties with different names. Properties cannot be overloaded.

A get- or set-accessor can contain arbitrary code, but should have no unexpected side-effects and should be fast; otherwise the resemblance of a property to a variable could lead to (performance) bugs.

## 10.14  Indexer Declarations

An indexer is used to get or set a value, using notations `C[i]` and `o[i]` and `C[i]=e` and `o[i]=e` similar to those for accessing or assigning an array element; see section 12.17. Indexers typically provide controlled access to elements of collections. An indexer may be *read-only* or *write-only* or *read-write*, according as it defines a get-accessor or a set-accessor or both. A declaration of an indexer has the form

```
indexer-modifiers t this[formal-list] {
   get get-body
   set set-body
}
```

The get-accessor or set-accessor, but not both, may be left out. The *indexer-modifiers* is a list of the modifiers `abstract`, `extern`, a legal combination of `new`, `override`, `sealed` and `virtual` (section 10.8), and a legal combination of access modifiers (section 10.3). An indexer cannot be static. The type `t` cannot be `void`. The *formal-list* is as for a method, but the list must be non-empty and cannot include `ref` or `out` parameters. A *get-body* is a *block-statement* which must return a value of type `t`; it can use the parameters in the *formal-list*. A *set-body* is a *block-statement* that cannot return a value. It can use the parameters in the *formal-list*, and the variable `value` of type `t` which initially holds the value of the right-hand side of an assignment to the indexer.

The get- and set-accessors of an indexer `this[formal-list]` of type `t` are methods `t get_Item(formal-list)` and `void set_Item(t value, formal-list)`. A get- or set-accessor can execute arbitrary code, but should have no unexpected side-effects and should be fast, as for properties.

Indexers can be overloaded, and different indexers may have different return types; see example 132.

**Example 59** Property Used to Access a Log

Class Log implements a simple log that stores the last SIZE strings written to it. The static property InstanceCount is the number of Log objects created. Property Count is the number of log entries written to this log. Property Last is the latest string logged to this log, if any. It has set- as well as get-accessors, so one can use assignment operators such as log.Last += "...". Property All returns an array of the last (up to) five strings logged. Example 89 uses these properties.

```
public class Log {
  private static int instanceCount = 0;
  private int count = 0;
  private String[] log = new String[SIZE];
  public Log() { instanceCount++; }
  public static int InstanceCount { get { return instanceCount; } }
  public void Add(String msg) { log[count++ % SIZE] = msg; }
  public int Count { get { return count; } }
  public String Last {
    get { // Return the last log entry, or null if nothing logged yet
      return count==0 ? null : log[(count-1)%SIZE];
    }
    set { // Update the last log entry, or create one if nothing logged yet
      if (count==0)
        log[count++] = value;
      else
        log[(count-1)%SIZE] = value;
    }
  }
  public String[] All { ... }
}
```

**Example 60** Sparse Matrix Indexing

A sparse matrix is a matrix that has many zeroes. A sparse matrix may be represented as an array of columns, where each column is a list of only the non-zero elements. Using a two-argument indexer, one can get and set its elements as A[i,j], as if it were an ordinary rectangular array. However, the indexer performs a linear search of column j for the element with index i, so element access is not constant time.

```
public double this[int i, int j] {
  get {
    NonZeroList colj = this[j];
    int k = 0;
    while (k < colj.Count && colj[k].i < i)
      k++;
    return k < colj.Count && colj[k].i == i ? colj[k].Mij : 0.0;
  }
  set {
    ...
  }
}
```

## 10.15 Operator Overloading

Some of the operators listed on page 57 can be overloaded in a user-defined type (class or struct) t. No new operator symbols can be defined, and the precedence of existing operators cannot be changed. An operator declaration must have one of these forms, according as the operator is binary or unary:

```
public static returntype operator operator-symbol(formal, formal)
    method-body
```

```
public static returntype operator operator-symbol(formal)
    method-body
```

The *returntype* cannot be void. The *operator-symbol* is an overloadable operator; see below. The *formal* parameters are as for a method declaration (section 10.7) but cannot be ref or out. The *method-body* is as in section 10.7. A class inherits the operator declarations of its base class. A class or struct cannot contain two operator declarations with the same signature. An operator declaration must follow these rules:

- When overloading a binary operator + - * / % & | ^ == != > < >= <= in type t, at least one argument must have type t. When overloading a shift operator << or >> the first argument must have type t and the second argument must have type int.

- When overloading a unary operator in type t, the permitted argument types and result types are:

| Operators | Argument Type | Result Type |
|---|---|---|
| + - ! ~ | t | any |
| ++ -- | t | t |
| true false | t | bool |

- There can be only one definition of the unary increment (++) and decrement (--) operators in a type. The same definition is used for prefix (++x) as well as postfix (x++) applications.

- Some operators go together in pairs; either none of them or both of them must be overloaded:

| Operator | Operator | Comment |
|---|---|---|
| true | false | |
| == | != | Methods Equals and GetHashCode must be overridden also |
| < | > | |
| <= | >= | |

- When a binary operator (say, +) is overloaded, then the corresponding compound assignment operator (+=) is automatically overloaded also (see example 128).

- An assignment operator (=, +=, and so on) cannot be overloaded separately, only as a consequence of overloading a binary operator. Nor can the operators &&, ||, ?? and ?: be overloaded.

- When any of the operators & or | is overloaded, then operators true and false must be overloaded also, and the corresponding sequential conditional && or || is automatically overloaded also.

Operator overloading is illustrated by examples 61, 128 and 166.

**Example 61** Operator Overloading

A Seq is a sequence of integers. For instance Seq(1,3) is the sequence 1  2  3. The operator (*) is overloaded so that k*seq is a sequence obtained by multiplying each element of seq by k, and the operator (+) is overloaded so that b+seq is a sequence obtained by adding b to each element of seq, when k and b have type int. The unary operator (!) creates a sequence that is the reverse of the given one.

Note how method ToString uses a foreach statement (section 13.6.2) to traverse a sequence. This is possible because Seq has a GetEnumerator method that returns an IEnumerator object (see example 57).

```
struct Seq : ISeq {
  private readonly int b, k, n;                      // Sequence b+k*[0..n-1]
  public Seq(int m, int n) : this(m, 1, n-m+1) { }   // Sequence [m..n]
  public Seq(int b, int k, int n) {
    this.b = b; this.k = k; this.n = n;
  }
  public static Seq operator +(int b, Seq seq) {
    return new Seq(seq.b+b, seq.k, seq.n);
  }
  public static Seq operator +(Seq seq, int b) {
    return new Seq(seq.b+b, seq.k, seq.n);
  }
  public static Seq operator *(int k, Seq seq) {
    return new Seq(seq.b*k, seq.k*k, seq.n);
  }
  public static Seq operator *(Seq seq, int k) {
    return new Seq(seq.b*k, seq.k*k, seq.n);
  }
  public static Seq operator !(Seq seq) {
    return new Seq(seq.b+(seq.n-1)*seq.k, -seq.k, seq.n);
  }
  public static bool operator ==(Seq s1, Seq s2) {
    return s1.n==s2.n && (s1.n==0 || s1.b==s2.b && (s1.n==1 || s1.k==s2.k));
  }
  public static bool operator !=(Seq s1, Seq s2) { return !(s1==s2); }
  public IEnumerator GetEnumerator() { return new SeqEnumerator(this); }
  private class SeqEnumerator : IEnumerator { ... }
  public override String ToString() {
    StringBuilder sb = new StringBuilder();
    foreach (int i in this)
      sb.Append(i).Append(" ");
    return sb.ToString();
  }
} }
...
Seq s1 = new Seq(1, 3);       // 1 2 3
Seq s2 = 2 * s1 + 5;          // 7 9 11
Seq s3 = s2 * 3;              // 21 27 33
Seq s4 = !s3;                 // 33 27 21
Console.WriteLine(s1==s2);    // False
Console.WriteLine(s3==!s4);   // True
```

## 10.16   User-Defined Conversion Operators

A class or struct may declare conversions to and from that class or struct. A user-defined conversion from type ts to type tt may be implicit or explicit; the declaration must have one of these forms:

```
public static implicit operator tt(ts x)
    method-body
public static explicit operator tt(ts x)
    method-body
```

The types ts and tt are the source and target types of the conversion. At least one of them must be the type of the enclosing class or struct; neither can be the class Object, nor an interface; and neither can be a base class of the other one. A class or struct cannot define both an implicit and an explicit conversion from type ts to tt.

The *method-body* must satisfy the same requirements as a method that has a single by-value parameter x of type ts and whose return type is tt; in particular all normally terminating execution paths should execute a return *expression* where *expression* is implicitly convertible to type tt. Although not enforced by the compiler, a user-defined conversion should have no unexpected side effects, and an implicit conversion should always terminate succesfully, whereas an explicit conversion may throw an exception.

User-defined implicit conversions are used in assignments, by-value parameter passing, and cast expressions, but not in instance tests (section 12.11).

User-defined implicit conversions can be subtle: The declaration of an implicit conversion may be accepted by the compiler but cause stack overflow at run-time, if the body of the conversion somehow uses the implicit conversion itself.

See example 62 opposite and example 128.

## 10.17   Events

An *event* E is a field holding related handlers, where a handler is a delegate; see section 17. An event is similar to a field of delegate type that can be invoked only from inside the declaring class, although new handlers can be added and removed from the outside also. A declaration of event E has one of two forms:

> *method-modifiers* event *delegate-type* E;
> *method-modifiers* event *delegate-type* E { add *add-body*   remove *remove-body* }

where the add and remove clauses must either both be absent (as in the first form) or both be present (as in the second form). The *delegate-type* is the type of event handlers associated with event E; it must be a delegate type. The *method-modifiers* are as for methods; the abstract modifier cannot be used with the second form. Outside the class declaring an event, it can be used only on the left-hand side of the operators += and -=, which have result type void. In particular, access to the event does not provide access to the individual handlers for the event.

In the first form of event declaration, the event E is just a field of delegate type (holding the event's handlers); the usual delegate operations (section 17) can be used on E inside the class or struct declaring it; and the operations += and -= are implemented as the corresponding delegate operations on E.

In the second form of event declaration, the operations += and -= are implemented as calls to the *add-body* and *remove-body*. These behave as methods with return type void and a single by-value parameter called value whose type is *delegate-type*, and they must satisfy the same requirements as such methods.

**Example 62** User-Defined Conversions

An implicit conversion of (byte)5 to Frac first makes a standard implicit conversion from byte to int and then an implicit conversion to Frac. An explicit conversion from Frac f2 to double first makes an explicit (possibly lossy) conversion from Frac to float and then a standard implicit conversion to double.

```
struct Frac : IComparable {
  public readonly long n, d;
  public Frac(long n, long d) { ... }
  public static implicit operator Frac(int n) { return new Frac(n, 1); }
  public static implicit operator Frac(long n) { return new Frac(n, 1); }
  public static explicit operator long(Frac r) { return r.n/r.d; }
  public static explicit operator float(Frac r) { return ((float)r.n)/r.d; }
}
...
Frac f1 = (byte)5;                        // Implicit int-->Frac
Frac f2 = 1234567890123L;                 // Implicit long-->Frac
int i1 = (int)f1;                         // Explicit Frac-->long
double d2 = (double)f2;                   // Explicit Frac-->float
```

**Example 63** Thermometer Readings As Events

A thermometer makes (simulated) temperature readings from time to time. Clients can add handlers (of type Handler) to the thermometer's Reading event; when a new (simulated) temperature reading is made, the thermometer calls these handlers. Only the thermometer can call the event's handlers.

```
delegate void Handler(double temperature);
class Thermometer {
  public event Handler Reading;
  private int temperature = 80;
  private static Random rnd = new Random();
  public Thermometer() { new Thread(new ThreadStart(Run)).Start(); }
  private void Run() {
    for (;;) {                              // Forever simulate new readings
      temperature += rnd.Next(-5, 6);       // Random number in range -5..5
      if (Reading != null)                  // If there are any handlers,
        Reading(temperature);               // call them with the new reading
      Thread.Sleep(rnd.Next(2000));
    }
  }
}
class MyTest {
  public static void Main(String[] args) {
    Thermometer t = new Thermometer();
    t.Reading += new Handler(PrintReading);
    t.Reading += new Handler(CountReading);
  }
  public static void PrintReading(double temperature) { ... }
  public static void CountReading(double temperature) { ... }
}
```

# 11   The Machine Model: Stack, Heap, and Garbage Collection

The machine model describes how data are stored and manipulated at run-time, during the execution of a C# program. It has two main components:

- The *stack*, which is divided into *frames*. A frame has room for the local variables and parameters of one invocation of a method. A new frame is created when the method is called, and thrown away when the method returns. Thus at any point in time, the frames on the stack correspond to those methods that have been called but have not yet returned.

- The *heap* stores objects, arrays and delegates created by the evaluation of new-expressions. These data are automatically removed from the heap by a *garbage collector* when they are no longer needed by the program. Then the space can be reused for other data. There is no way to explicitly remove anything from the heap, not even by calling a so-called destructor (which is not the same as in C++).

In fact, there is a separate stack for each thread (section 20), but only one heap shared among all threads. The various values used in C# are stored as follows:

- All objects, arrays and delegates are stored in the heap. If an array has element type t which is a simple type, then each array element directly contains its value; if t is a reference type, then each array element contains either null or a reference to an object, array or delegate stored elsewhere in the heap; if t is a struct type, then each array element directly contains the struct value, that is, has room for its instance fields.

- Local variables and parameters are stored on the stack. A local variable of simple type directly contains its value. A local variable of reference type contains null or a reference to an object or array or delegate stored in the heap. A local variable of struct type directly contains the struct, that is, has room for its instance fields.

## 11.1   Class and Object versus Struct Type and Struct Value

At run-time, a class is represented by a chunk of storage, set aside when the class is loaded. The representation of a class contains the name of the class and all the static fields of the class; see the illustration in example 48. At run-time, an object (instance of a class) is allocated in the heap and has two parts: an identification of the *class* C of the object, which is the class C used when creating it; and room for all the instance fields of the object. The class identification is used when evaluating instance test expressions (section 12.11), cast expressions (section 12.18), and array element assignments (section 9.1).

At run-time, a struct type is represented very much like a class: the representation of a struct type contains the name of the struct and all the static fields of the struct type. At run-time a struct value (instance of a struct type) is allocated on the stack or as part of an array or object in the heap. Like an object the struct value has room for the instance fields of the struct, but unlike an object it contains no indication of the struct type.

**Example 64** Stack, Heap, Objects, Arrays, Structs, and Assignment

The assignment p = q of a variable of reference type (class Point, example 40) copies only the reference. Afterwards p and q point to the same object, so the assignment to p.x affects q.x also. Likewise for the array assignment arr2 = arr1. By contrast, an assignment r = s of a variable of struct type (SPoint, example 125) copies the entire struct from s to r; hence the later assignment to r.x does not affect s.x.

When a method M2 calls itself recursively, the stack contains a separate copy of local variables and parameters (here just i) for each unfinished call of the method:

```
public static void M1() {
  Point p = new Point(11, 111), q = new Point(22, 222);
  p = q;
  p.x = 33;
  SPoint r = new SPoint(44, 444), s = new SPoint(55, 555);
  r = s;
  r.x = 66;
  int[] iarr1 = new int[4];
  int[] iarr2 = iarr1;
  iarr1[0] = 77;
  SPoint[] sarr = new SPoint[3];
  sarr[0].x = 88;
  M2(2);
}
public static void M2(int i) {
  if (i > 0)
    M2(i-1);
}
```

After executing the body of M1 and three calls of M2, just before M2(0) returns, the stack contains three frames for M2. The left-most Point object in the heap is not referred to by a variable any longer and will be removed by the garbage collector:

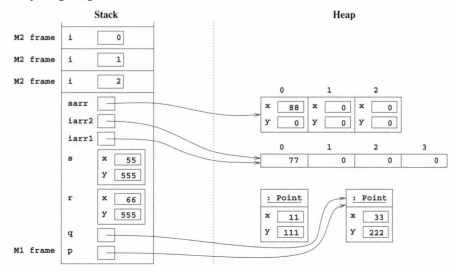

# 12   Expressions

An expression is evaluated to obtain a value such as 117 or true. In addition, evaluation of an expression may change the computer's *state*: the values of variables, fields and array elements, the contents of files, and so on. More precisely, evaluation of an expression either:

- terminates normally, producing a value, or
- terminates abruptly by throwing an exception, or
- does not terminate at all (for instance, because it calls a method that does not terminate).

Expressions are built from anonymous constants (literals), variables, fields, operators, method calls, array accesses, conditional expressions, the new operator, and so on; see the table opposite.

One should distinguish the *compile-time type of an expression* from the *run-time type of its value*. An expression has a compile-time type inferred by the compiler. When this is a reference type t, and the run-time value of the expression is an object o, then the run-time type of o is a class that is implicitly convertible to t, but not necessarily equal to t. For instance, the expression (Object)"foo" has compile-time type Object, but its run-time value is an object of class String, a subclass of Object.

## 12.1   Table of Expression Forms and Predefined Operators

The table opposite shows the form, meaning, associativity, argument (operand) types and result types for expressions. The expressions are grouped according to precedence as indicated by the horizontal lines, from high precedence (top) to low precedence (bottom). Higher-precedence forms are evaluated before lower precedence forms. Left-hand argument expressions are evaluated before right-hand argument expressions. Parentheses may be used to emphasize or force a particular order of evaluation of operators.

When an operator such as (+) is left associative, then a sequence e1 + e2 + e3 of operators is evaluated as if parenthesized (e1 + e2) + e3. When an operator such as (=) is right associative, then a sequence e1 = e2 = e3 of operators is evaluated as if parenthesized e1 = (e2 = e3).

In the argument type and result type columns of the table, the kind integer stands for any of char, sbyte, byte, short, ushort, int, uint, ulong or long; and numeric stands for integer or float or double or decimal.

Before the operation is performed, its operands are promoted, that is, converted to the *promotion type* described below, by an implicit conversion (section 5.3.1).

For the unary operators  + - ~  the promotion type is int if the type of the operand is char, sbyte, byte, short or ushort; and for the operator  -  the promotion type is long if the type of the operand is uint. Otherwise the promotion type of the operand is the type of the operand.

For an operator with two numeric operands (except the shift operators, section 12.5, and enum operands, section 16), the promotion type is decimal if any operand has type decimal (the other cannot be double or float); otherwise, it is double if any operand has type double; otherwise, it is float if any operand has type float; otherwise, it is ulong if any operand has type ulong (the other operator cannot have a signed type); otherwise, it is long if any operand has type long, or if one operand has type uint and the other has a signed type; otherwise it is uint if any operand has type uint; otherwise it is int.

If the result type is given as numeric also, it equals the promotion type. For example, 10 / 3 has type int, whereas 10 / 3.0 has type double, and c + (byte)1 has type int when c has type char.

| Expression | Meaning | Section | Assoc'ty | Argument(s) | Result type |
|---|---|---|---|---|---|
| `a[...]` | array access | 9 | | `t[]`, integer | `t` |
| `o[...]` | indexer access | 12.17 | | object | `t` |
| `o.f` | field or property access | 12.13, 12.16 | | object | type of `f` |
| `C.f` | static field or property | 12.13, 12.16 | | class/struct | type of `f` |
| `o.M(...)` | method call | 12.15 | | object | return type of `M` |
| `C.M(...)` | static method call | 12.15 | | class/struct | return type of `M` |
| `new t[...]` | create array | 9 | | type | `t[]` |
| `new t(...)` | create object/struct/delegate | 12.9, 17 | | class/struct/delegate | `t` |
| `default(t)` | default value for type `t` | 6.2 | | type | `t` |
| `typeof(t)` | type determination | 12.19 | | type/void | Type |
| `checked(e)` | overflow checking | 12.3 | | integer | integer |
| `unchecked(e)` | no overflow checking | 12.3 | | integer | integer |
| `delegate ...` | anonymous method | 12.20 | | | delegate |
| `x++` | postincrement | 12.2 | | numeric | numeric |
| `x--` | postdecrement | 12.2 | | numeric | numeric |
| `++x` | preincrement | 12.2 | | numeric | numeric |
| `--x` | predecrement | 12.2 | | numeric | numeric |
| `-x` | negation (minus sign) | 12.2 | right | numeric | int/long |
| `~e` | bitwise complement | 12.5 | right | integer | `(u)int/(u)long` |
| `!e` | logical negation | 12.4 | right | bool | bool |
| `(t)e` | type cast | 12.18 | | type, any | `t` |
| `e1 * e2` | multiplication | 12.2 | left | numeric, numeric | numeric |
| `e1 / e2` | division | 12.2 | left | numeric, numeric | numeric |
| `e1 % e2` | remainder | 12.2 | left | numeric, numeric | numeric |
| `e1 + e2` | addition | 12.2 | left | numeric, numeric | numeric |
| `e1 + e2` | string concatenation | 7 | left | String, any | String |
| `e1 + e2` | string concatenation | 7 | left | any, String | String |
| `e1 + e2` | delegate combination | 17 | left | delegate, delegate | delegate |
| `e1 - e2` | subtraction | 12.2 | left | numeric | numeric |
| `e1 - e2` | delegate removal | 17 | left | delegates | delegate |
| `e1 << e2` | left shift | 12.5 | left | integer, int | `(u)int/(u)long` |
| `e1 >> e2` | right shift | 12.5 | left | integer, int | `(u)int/(u)long` |
| `e1 < e2` | less than | 12.6 | | numeric | bool |
| `e1 <= e2` | less than or equal to | 12.6 | | numeric | bool |
| `e1 >= e2` | greater than or equal to | 12.6 | | numeric | bool |
| `e1 > e2` | greater than | 12.6 | | numeric | bool |
| `e is t` | instance test | 12.11 | | any, type | bool |
| `e as t` | instance test and cast | 12.12 | | any, type | `t` |
| `e1 == e2` | equal | 12.6 | left | compatible | bool |
| `e1 != e2` | not equal | 12.6 | left | compatible | bool |
| `e1 & e2` | bitwise and | 12.5 | left | integer, integer | `(u)int/(u)long` |
| `e1 & e2` | logical strict and | 12.4 | left | bool, bool | bool |
| `e1 ^ e2` | bitwise exclusive-or | 12.5 | left | integer, integer | `(u)int/(u)long` |
| `e1 ^ e2` | logical strict exclusive-or | 12.4 | left | bool, bool | bool |
| `e1 | e2` | bitwise or | 12.5 | left | integer | `(u)int/(u)long` |
| `e1 | e2` | logical strict or | 12.4 | left | bool | bool |
| `e1 && e2` | logical and | 12.4 | left | bool | bool |
| `e1 || e2` | logical or | 12.4 | left | bool | bool |
| `e1 ?? e2` | null-coalescing | 18 | right | nullable/reftype, any | any |
| `e1 ? e2 : e3` | conditional | 12.8 | right | bool, any, any | any |
| `x = e` | assignment | 12.7 | right | e impl. conv. to x | type of `x` |
| `x += e` | compound assignment | 12.7 | right | compatible | type of `x` |
| `x += e` | event assignment | 10.17 | right | event, delegate | void |
| `x -= e` | event assignment | 10.17 | right | event, delegate | void |

## 12.2    Arithmetic Operators

The value of the postincrement expression x++ is that of x, and its effect is to increment x by one; and similarly for postdecrement x--. The value of the preincrement expression ++x is that of x+1, and its effect is to increment x by one; and similarly for predecrement.

Integer division e1/e2 truncates, that is, rounds towards 0, so 10/3 is 3, and (-10)/3 is −3. The integer remainder x%y equals x-(x/y)*y when y is non-zero; it has the same sign as x. Integer and decimal division or remainder by zero throws DivideByZeroException. Integer overflow does not throw an exception (unless in a checked context; see section 12.3) but wraps around. That is, the result is truncated by discarding any higher order bits that do not fit in the type. Overflow in expressions of type decimal always throws OverflowException.

The floating-point remainder x%y equals x-((int)(x/y))*y. Floating-point division by zero and floating-point overflow never throw exceptions, but produce special IEEE754 values (of type float or double) such as Infinity or NaN, that is, "not a number".

## 12.3    The checked and unchecked Operators

In a *checked context*, run-time integer overflow will not wrap around but throw an OverflowException, and compile-time overflow will produce a compile-time error. In an *unchecked context*, both compile-time and run-time integer overflow will wrap around, not throw any exception nor be a compile-time error.

The default context for run-time integer arithmetic operations is *unchecked* (overflow wraps around), and the default context for compile-time constant operations is *checked* (overflow produces a compile-time error).

The overflow checking context for integer arithmetic operations is explicitly set using the checked or unchecked operators. Only the following operations are affected by the checked and unchecked operators:  ++ -- + - * /  on integer types and explicit conversions from double, float or integer types to integer types. Note that the negation operator -i will produce overflow when i is the integer type's MinValue; see table on page 5.1.

For arithmetics on enum types (section 16) it is checked only that the result is within in the underlying representation type; it is not checked that the result corresponds to any declared enum member.

## 12.4    Logical Operators

The conditional logical operators && and || perform *short-cut evaluation*: if e1 evaluates to true in e1&&e2, then e2 is evaluated to obtain the value of the expression; but if e1 evalutes to false, then e2 is ignored and the value of the expression is false. Conversely, if e1 evaluates to false in e1||e2, then e2 is evaluated to obtain the value of the expression; but if e1 evaluates to true, then e2 is ignored and the expression is true. In fact, e1 && e2 is equivalent to e1 ? e2 : false, and e1 || e2 is equivalent to e1 ? true : e2.

By contrast, the operators & (logical strict and) and ^ (logical strict exclusive-or) and | (logical strict or) always evaluate both operands, regardless of the value of the left-hand operand. On the nullable logical type bool? the operators & and | have special definitions; see section 18.

The logical negation operator !e evaluates its argument to true or false and returns false or true.

**Example 65**  Arithmetic Operators

```
public static void Main() {
  int max = 2147483647;                     // = int.MaxValue
  int min = -2147483648;                    // = int.MinValue
  WriteLine(max+1);                         // Prints -2147483648
  WriteLine(min-1);                         // Prints  2147483647
  WriteLine(-min);                          // Prints -2147483648
  Write(   10/3); WriteLine(   10/(-3));    // Prints  3 -3
  Write((-10)/3); WriteLine((-10)/(-3));    // Writes -3  3
  Write(   10%3); WriteLine(   10%(-3));    // Prints  1  1
  Write((-10)%3); WriteLine((-10)%(-3));    // Prints -1 -1
}
static void Write(int i)     { Console.Write(i + " "); }
static void WriteLine(int i) { Console.WriteLine(i); }
```

**Example 66**  The checked and unchecked Operators
Overflow of run-time evaluated expression of type int:

```
int max = int.MaxValue;
int j = max+1;                  // j = -2147483648
int k = checked(max+1);         // Throws OverflowException
int l = checked(Add(max,1));    // l = -2147483648
```

Overflow of compile-time constant expression of type int:

```
int m = int.MaxValue+1;         // Compile-time error!
int n = unchecked(int.MaxValue+1); // n = -2147483648
int p = checked(int.MaxValue+1);   // Compile-time error!
```

Overflow in the explicit conversion from int to char, evaluated at run-time:

```
char a = char.MaxValue;
char b = (char)(a + 66);        // b = 'A'
char c = checked((char)(a + 66)); // Throws OverflowException
```

**Example 67**  Logical Operators
Due to short-cut evaluation of &&, this expression from example 32 does not evaluate the array access days[mth-1] unless $1 \leq$ mth $\leq 12$, so the index is never out of bounds:

```
(mth >= 1) && (mth <= 12) && (day >= 1) && (day <= days[mth-1]);
```

This method returns true if y is a leap year: if y is a multiple of 4 but not of 100, or is a multiple of 400:

```
static bool LeapYear(int y)
{ return y % 4 == 0 && y % 100 != 0 || y % 400 == 0; }
```

## 12.5 Bitwise Operators and Shift Operators

The operators ~ (bitwise complement) and & (bitwise and) and ^ (bitwise exclusive-or) and | (bitwise or) may be used on operands of enum type or integer type. The operators work in parallel on all bits of the operands and never cause overflow, not even in a checked context. The two's complement representation is used for signed integer types, so ~n equals (-n)-1 and also equals (-1)^n.

The shift operators << and >> shift the bits of the two's complement representation of the first argument; they never cause overflow, not even in a checked context. The two operands are promoted (page 56) separately, and the result type is the promotion type of the first argument.

Thus the shift operation is always performed on a 32-bit (int or uint) or a 64-bit (long or ulong) value. In the former case, the length of the shift is between 0 and 31 as determined by the 5 least significant bits of the second argument; in the latter case, the length of the shift is between 0 and 63 as determined by the 6 least significant bits of the second argument. This holds also when the second argument is negative: the length of the shift is the non-negative number determined by the 5 or 6 least significant bits of its two's complement representation.

Thus the left shift n<<s equals n*2*2*...*2 where the number of multiplications is determined by the 5 or 6 least significant bits of s, according as n was promoted to a 32-bit value or to a 64-bit value.

For signed integer types, the operator >> performs right shift with sign-bit extension: the right shift n>>s of a non-negative n equals n/2/2/.../2 where the number of divisions is determined by the 5 or 6 least significant bits of s. The right shift of a negative n equals ~((~n)>>s). In other words, the low-order s bits of n are discarded, the remaining bits are shifted right, and the high-order empty bit positions are set to zero if n is non-negative and set to one if n is negative.

For unsigned integer types, the operator >> performs right shift with zero extension: the right shift n>>s equals n/2/2/.../2 where the number of divisions is determined by the 5 or 6 least significant bits of s. In other words, the low-order bits of n are discarded, the remaining bits are shifted right, and the high-order empty bit positions are set to zero.

See example 205 for clever and intricate use of bitwise operators. This may be efficient and good style on a tiny embedded processor, but not in general programming.

## 12.6 Comparison Operators

The *comparison operators* == and != require the operand types to be *compatible*: one must be implicitly convertible to the other. Two values of simple type are equal (by ==) if they represent the same value after conversion. For instance, 10 and 10.0 are equal. Two values of a reference type that does not override the default implementation of the operators are equal (by ==) if both are null, or both are references to the same object or array, created by the same execution of the new-operator.

Class String redefines the == and != operators so that they compare the characters in the strings. Hence two strings s1 and s2 may be equal by s1==s2, yet be distinct objects (and therefore unequal by (Object)s1==(Object)s2); see example 15.

Values of struct type can be compared using == and != only if the operators have been explicitly defined for that struct type. The default Equals method (section 5.2) compares struct values field by field.

The four comparison operators < <= >= > can be used only on numeric types (and on user-defined types; see section 10.15). On signed integer types they perform signed comparison; on unsigned integer types they perform unsigned comparison.

**Example 68**  Bitwise Operators and Shift Operators

In a shift operation such as n << 48 or n >> 40 or n << -2 the type of the first argument n determines whether the shift will be performed on a 32-bit or a 64-bit value. The 5 least significant bits of 48, 40 and −2 represent the numbers 16, 8, and 30 respectively. Hence the result of 1 << 48 is $2^{16} = 65535$, the result of 1024 >> 40 is $2^{10}/2^8 = 2^2 = 4$, and the result of 1 << -2 is $2^{30} = 1073741824$.

```
public static void Main() {
  int a = 0x3;                      // Bit pattern  0011
  int b = 0x5;                      // Bit pattern  0101
  WriteLine4(a);                    // Prints       0011
  WriteLine4(b);                    // Prints       0101
  WriteLine4(~a);                   // Prints       1100
  WriteLine4(~b);                   // Prints       1010
  WriteLine4(a & b);                // Prints       0001
  WriteLine4(a ^ b);                // Prints       0110
  WriteLine4(a | b);                // Prints       0111
  Console.WriteLine(1 << 48);       // Prints          65536
  Console.WriteLine(1L << 48);      // Prints 281474976710656
  Console.WriteLine(1024 >> 40);    // Prints              4
  Console.WriteLine(1024L >> 40);   // Prints              0
  Console.WriteLine(1 << -2);       // Prints     1073741824
}
static void WriteLine4(int n) {
  for (int i=3; i>=0; i--)   Console.Write(n >> i & 1);
  Console.WriteLine();
}
```

**Example 69**  Bitwise Operators on Enum Values

Bitwise operators ( |, &) and shifts (<<) can be applied to enum values (section 16) as if they were integers. This is useful for combining enum values that represent permissions, such as file access permissions. Bitwise or ( |) is used to combine permissions. Bitwise and (&) is used to test for a particular permission. The [Flags] attribute just causes enum value combinations to be printed symbolically; see section 28.

```
[Flags]                             // Print enum combinations symbolically
public enum FileAccess {
  Read = 1 << 0,
  Write = 1 << 1
}
...
public static void Write(FileAccess access) {
  if (0 != (access & FileAccess.Write))
    Console.WriteLine("You have write permission");
}
public static void Main(String[] args) {
  FileAccess access = FileAccess.Read | FileAccess.Write;
  Console.WriteLine(access);                           // Prints: Read, Write
  Write(access);
}
```

## 12.7    Assignment Expression

In the *assignment expression* x = e, the type of e must be implicitly convertible to the type of x; see section 5.3. The type of the expression x = e is the same as the type of x. The assignment is executed by evaluating expression x, then evaluating expression e and implicitly converting the value to the type of x (if necessary; section 5.3), and finally storing the result in variable x. The value of the expression x = e is the value that was stored in x.

The left-hand side x may be a local variable or parameter, or a field such as o.f, or an array element such as a[i], or a property or indexer. See sections 12.16 and 12.17 for the latter case.

When x is an element of an array whose element type is a reference type t, it is checked at run-time that there is an implicit reference conversion from the value of e to t; see section 9.1.

When e is a compile-time constant of type int, and x has type sbyte, byte, short, ushort, uint or ulong then conversion is performed automatically, provided the value of e is within the range representable in x (section 5.1), and similarly when e has type long and x has type ulong.

The assignment operator is right associative, so the multiple assignment x = y = e has the same meaning as x = (y = e), that is, evaluate the expression e, assign its value to y, and then to x.

When e has reference type, then only a reference to the object or array is stored in x. Thus the assignment x = e does not copy the object or array; see example 64. When e has value type, the assignment copies the value of e. Example 64 shows that assignment of a struct type variable copies the entire struct value.

A *compound assignment* has the form x += e, and is legal in two cases: Either x+e must be implicitly convertible to the type of x, in which case the compound assignment x+=e is equivalent to x = x+e. Otherwise x+e must be explicitly convertible to the type t of x, and e must be implicitly convertible to t, in which case the compound assignment x += e is equivalent to x = (t)(x+e). In both cases, x is evaluated only once; for instance, in a[i++] += e the variable i is incremented only once.

The second case ensures that x += e is legal when both x+e and x = e are legal; see example 70.

Since the value of the expression x += e is that of x after the assignment, and the assignment operators associate to the right, one can write ps[i] = sum += e to first increment sum by e and then store the result in ps[i]; see example 53.

The rules for += apply to the compound assignment operators += -= *= /= %= &= |= ^= but not to the compound shift operators <<= and >>=.

When a new user-defined overloading of an operator such as (+) is defined, the corresponding compound assignment operator (+=) is automatically overloaded also; see section 10.15.

## 12.8    Conditional Expression

The *conditional expression* e1 ? e2 : e3 is legal if e1 has type bool, a type with an implicit conversion to bool, or a type that implements the true operator, and e2 and e3 have the same types, or an implicit conversion exists from one of the types to the other. The conditional expression is evaluated by first evaluating e1. If e1 evaluates to true, then e2 is evaluated (and not e3); otherwise e3 is evaluated (and not e2). The resulting value is the value of the conditional expression.

**Example 70**  Assignment Expression: Implicit and Automatic Explicit Conversion
The assignment d = 12 performs an implicit conversion from int to double. The assignment b=252+1 performs an automatic (explicit, but invisible) conversion from int to byte because 252+1 is a compile-time constant within the range 0…255 of byte, but the assignment b=252+5 is illegal because 252+5 is not within that range. The assignment b=b+2 is illegal because the right-hand side b+2 has type int, but b=(byte)(b+2) is legal because the right-hand side has type byte. The assignment b+=2 is legal because it is equivalent to the preceding one, and 2 is within the range of byte, but b+=257 is illegal because 257 is not within the range of byte.

```
double d;
d = 12;                 // legal:   implicit conversion from int to double
byte b;
b = 252 + 1;            // legal:   252 + 1 is a compile-time constant
// b = 252 + 5;         // illegal: 252 + 5 is too large
// b = b + 2;           // illegal: b + 2 has type int
b = (byte)(b + 2);      // legal:   right-hand side has type byte
b += 2;                 // legal:   equivalent to b = (byte)(b + 2)
// b += 257;            // illegal: b = 257 would be illegal
```

**Example 71**  Compound Assignment Operators
Compute the product of all elements of array xs:

```
static double Multiply(double[] xs) {
  double prod = 1.0;
  for (int i=0; i<xs.Length; i++)
    prod *= xs[i];                          // equivalent to: prod = prod * xs[i]
  return prod;
}
```

**Example 72**  The Conditional Expression
Return the absolute value of x, always non-negative:

```
static double Absolute(double x)
{ return (x >= 0 ? x : -x); }
```

**Example 73**  Nested Conditional Expressions
Nested conditional expressions are useful for making three-way comparisons, as in a Compare method (section 24.3). Note that the conditional operator (?:) associates to the right. Implementing Compare by computing the difference v1-v2 does not work because the subtraction may overflow.

```
class LongComparer : IComparer {
  public int Compare(Object o1, Object o2) {
    long v1 = (long)o1, v2 = (long)o2;
    return v1<v2 ? -1 : v1>v2 ? +1 : 0;
  }
}
```

## 12.9    Object Creation Expression

The *object creation expression*

    new C(*actual-list*)

creates a new object of non-abstract class C, and then calls that constructor in class C whose signature matches the argument types in *actual-list*, a (possibly empty) comma-separated list of expressions.

The *actual-list* is evaluated from left to right to obtain a list of argument values. These argument values are bound to the matching constructor's parameters, an object of the class is created in the computer's store, the instance fields are given default initial values according to their type, a base class constructor is called (explicitly or implicitly, see examples 55 and 88), all instance field initializers are executed in order of appearance, and finally the constructor body is executed to initialize the object. The value of the constructor call expression is the newly created object, whose class is C.

## 12.10    Struct Value Creation Expression

To create and initialize a value of struct type (section 14), use the *struct value creation expression*:

    new S(*actual-list*)

It creates a new struct value of struct type S and then calls that constructor in struct S whose signature matches the argument types in *actual-list*, a possibly empty comma-separated list of expressions.

The *actual-list* is evaluated from left to right to obtain a list of argument values. If this list is empty, the default constructor is called, otherwise a matching constructor is found, and the argument values are bound to the constructor's parameters. A struct value of type S is created in the computer's store, a base class constructor is implicitly called, and finally the constructor body is executed to initialize the struct value. The value of the constructor call expression is the newly created struct value, whose type is S.

## 12.11    Instance Test Expression

The *instance test* e is t tests whether the value of e can be converted to type t by a reference conversion, a boxing conversion, or an unboxing conversion. It is evaluated by first evaluating e to a value v. If v is not null and is a reference to an object of class C, where C can be converted to t, the result is true; otherwise if e evaluates to a value that can be boxed or unboxed to obtain a value of type t, the result is true; otherwise false. In particular, if e has reference type and evaluates to null, the result is false. The instance test considers only reference conversions, boxing conversions, and unboxing conversions (section 5.3); but not user-defined conversions (section 10.16) or conversions between simple types (section 5.3.1).

The type t may be a struct type or another value type. This is useful only if expression v has reference type, possibly being a reference to a boxed value (see section 14.1); if v had value type too, the expression would be either constant true or constant false.

## 12.12    Instance Test and Cast Expression

The expression x as t is equivalent to a combined test and cast: (x is t ? (t)x : (t)null) but evaluates x only once. It has type t. The type t must be a reference type.

**Example 74** Struct Value Creation

Two ways of creating new struct values of type Frac from example 128. The first one calls the default argumentless constructor, and the second one calls the user-defined constructor Frac(long,long).

```
Frac f1 = new Frac();
Frac f2 = new Frac(1,2);
```

**Example 75** Object Creation and Instance Test

```
interface I1 { }
interface I2 : I1 { }
class B : I2 { }
class C : B { }
...
Object n1 = new Exception(), n2 = "foo", n3 = null, n4 = 4711;
Object n5 = new B(), n6 = new C();
Object n7 = new C[10];
Print("n1 is a String:      " + (n1 is String));     // False
Print("n2 is a String:      " + (n2 is String));     // True
Print("null is a String:    " + (n3 is String));     // False
Print("4711 is an int:      " + (n4 is int));        // True
Print("4711 is a long:      " + (n4 is long));       // False
Print("4711 is a ValueType: " + (n4 is ValueType));  // True
Print("n5 is an I1:         " + (n5 is I1));          // True
Print("n5 is an I2:         " + (n5 is I2));          // True
Print("n5 is a B:           " + (n5 is B));           // True
Print("n5 is a C:           " + (n5 is C));           // False
Print("n6 is a B:           " + (n6 is B));           // True
Print("n6 is a C:           " + (n6 is C));           // True
Print("n7 is an Array:      " + (n7 is Array));       // True
Print("n7 is a B[]:         " + (n7 is B[]));         // True
Print("n7 is a C[]:         " + (n7 is C[]));         // True
```

**Example 76** Instance Test and Cast: the as Operator

If parameter o cannot be converted to class Point (declared in example 40), then the result p is null. The test for null in the if statement therefore effectively checks both that o is non-null and that it is a Point.

```
public static void IsNearPoint(Object o) {
  Point p = o as Point;
  if (p != null && p.x*p.x + p.y*p.y <= 100)
    Console.WriteLine(p + " is a Point near (0,0)");
  else
    Console.WriteLine(o + " is not a Point or not near (0,0)");
}
```

Example 107 shows another typical use of the as operator.

## 12.13   Field Access Expression

A *field access* must have one of these four forms

```
f
C.f
o.f
base.f
```

where C is a class and o an expression of reference type. Note that an object of a class may have several fields of the same name f, distinguished by the name of the class that declared the field; see section 10.5, example 47, and example 77 opposite. Field accesses are evaluated as follows:

- A field access of form f refers to a static or instance field of the innermost enclosing class that declares or inherits a field named f.

- A field access of form C.f refers to a static field declared in or inherited by class C.

- A field access of form o.f, where expression o has compile-time type C, refers to an instance field declared in or inherited by class C. To evaluate the field access, the expression o is evaluated to obtain an object. The value of o.f is found as the value of the C-field f in object o. Throws NullReferenceException if o is null.

- A field access of form base.f refers to an instance field in the base class of the innermost class whose declaration encloses the field access expression.

Note that the resolution of an instance field access o.f is similar to a *non-virtual* instance method call o.M(...); see also section 12.15:

- In an instance field access o.f, the field referred to is determined by the *compile-time type* of the object expression o; see example 77.

- In a call to a non-virtual instance method o.M(...), the method called is determined by the *compile-time type* (which must be a class or struct type) of the object expression o; see example 87.

- In a call to a virtual instance method o.M(...), the method called is determined by the *run-time type* (which must be a class) of the object to which o evaluates; see example 87.

## 12.14   The Current Object Reference `this`

The name this may be used in non-static code to refer to the current object (section 10.1). When non-static code in a given object is executed, the object reference this refers to the object as a whole. Hence, if m is an instance (non-static) member, this.m means the same as m when the member m has not been shadowed by a variable or parameter of the same name.

In a class, the this reference is not assignable; in a struct method it is (section 14.2).

**Example 77** Field Access

Here we illustrate static and instance field access in the classes B, C and D from example 47. Note that the field referred to by an expression of form o.nf is determined by the compile-time type of expression o, not the run-time class of the object to which o evaluates.

```
C c1 = new C(100);              // c1 has type C; object has class C
B b1 = c1;                      // b1 has type B; object has class C
Print(C.sf,  B.sf);            // Prints 102 121
Print(c1.nf, b1.nf);           // Prints 100 120
C c2 = new C(200);              // c2 has type C; object has class C
B b2 = c2;                      // b2 has type B; object has class C
Print(c2.nf, b2.nf);           // Prints 200 220
Print(c1.nf, b1.nf);           // Prints 100 120
D d3 = new D(300);              // d3 has type D; object has class D
C c3 = d3;                      // c3 has type C; object has class D
B b3 = d3;                      // b3 has type B; object has class D
Print(D.sf,  C.sf,  B.sf);     // Prints 304 304 361
Print(d3.nf, c3.nf, b3.nf);    // Prints 300 340 360
```

**Example 78** Using this When Referring to Shadowed Fields

A common use of this is to refer to fields (this.x and this.y) that have been shadowed by parameters (x and y), especially in constructors; see the Point class (example 40):

```
class Point {
  protected internal int x, y;
  public Point(int x, int y) { this.x = x; this.y = y; }
  ...
}
```

**Example 79** Using this to Pass the Current Object to a Method

In the APoint class (example 41), the current object reference this is used in the constructor to add the newly created object to the arraylist allpoints, and it is used in the method GetIndex to look up the current object in the arraylist:

```
public class APoint {
  private static ArrayList allpoints = new ArrayList();
  private int x, y;
  public APoint(int x, int y) {
    allpoints.Add(this); this.x = x; this.y = y;
  }
  public int GetIndex() {
    return allpoints.IndexOf(this);
  }
  ...
}
```

## 12.15    Method Call Expression

A *method call* expression, or *method invocation*, must have one of these four forms:

```
M(actual-list)
base.M(actual-list)
C.M(actual-list)
o.M(actual-list)
```

where M is a method name, C is a class name, and o is an expression. The *actual-list* is a possibly empty comma-separated list of expressions, called the *arguments* or *actual parameters*. Each expression in the *actual-list* may be prefixed by ref or out; the called method's *formal-list* must have ref and out in exactly the same parameter positions.

The call's signature is $M(t_1, \ldots, t_n)$ where $(t_1, \ldots, t_n)$ is the list of types of the $n$ arguments in the *actual-list*, including any ref and out modifiers.

Determining which method is actually called by a method call requires several steps, described in sections 12.15.4 and 12.15.5. The steps done at compile-time are:

- Find the accessible methods, including signatures. If the current class does not declare or inherit a member named M, look for M in the enclosing class, if any (and so on recursively). See example 80.

- Given the call's signature, find the applicable method signatures from among the accessible ones.

- Then find the best method signature among the applicable signatures. If there is no best signature, or no accessible and applicable method, the call is rejected by the compiler.

For static methods and non-virtual instance methods, the above steps determine which method to call. For virtual instance methods, a search must be done at run-time also; see section 12.15.5.

Section 12.15.2 describes argument evaluation and parameter passing at run-time, assuming it is clear which method M is being called.

### 12.15.1    Better and Best Method Signature

This section defines the concept of best method signature, used in compile-time overloading resolution (section 12.15.4). When either t or u is a non-simple type, we say that type t is *better* than type u if t is implicitly convertible to u but not the other way around; see section 5.3. For instance, array type String[] is better than Object[] which is better than Array which is better than Object. Also, any type other than Object is better than Object. Informally, a more specific type is a better type.

For simple types, special rules apply: t is better than u if there is a sequence of (thick or thin) arrows from t to u in the graph shown on page 11. For instance, sbyte is better than short which is better than int which is better than long, and so on; and sbyte is better than byte, and so on.

When deciding whether signature $sig_t = M(t_1, \ldots, t_n)$ is better than signature $sig_u = M(u_1, \ldots, u_n)$, only positions that correspond to by-value parameters are taken into account; the types of ref and out parameters must match exactly. Signature $sig_t$ is *better* than signature $sig_u$ if some $t_i$ is better than $u_i$ and no $u_i$ is better than $t_i$ when considering only by-value parameter positions. The method name M and the number $n$ of types must be the same in the two signatures. Informally, a better signature is a more specific signature. In a set of signatures there may be one which is better than all other signatures in the set; this is then called a *best signature*.

**Example 80** Inherited Members are Preferred over Members of Enclosing Types
The call M() in C calls method B.M() because members of C, even inherited ones, are preferred over
members of enclosing classes. If B.M() were private it is not inherited by C, and method E.M() is
called instead. If furthermore B.M(int) were public, then C has an accessible method M(int) and so
the members of enclosing classes are ignored, but B.M(int) is not applicable and the call M() is not legal.

```
class B {
  public static void M() { Console.WriteLine("B.M"); }
  private static void M(int i) { Console.WriteLine("B.M(int)"); }
}
class E {
  static void M() { Console.WriteLine("E.M"); }
  static void M(int i) { Console.WriteLine("E.M(int)"); }
  class C : B {
    public static void Main(String[] args) { M(); }
  }
}
```

**Example 81** Calling Non-overloaded, Non-overridden Methods
This program uses the APoint class from example 41. The static methods GetSize and GetPoint can
be called only by prefixing them with the class name APoint. They may be called before any objects
of class APoint have been created. The instance method GetIndex must be called with an object, as in
r.GetIndex(); then the method is executed with the current object reference this bound to r.

```
Console.WriteLine("Number of points created: " + APoint.GetSize());
APoint p = new APoint(12, 123), q = new APoint(200, 10), r = new APoint(99, 12);
APoint s = p;
q = null;
Console.WriteLine("Number of points created: " + APoint.GetSize());
Console.WriteLine("r is point number " + r.GetIndex());
for (int i=0; i<APoint.GetSize(); i++)
  Console.WriteLine("APoint number " + i + " is " + APoint.GetPoint(i));
```

**Example 82** Calling Overloaded Methods
The overloading resolution for the four method calls in example 49 may be explained as follows. The call
M(10, 20) has call signature M(int, int) and thus calls the method with signature M(int, double),
which is the best applicable one; and similarly for M(10, 20.0). For M(10.0, 20) and M(10.0, 20.0),
the best applicable method signature is M(double, double).

**Example 83** Better and Best Method Signatures

- M(int,int) is better than M(double,int), M(int,double), M(double,double),...
- M(long,long) is better than M(long, ulong), M(ulong, long), M(float, long),...
- M(double,int) is not better than M(int,double), nor the other way round.
- The set M(double,int), M(int,int), M(int,double) has best signature M(int,int).
- The set M(double,int), M(int,double) has no best signature.

### 12.15.2   Method Call: Run-Time Parameter Passing By-Value, Ref or Out

This section and the next one consider the run-time evaluation of a method call M(*actual-list*) when it is clear which method M is called, and focuses on the parameter passing mechanism.

The call is evaluated by evaluating the expressions in the *actual-list* from left to right to obtain the argument values. These argument values are then associated with the corresponding parameters in the method's *formal-list*, in order of appearance.

A *by-value* argument is one not marked ref or out. The type of a by-value argument expression must be implicitly convertible (see section 5.3) to the type of the method's corresponding formal parameter. When executing the method call, a copy of the argument's converted value is bound to the formal parameter, which is similar to an initialized local variable. For formal parameters of value type (simple types and struct types) this means that even if the method changes the value of the formal parameter, this change does not affect the value of the argument expression. For formal parameters of reference type, this means that the formal parameter refers to the same object or array as the argument expression, and any changes made by the method to that object or array will be visible after the method returns (see examples 84 and 86).

A ref argument must be a variable x, a non-readonly field f, this, or an array access a[i]: it must denote a storage location. The storage location must be definitely assigned before the call. The type of a ref argument expression must be exactly the same as the method's corresponding formal parameter. When executing the method call, the formal parameter is the same storage location as the argument expression, so any assignment to the formal parameter immediately modifies the argument.

An out argument is very similar to a ref argument. The only differences are that the storage location denoted by an out argument need not be definitely assigned before the call, and that every execution path in the method must definitely assign a value to the out formal parameter.

When the argument values have been bound to the formal parameters as described above, then the method body is executed. If the method's return type is non-void, the value of the method call expression is the value returned by the method. If the method's return type is void, the method call expression has no value, and cannot be used in an expression. When the method returns, all parameters and local variables in the method are discarded.

### 12.15.3   Method Call: Parameter Arrays

The formal parameter list of a method, constructor or indexer may end with a parameter array: a formal parameter of array type preceded by the params modifier (section 10.7). Assume that this parameter is declared as params t[] xs. In a call to such a method, the actual arguments corresponding to the parameter array can either be zero or more actual by-value parameters of a type implicitly convertible to t, or an array that is implicitly convertible to t[]. In the former case, a new array of type t[] is allocated, the argument expressions are evaluated and converted, their converted values are stored in the array, and the formal parameter xs is bound to the newly created array.

For overloading resolution, an explicit overload such as Max(int, int, int) is preferred over an expansion of a formal parameter array such as Max(int, params int[]). An expansion of a formal parameter array is preferred over a signature that requires an implicit conversion. See examples 51 and 85.

**Example 84** Pass by Value and by Pass by Reference for Simple Types and Arrays

The call M(d1, ref d2, a1, ref a2) passes a double, a reference to the variable d2 holding a double, a reference to an array, and a reference to the variable a2 holding a reference to an array:

```
double d1 = 1.1, d2 = 2.2;
int[] a1 = new int[4], a2 = new int[4];
M(d1, ref d2, a1, ref a2);
...
static void M(double dd1, ref double dd2, int[] aa1, ref int[] aa2) {
  dd1 = 3.3; dd2 = 4.4;
  aa1[0] = 17;
  aa2[0] = 18;
  aa2 = new int[3];
  aa1 = aa2;
}
```

The full arrows show the state before the method call; the dashed arrow are references caused by parameter passing; and the dotted arrows show the state just before method return:

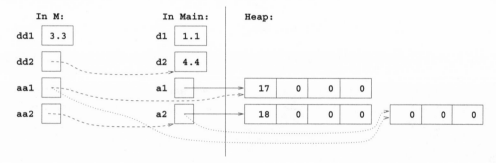

After method return the parameters dd1, dd2, aa1 and aa2 are discarded. In Main, the ref arguments d2 and a2 have been modified. The by-value arguments d1 and a1 are unmodified, but an element in the array pointed to by a1 has been modified.

**Example 85** Calling a Method with a Parameter Array and Overloading

This example shows six calls to the three overloads of the Max method in example 51. For one and four arguments, the params-overload is called because it is the only applicable one. For two arguments the Max(int, int[]) overload is called because its expanded form Max(int, int) is a better overload than Max(int, double). For three arguments, the Max(int, int, int) overload is called because an explicit overload is preferred to an expanded form of a parameter array.

```
Console.WriteLine(Max(2, 1));              // Calls Max(int, int[])
Console.WriteLine(Max(4));                 // Calls Max(int, int[])
Console.WriteLine(Max(5, 8, 7));           // Calls Max(int, int, int)
Console.WriteLine(Max(8, 16, 10, 11));     // Calls Max(int, int[])
int[] xr = { 13, 32, 15 };
Console.WriteLine(Max(12, xr));            // Calls Max(int, int[])
// Console.WriteLine(Max(16, ref xr[0])); // Illegal: params are by-value
```

### 12.15.4   Compile-Time Processing of Method Calls

All methods may be overloaded, and virtual instance methods may be overridden. Overloading is resolved at compile-time by finding the best method signature among the those applicable for the call's signature. Overriding of virtual instance methods is handled by a run-time search, based on the run-time class of the object on which the instance method is called (next section).

#### Compile-Time Step 1: Find Candidate Methods

The first step is to find a set of candidate methods. The notion of a candidate method TT.M(*sig*) includes the type TT that contains its declaration, its name M, and its signature *sig*.

If the method call has the form M(*actual-list*) then candidate methods are the methods named M in the innermost enclosing class that has (declares or inherits) a member named M. If no enclosing class has a member named M, or the member named M in the innermost enclosing class is not a method, then the call is illegal.

If the method call has the form base.M(*actual-list*) the candidate methods are the non-private methods named M in the base class of the current class.

If the method call has the form C.M(*actual-list*) where C is a class or struct type, then the candidate methods are the accessible methods in C named M.

If the method call has the form o.M(*actual-list*) where the compile-time type of expression o is a class or struct type, then the candidate methods are the accessible methods named M in the compile-time type of the expression o.

If the method call has the form o.M(*actual-list*) where the compile-time type of expression o is an interface, then the call is an interface method call and is handled specially at run-time; see below.

#### Compile-Time Step 2: Find Best Applicable Method

The second step is to find those of the candidate methods that are applicable, and then to find the best (most specific) one of these methods.

A candidate method is *applicable* if its *formal-list* has the same length as the call's *actual-list*, corresponding positions agree on parameter passing (by-value or ref or out), corresponding ref and out positions have exactly the same type, and for corresponding by-value positions there is an implicit conversion from the actual argument's type to the corresponding formal parameter's type at that position. In addition, a candidate method whose *formal-list* ends with a parameter array params t[] xs is applicable if replacing the parameter array by zero or more by-value parameters of type t would make it applicable, and if there is no candidate method with the resulting signature already.

Now consider the set of applicable candidate methods. If the set is empty, then the call is illegal (no such method). Otherwise, use the rules of section 12.15.1 to find the method with the best signature. If there is no best signature, or more than one best signature, then the call is illegal (ambiguous).

Thus if the call is legal there is exactly one best signature which identifies a method TT.M(*sig*) from a particular class TT with a particular signature *sig*. This is used for further processing of the method call at run-time; see section 12.15.5.

**Example 86** Pass by Value and Pass by Reference for Classes and Struct Types
The call M(pc1, ref pc2, ps1, ref ps2) passes an object reference, a reference to a variable holding
an object reference, a struct value, and a reference to a variable holding a struct value:

```
Point pc1 = new Point(55, 555), pc2 = new Point(66, 666);
SPoint ps1 = new SPoint(77, 777), ps2 = new SPoint(88, 888);
M(pc1, ref pc2, ps1, ref ps2);
...
static void M(Point ppc1, ref Point ppc2, SPoint pps1, ref SPoint pps2) {
  ppc1.x = 97;
  ppc2 = new Point(16, 17);
  ppc1 = ppc2;
  pps1.x = 98;
  pps1 = new SPoint(18, 19);
  pps2.x = 99;
}
```

The full arrows show the state before the method call; the dashed arrow are references caused by parameter
passing; and the dotted arrows show the state just before method return:

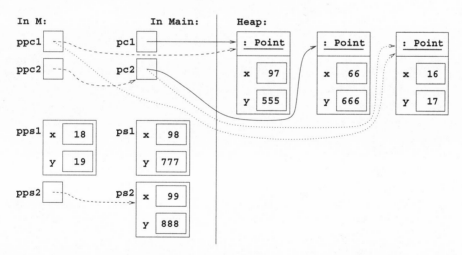

When method M returns, its parameters ppc1, ppc2, pps1 and pps2 are discarded. In Main, the ref
arguments pc2 and ps2 have been modified. The by-value arguments pc1 and ps1 are unmodified, but a
field of the object pointed to by pc1 has been modified.

### 12.15.5   Run-Time Processing of Method Calls

**Run-Time Step 1: Compute the Target Object (for Instance Methods)**

In a call to an instance method, a target object or target struct is needed, to be bound to this during execution of the method.

In the case of M(*actual-list*) or base.M(*actual-list*), the target object is this.

In the case of o.M(*actual-list*) where the compile-time type of o is a *reference type*, expression o in o.M(*actual-list*) must evaluate to an object reference. If non-null, that object is the target object; otherwise the exception NullReferenceException is thrown.

In the case of o.M(*actual-list*) where the compile-time type of o is a struct type and o is a variable (or field or this or array access), the method's this reference will be bound to o during execution of the method. Thus the method may modify the fields of the struct held in the o variable. If o is not a variable, then this is bound to a copy of the value during evaluation of the method, which therefore cannot make any observable modifications to the fields of the struct. See sections 14.2 and 14.3 and example 127. The method must be non-virtual when the compile-time type of o is a struct type.

**Run-Time Step 2: Find the Method to Execute**

If the method TT.M(*sig*) is static, then no search is needed: the method to call is the method M with signature *sig* in class TT.

If the method TT.M(*sig*) is a *non-virtual instance method*, then the method to call is M(*sig*) in TT.

Otherwise, if TT.M(*sig*) is a *virtual instance method*, then the method to call is the most derived implementation of TT.M(*sig*) with respect to the run-time type RT of the value of o. The *most derived implementation* of TT.M(*sig*) with respect to RT is found as follows. If RT contains the virtual declaration of TT's M(*sig*), or an override of TT's M(*sig*), then the most derived implementation is RT's M. Otherwise, it is the most derived implementation of M with respect to the base class of RT.

Note that if some class in the inheritance path from RT up to TT hides TT.M(*sig*), then the most derived implementation of TT.M(*sig*) must be found in that class or a class above it in the inheritance hierarchy. See method M3 in examples 52 and 87.

If the compile-time type of o in the call o.M(*actual-list*) is an interface I, then the method called is the implementation of M provided by the run-time type RT of the value of o. This implementation is found as follows: If RT declares an explicit interface member implementation of I.M with a matching signature (identical names, return types and formal parameter lists), then that is the method to call. Otherwise, if RT declares a public instance method with a matching signature, then that is the method to call. Otherwise, look for the implementation of M in the base class of RT, recursively.

Note that explicit interface member implementations take precedence over ordinary method declarations; see section 15.3 and example 133.

**Run-Time Step 3: Evaluate and bind the arguments**

This is explained in section 12.15.2.

**Example 87** Calling Overridden Methods

Here we use the classes A, B, C, D and E from example 52. In a call such as ae.M2() the compile-time target type is A and the target object's run-time class is E. As can be seen, if a method is a non-virtual instance method in the compile-time target type, then only the compile-time target type matters: ae.M2() calls M2 in class A although the target object's run-time class is E. When the method is virtual or abstract in the compile-time target type, the target object's class matters: de.M2() calls M2 in class E because M2 is abstract in the compile-time target type D, and the target object's class is E.

For virtual instance methods, note that method M3 in E is an override of M3 in D, but not of M3 in C. The reason is the modifier new virtual in class D which hides the method inherited from C.

```
A.M1(); B.M1(); C.M1(); D.M1(); E.M1();          // A.M1 A.M1 C.M1 C.M1 C.M1
E ee = new E(); D de = ee; C ce = ee; B be = ee; A ae = ee;
ae.M2(); be.M2(); ce.M2(); de.M2(); ee.M2();     // A.M2 A.M2 C.M2 E.M2 E.M2
ae.M3(); be.M3(); ce.M3(); de.M3(); ee.M3();     // C.M3 C.M3 C.M3 E.M3 E.M3
A ab = new B(); A ac = new C();
ab.M2(); ac.M2(); ae.M2();                       // A.M2 A.M2 A.M2
ab.M3(); ac.M3(); ae.M3();                       // A.M3 C.M3 C.M3
ab.M4(); ac.M4(); ae.M4();                       // B.M4 B.M4 E.M4
```

**Example 88** Calling Overridden Methods from a Constructor

If d2 is an object of class D2 below, then calling d2.M2() will call the method M2 inherited from base class D1. The call M1() in M2 is equivalent to this.M1(), where this equals d2, so the method M1 declared in class D2 is called. Hence the call d2.M2() will print D1.M2 and then D2.M1:7. It prints 7 because field f is initialized to 7 in constructor D2().

Perhaps more surprisingly, the creation d2 = new D2() of an object of class D2 will print D1.M2 and then D2.M1:0. Why does it print 0, not 7? The very first action of constructor D2() is to make an implicit call to the base class constructor D1(), even *before* executing the assignment f = 7. Hence f will still have its default value 0 when method M1 in D2 is called from method M2 in D1, which in turn is called from constructor D1().

```
class D1 {
  public D1() { M2(); }
  public virtual void M1() { Console.WriteLine("D1.M1 "); }
  public virtual void M2() { Console.Write("D1.M2 "); M1(); }
}

class D2 : D1 {
  int f;
  public D2() { f = 7; }
  public override void M1() { Console.WriteLine("D2.M1:" + f); }
}
```

## 12.16   Property Access Expression

A *property get-access* must have one of these three forms

```
P
C.P
o.P
base.P
```

where C is a class and o an expression of reference type. In the first case, P must be a static or instance property declared in an enclosing class. In the second case, P must be a static property declared in class C. In the third case, P must be an instance property declared in the type of o, where o is a value. In the fourth case, the property P must be an instance property in the base class. Property declarations are described in section 10.13.

In each case, the type of the property get-access expression is the declared type of the property P. A property get-access is evaluated by evaluating o, if present, and then executing the body of the get-accessor. The value of the expression is the value returned by the return-statement that terminates the execution of the get-accessor's body. Such a return-statement will eventually be executed, provided the get-accessor terminates normally; see section 10.13. If o is present but evaluates to null, NullReference-Exception is thrown.

A *property set-access* must have one of these three forms

```
P = expression
C.P = expression
o.P = expression
base.P = expression
```

where C is a class and o an expression of reference type. Each case must satisfy the same requirements as for get-access above. In each case, the type of the entire expression is the declared type of the property P. The type of the right-hand side *expression* must be implicitly convertible to the declared type of the property. A property set-access is evaluated by evaluating o, if present, and then evaluating *expression* to a value which is implicitly converted to obtain a value v of the declared type of P. Then parameter value is bound to v and the body of the set-accessor is executed. If o is present but evaluates to null, NullReferenceException is thrown. The value of the property set-access expression is the value passed to the set-accessor of P.

A read-write property P may be used in a compound assignment such as o.P *= 2 or with increment and decrement operators as in o.P++. First the get-accessor is called to get the value of P, and then the set-accessor is called to set it. The expression o is evaluated only once.

A property cannot be used as a ref or out parameter.

**Example 89**  Using Properties from the Log Class

This example uses the Log properties `InstanceCount`, `Last`, `Count` and `All` from example 59. Note the use of (+=) on the `Last` property, which invokes its get-accessor and then its set-accessor.

```
Log log1 = new Log(), log2 = new Log();
Console.WriteLine("Number of logs = " + Log.InstanceCount);
log1.Add("Alarm"); log1.Add("Shower"); log1.Add("Coffee");
log1.Add("Bus"); log1.Add("Work"); log1.Add("Lunch");
Console.WriteLine(log1.Last);
log1.Last += " nap";
Console.WriteLine(log1.Last);
log1.Add("More work");
Console.WriteLine("Logged entries = " + log1.Count);
foreach (String s in log1.All)
  Console.WriteLine(s);
```

**Example 90**  Static, Instance, and Virtual Properties

A class may declare abstract, static, instance, and virtual properties; they behave like the corresponding kinds of methods. A subclass may hide (with new) or override properties inherited from the base class.

```
abstract class A {
  public abstract String Cl { get; }
}
class B : A {
  public static String Name { get { return "B"; } }
  public String Ty { get { return "B"; } }
  public override String Cl { get { return "B"; } }
}
class C : B {
  public new static String Name { get { return "C"; } }
  public new String Ty { get { return "C:" + base.Ty; } }
  public override String Cl { get { return "C:" + base.Cl; } }
}
...
B b1 = new B();
C c2 = new C();
B b2 = c2;
Console.WriteLine("B.Name = {0}, C.Name = {1}", B.Name, C.Name);  // B C
Console.WriteLine("b1.Ty = {0}, b2.Ty = {1}, c2.Ty = {2}",         // B B C:B
                  b1.Ty, b2.Ty, c2.Ty);
Console.WriteLine("b1.Cl = {0}, b2.Cl = {1}, c2.Cl = {2}",         // B C:B C:B
                  b1.Cl, b2.Cl, c2.Cl);
```

## 12.17 Indexer Access Expression

An *indexer get-access* must have one of these three forms

```
o[actual-list]
this[actual-list]
base[actual-list]
```

where o an expression of reference type. In the first case, the type of o must have an indexer with the given argument types. In the second case, the current class must have (declare or inherit) an indexer with the given argument types. In the third case, the base class of the current class must have an indexer with the given argument types. In each case, the type of the expression is the declared type of the indexer. An indexer get-access is evaluated by evaluating o, if present, and then evaluating the expressions in the *actual-list* to obtain argument values, implicitly converting them to the types of the formal parameters of the indexer, and then executing the body of the indexer's get-accessor. The value of the expression is the value returned by the return-statement that terminates the execution of the get-accessor's body. Such a return-statement will eventually be executed, provided the get-accessor terminates normally; see section 10.14. If o is present but evaluates to null, NullReferenceException is thrown.

An *indexer set-access* must have one of these three forms

```
o[actual-list] = expression
this[actual-list] = expression
base[actual-list] = expression
```

where o is an expression of reference type. Each case must satisfy the same requirements as for get-access above. In each case, the type of the entire expression is the declared type of the indexer. The type of the right-hand side *expression* must be implicitly convertible to the declared type of the indexer. To evaluate an indexer set-access, first evaluate o, if present; evaluate the expressions in the *actual-list* to obtain argument values, implicitly converting them to the types of the formal parameters of the indexer; evaluate *expression* to a value which is implicitly converted to obtain a value v of the declared type of the indexer; bind parameter value to v; and finally execute the body of the set-accessor. If o is present but evaluates to null, NullReferenceException is thrown.

An indexer may be used in a compound assignment such as o[e] *= 2 or with increment and decrement operators as in o[e]++. First the get-accessor is called to get the indexer's value, and then the set-accessor is called to set it. The expression o and the argument expressions are evaluated only once.

An indexer cannot be used as a ref or out parameter.

**Example 91** Using a Sparse Matrix Indexer
This example uses the sparse matrix indexer this[int i, int j] from example 60.

```
SparseMatrix A = new SparseMatrix(4, 5), B = new SparseMatrix(4, 5);
A[0,2] = 102; A[0,3] = 103; A[1,0] = 110; A[3,4] = 134;
B[0,2] = 202; B[1,3] = 213; B[2,0] = 220; B[3,4] = 234;
Console.WriteLine("A =\n{0}", A);
Console.WriteLine("B =\n{0}", B);
Console.WriteLine("A+B =\n{0}", SparseMatrix.Add(A,B));
```

**Example 92** Hiding Base Class's Indexer with a New One for Type Safety
Class StringList is meant to be a class of lists of strings; it is declared as a subclass of ArrayList (from namespace System.Collections) so that it inherits the Count property, the Add method, and so on. It declares an indexer that hides the inherited int-argument indexer but calls it explicitly by base[i] and casts the result to String. The other indexer this(String) calls this class's indexer using this[...] on the integer (if any) parsed from the string. In C# 2.0, it is better to use a generic collection class (section 24.6) instead, for type safety and efficiency.

Note the use of += on ss[0]; this first calls the indexer's get-accessor and then its set-accessor.

```
class StringList : ArrayList {
  public new String this[int i] {
    get { return (String)base[i]; }
    set { base[i] = value; }
  }
  public String this[String s] {
    get { return this[int.Parse(s)]; }
  }
}
...
StringList ss = new StringList();
ss.Add("Cop"); ss.Add("en"); ss.Add("cabana");
ss[2] = "hagen";
ss[0] += "en" + ss[2];
Console.WriteLine("A total of {0} strings", ss.Count);
String last = ss[2];                       // Correct type
Console.WriteLine(ss["0"] + "/" + last);   // Prints: Copenhagen/hagen
```

## 12.18   Type Cast Expression

A *type cast expression* is used to perform an explicit conversion (section 5.3) of a value from one type to another type. When e is an expression and t is a type, then a *type cast* of e to t is done using the expression

```
(t)e
```

This expression, when legal, has type t. It is evaluated by evaluating e to a value v. If e has a simple type and t is a simple type, then the conversion is performed as described in section 5.3.1.

If e has a reference type and there is a standard conversion from that type to t, then if v is null or is a reference to an object or array whose class is implicitly convertible to t, then the conversion succeeds with result v; otherwise the exception InvalidCastException is thrown.

If e has a struct type and there is a standard conversion from that type to t (where t must be an interface, or Object, or ValueType), then the conversion succeeds with a result which is a boxed copy of v (section 5.3.3).

If e has a class or struct type and that type or type t declares a conversion to type t, then that conversion is used to obtain the result.

If e has a simple type, and type t declares a conversion from that type to type t, that conversion is used to obtain the result.

The type cast is illegal and is rejected at compile-time when it can be determined at compile-time that it cannot possibly succeed at run-time; for instance, when e has type String and t is Array. When one or both is an interface, this usually cannot be determined at compile-time.

If the instance test  e is t  described in section 12.11 returns true, then the type cast (t)e will succeed without throwing an exception. The converse does not hold. For example, the cast (t)e may succeed although e evaluates to null; it takes user-defined conversions into account, and it takes implicit and explicit conversions of simple types into account, whereas the instance test e is t does not.

## 12.19   The `typeof` operator

All types can be represented by an object of the predefined class Type from namespace System. This holds also for the pseudo-type void and for types constructed from generic types (section 23.2). There is a single unique Type object for any given type.

The expression typeof(t) evaluates to the Type object representing the type t, and typeof(void) evaluates to the type object representing void. The typeof operator can be applied to all types, even to types involving type parameters (section 23.6).

Note that whereas typeof(t) returns the Type object for a given type t, the method call e.GetType() returns the Type object for the run-time type of a given value e. The GetType method is declared in class Object and is therefore available on all kinds of values (except anonymous methods); see section 5.2 and example 8.

**Example 93** Type Casts

The cast `(long)i` succeeds although `i is long` is false. In a cast such as `(C)s` that involves a user-defined conversion, the type of `s` must be exactly the declared argument type of the conversion operator.

```
class B { }
class C : B {
  private String s;
  public C(String s) { this.s = s; }
  public static explicit operator C(String s) { return new C(s + s); }
}
...
int i = 4711;
long ll = (byte)i + (long)i;        // Simple type conversions
String s = "ole";
B b1 = new C("foo"), b2 = new B();
C c1 = (C)b1;                        // Succeeds, b1 has class C
C c2 = (C)b2;                        // Fails, b2 has class B
C c3 = (C)s;                         // User-defined conversion String-->C
Object o = (Object)s;               // Always succeeds
C c4 = (C)(String)o;                // Succeeds, Object-->String-->C
C c5 = (C)o;                         // Fails, no Object-->C conversion
// Array arr = (Array)s;            // Rejected at compile-time
```

**Example 94** Type `typeof` Operator

```
interface I { }
class B { }
class C : B, I { }
delegate int D(int i);
struct S : I { }
class G<T> { public static void WriteType() { Console.WriteLine(typeof(T)); } }
...
Console.WriteLine(typeof(String));          // System.String
Console.WriteLine(typeof(int));             // System.Int32   (int)
Console.WriteLine(typeof(double));          // System.Double (double)
Console.WriteLine(typeof(int[]));           // System.Int32[]
Console.WriteLine(typeof(int[][]));         // System.Int32[][]
Console.WriteLine(typeof(int[,]));          // System.Int32[,]
Console.WriteLine(typeof(void));            // System.Void
Console.WriteLine(typeof(B));               // B
Console.WriteLine(typeof(C));               // C
Console.WriteLine(typeof(I));               // I
Console.WriteLine(typeof(D));               // D
Console.WriteLine(typeof(S));               // S
Console.WriteLine(typeof(G<int>));          // G[System.Int32]
Console.WriteLine(typeof(G<String>));       // G[System.String]
G<int>.WriteType();                         // System.Int32
Console.WriteLine(typeof(int)==typeof(Int32));  // True
```

## 12.20   Anonymous Method Expression (C# 2.0)

An *anonymous method expression* is an expression that evaluates to a nameless method. This is similar to nameless functions as known from Lisp and Scheme (lambda), Standard ML (fn), and other functional languages. Anonymous methods are convenient for passing behaviors, such as comparers (example 136), to a library or similar; in Java the same purpose is served by anonymous inner classes. An anonymous method expression must have one of these forms:

```
delegate block-statement
delegate(formal-list) block-statement
```

The *formal-list* is as for a method (section 10.7) except that it cannot include a parameter array (params), and no formal parameter in the list can have the same name as a variable or parameter of an enclosing function. The *block-statement* is the anonymous method's body. No goto or continue or break statement can leave the *block-statement*. A return statement in the *block-statement* terminates the anonymous method, not any enclosing function. The *block-statement* cannot contain a yield statement.

An anonymous method expression can use local variables as well as non-ref and non-out parameters of any enclosing function, and static members of all enclosing classes or struct types. In addition, an anonymous method expression that appears in non-static code in a class C can use C's instance members and the current object reference this. An anonymous method expression that appears in a struct cannot use the current struct instance reference this, which is assignable (section 14.2).

An anonymous method can be implicitly converted to a compatible delegate type (section 17): An anonymous method of the first form is compatible with any delegate type D whose *formal-list* contains no out parameter. An anonymous method of the second form is compatible with a delegate type D if their *formal-list*s have the same parameter types and ref/out modifiers; moreover, the delegate type D may have a parameter array (params) that matches nothing in the anonymous method. In both cases, if D's return type is void, then no return statement directly contained in the *block-statement* can return a value. Conversely, if D's return type is t, then every return statement directly contained in the *block-statement* must have an argument expression that is implicitly convertible to t, and the end of the *block-statement* must not be reachable.

After an anonymous method has been converted to a delegate, it can be called just like a delegate; see section 17. The delegate call's arguments will be evaluated. In the first form of anonymous method, the argument values will be ignored; in the second form they will be bound to the anonymous method's formal parameters as usual in method calls. The anonymous method's body will be evaluated, and if it executes a return statement, the anonymous method will terminate.

The body of an anonymous method may contain occurrences of so-called captured variables: local variables and parameters that are bound in the enclosing function. It is possible for an anonymous method to persist after the enclosing function has returned. In that case, captured variables are stored in a *closure* rather than in the enclosing function's stack frame (section 11). A closure is a data structure allocated in the heap; its purpose is to make sure that captured variables exist as long as the anonymous method needs them. Note that captured variables are shared between the enclosing function and the anonymous method, may be shared between several anonymous methods, and even between separate threads (section 20). This is the only way local variables can be shared between threads.

If an anonymous method expression occurs within a loop and captures a local variable declared within the loop, then a new closure and an instance of the local variable is created for each iteration of the loop.

**Example 95** Anonymous Method Compatibility

The anonymous method d11 is compatible with D1 but not D2; the anonymous method d21 is compatible with D2 but not D1; and d22 is compatible with D2 and D3 but not D1. None of the anonymous methods are compatible with D4. The foreach loop calls five anonymous methods; each of the calls to d21 and the anonymous method created by M(4) increments the ref parameter y by one.

```
delegate int D1(int x, ref int y, out int z);
delegate int D2(int x, ref int y);
delegate int D3(int x);
delegate void D4(int x, ref int y);
class Test {
  static D1 d11 = delegate(int x, ref int y, out int z) { z = y++; return x + y; };
  static D2 d21 = delegate(int x, ref int y) { y+=2; return x + y; };
  static D2 d22 = delegate { return 5; };
  public static D2 M(int mx) {
    if (mx < 6)
      return delegate(int x, ref int y) { y+=2; return x + y; };
    else
      return delegate { return mx; };
  }
  public static void Main(String[] args) {
    D2[] ds = { d21, d22, M(4), M(7), delegate { return 8; } };
    int y = 0;
    foreach (D2 d in ds)
      Console.WriteLine(d(2, ref y));    // Prints 4 5 6 7 8
    Console.WriteLine(y);                // Prints 4
} }
```

**Example 96** Local Variables Captured in an Anonymous Method

The local variables u and v get captured in the anonymous methods in the loop body. Since u is declared outside the for-loop, only one instance of the variable is created, and all anonymous methods in udlgs refer to that one instance. Since v is declared inside the loop, a separate instance of the variable is created for each iteration of the loop, and each anonymous method in vdlgs refers to its own instance. Thus the single u instance is incremented five times, and each v instance is incremented once.

```
public static void Main(String[] args) {
  D[] udlgs = new D[5], vdlgs = new D[5];
  int u = 0;
  for (int i=0; i<5; i++) {
    int v = 0;
    udlgs[i] = delegate() { u++; Console.Write(u); };
    vdlgs[i] = delegate() { v++; Console.Write(v); };
  }
  foreach (D dlg in udlgs) dlg();            // Prints 12345
  foreach (D dlg in vdlgs) dlg();            // Prints 11111
}
public delegate void D();
```

# 13  Statements

The execution of a *statement* may change the computer's *state*: the value of variables, fields, etc.

## 13.1  Expression Statement

An *expression statement* is an *expression* followed by a semicolon:

> *expression* ;

It is executed by evaluating the *expression* and ignoring its value. The only forms of *expression* that may be legally used in this way are assignment expressions (section 12.7), increment and decrement expressions (section 12.2), method call expressions (section 12.15), and object creation expressions (section 12.9).

## 13.2  Block Statement

A *block-statement* is a sequence of zero or more *statements* enclosed in braces:

> { *statements* }

## 13.3  The Empty Statement

The *empty statement* consists of a semicolon only, and has no effect at all. If you ever need an empty statement, it is clearer to use the equivalent empty block statement { } that contains no statements.

> ;

## 13.4  Declaration Statement

The purpose of a declaration statement is to declare and initialize local variables and constants.

A *local variable declaration* has one of these forms

> *type  local-variable-declarator* ;
> *type  local-variable-declarator$_1$,  local-variable-declarator$_2$,  ... ;*

where *type* is the type of variable being declared, and the *local-variable-declarator* has one of these forms

> *identifier*
> *identifier = local-variable-initializer*

where *identifier* is the name of the variable, and the *local-variable-initializer* must be an expression or an array initializer whose value is implicit convertible to *type*. Thus, the initialization of a local variable is optional at declaration. A declaration of a variable with an initialization, int x = 1; is semantically equivalent to a declaration statement without initialization int x; followed by an assignment, x = 1;.

A *local constant declaration* is a local variable declaration of the second form preceded by const; the *local-variable-initializer* must be a compile-time constant. A local constant may have simple type (section 5.1), enum type (section 16), or reference type (section 5.2) in which case it must be null.

**Example 97** Statement Termination

Execution of a statement may (1) terminate normally, meaning execution will continue with the next statement, if any; or (2) terminate abruptly by throwing an exception; or (3) exit by executing a `return` statement, if inside a method or constructor; or (4) exit a switch or loop by executing a `break` statement; or (5) exit the current iteration of a loop and start a new iteration by executing a `continue` statement; or (6) exit by executing a `goto` statement; or (7) not terminate at all — for instance, by executing `while (true) {}`.

```
public static void Statement(int choice) {
  bool again = true;
  while (again) {
    again = !again;
    if (choice == 1)                    // Terminate normally
      Console.WriteLine("Choice 1");
    else if (choice == 2)               // Throw exception
      throw new Exception();
    else if (choice == 3)               // Return from method
      return;
    else if (choice == 4)               // Break out of loop
      break;
    else if (choice == 5)               // Continue at loop test
      continue;
    else if (choice == 6)               // Jump out of loop
      goto end;
    else                                // Loop forever
      while (true) { }
    Console.WriteLine("At end of loop");
  }
  Console.WriteLine("After loop");
end:
  Console.WriteLine("At end of method");
}
```

**Example 98** Common Expression Statements: Assignment and Method Call

An assignment statement `x=e;` is an assignment expression `x=e` followed by a semicolon. A method call statement `M(...);` is a method call expression `M(...)` followed by a semicolon. The value returned by the method, if any, is discarded; the method is executed only for its side effect.

**Example 99** Variable Declarations

Variable and constant declaration statements may appear anywhere inside a block statement. Initializer expressions may use (initialized) variables declared previously, possibly in the same statement.

```
int a;
const int year = 365, week = 7, weekMax = year / week + 1;
Console.WriteLine(weekMax);
int x, y = year, z = 3, ratio = z/y;
const double pi = 3.141592653589;
bool found = false;
```

## 13.5   Choice Statements

### 13.5.1   The `if` Statement

An if statement has the form:

```
if (condition)
    truebranch
```

The *condition* must have type bool, and the *truebranch* is a statement but not a declaration statement or a labeled statement. If the *condition* evaluates to true, then the *truebranch* is executed, otherwise not.

### 13.5.2   The `if-else` Statement

An if-else statement has the form:

```
if (condition)
    truebranch
else
    falsebranch
```

The *condition* must have type bool, and *truebranch* and *falsebranch* are statements but not declaration statements or labeled statements. If the *condition* evaluates to true, then the *truebranch* is executed; otherwise the *falsebranch* is executed.

### 13.5.3   The `switch` Statement

A switch statement has the form:

```
switch (expression) {
case constant₁: branch₁
case constant₂: branch₂
...
default: branchₙ
}
```

The *expression* must have type sbyte, byte, short, ushort, int, uint, long, ulong, char, String, an enum type, or a user defined type with exactly one implicit conversion to one of these types (except to an enum type). This is called the *governing type* of the switch statement. Each *constant* must be a compile-time constant expression. No two *constant*s may have the same value. The type of each *constant* must be implicitly convertible to the type of *expression*.

Each *branch* is preceded by one or more case clauses, contains a possibly empty sequence of statements, and must be terminated by return (if inside a method or constructor) or continue (if inside a loop) or goto or throw or break or any other combination of statements that ensures that the end of the *branch* is never reached. This is checked by the compiler. The default clause may be left out. It can appear anywhere among the other clauses, but first or last seem to be the most sensible choices.

The switch statement is executed as follows: The *expression* is evaluated to obtain a value v. If the result v equals one of the *constants*, then the corresponding *branch* is executed. If v does not equal any of the *constants*, then the *branch* following default is executed; if there is no default clause, nothing is executed. A *branch* may contain goto case and goto default statements; see section 13.7.5.

**Example 100** Block Statements

All method bodies and constructor bodies are block statements. In method Sum from example 6, the *truebranch* of the second if statement is a block statement. Method M5 in example 12 contains two block statements, each of which contains a declaration of variable x local to the block statement.

**Example 101** Single if-else Statement

This method behaves the same as Absolute in example 72:

```
static double Absolute(double x) {
  if (x >= 0)
    return x;
  else
    return -x;
}
```

**Example 102** A Sequence of if-else Statements

A sequence of if-else statements is useful for finding the interval to which a value belongs:

```
static String AgeGroup(int age) {
  if (age <= 12)      return "child";
  else if (age <= 19) return "teenager";
  else if (age <= 45) return "young";
  else if (age <= 60) return "middle-age";
  else                return "old";
}
```

**Example 103** switch Statement

Method FindCountry finds the country corresponding to a given international phone number prefix. This can have been done using a sequence of if-else statements, but a switch is both faster and clearer. Note that the default clause need not be the last one.

```
static String FindCountry(int prefix) {
  switch (prefix) {
  default:  return "Unknown";
  case 1:   return "North America";
  case 44:  return "Great Britain";
  case 45:  return "Denmark";
  case 299: return "Greenland";
  case 46:  return "Sweden";
  case 7:   return "Russia";
  case 972: return "Israel";
  }
}
```

## 13.6   Loop Statements

### 13.6.1   The `for` Statement

A `for` statement has the form

```
for (initialization; condition; step)
    body
```

where the *initialization* is a local variable declaration (section 13.4) or a possibly empty comma-separated list of method call expressions, assignment expressions, object creation expressions, increment expressions, and decrement expressions; *condition* is an expression of type `bool`; *step* is a possibly empty comma-separated list of the same kinds of expressions allowed for the *initialization*; and *body* is a statement, but not a declaration statement or a labeled statement. Comma-separated lists of expressions are evaluated from left to right when the list is evaluated. The *initialization*, *condition* and *step* may be empty. An empty *condition* is equivalent to `true`. Thus `for (;;)` *body* means "forever execute *body*".

The `for` statement is executed as follows:

1. The *initialization* is executed
2. The *condition* is evaluated. If it is false, the loop terminates.
3. If it is true, then
   (a) The *body* is executed.
   (b) The *step* is executed.
   (c) Execution continues at 2.

### 13.6.2   The `foreach` Statement

A `foreach` statement has the form

```
foreach (type x in expression)
    body
```

where the *expression* must be enumerable and its enumerators must produce elements that can be explicitly converted to *type*. The *body* must be a *statement* but not a declaration statement or a labeled statement.

First the *expression* is evaluated to obtain an enumerator. Then the *body* is evaluated for each element produced by the enumerator, with variable x bound to the result of explicitly converting the element to *type*, possibly by an unboxing conversion. If the element cannot be converted to *type*, an InvalidCastException is thrown. The scope of local variable x is *body*, and the variable is read-only: it cannot be assigned to or passed as a `ref` or `out` parameter. The *body* should not modify the enumerator obtained from the *expression*, or any data underlying the enumerator. The *expression* of type t is enumerable:

- If t implements the interface IEnumerable or IEnumerable<T> (section 24.2). In particular, class Array and hence all array types (section 9) implement IEnumerable, and array type T[] implements IList<U> hence IEnumerable<U> whenever T[] is implicitly convertible to U[].

- Or, if t implements a `public` instance method `GetEnumerator()` with a return type that must implement both a `public` instance method `MoveNext()` with return type `bool` and a `public` instance property `Current`, as required by interface IEnumerator (section 24.2). See examples 57 and 61.

Examples 20, 61, 106, 107, 114, 115, 170, 177, 183, and 209 illustrate the `foreach` statement.

**Example 104** Nested `for` Loops to Print a Triangle of Asterisks

```
for (int i=1; i<=4; i++) {                          // Output:
  for (int j=1; j<=i; j++)                           // *
    Console.Write("*");                              // **
  Console.WriteLine();                               // ***
}                                                    // ****
```

**Example 105** Multiple Initialization and Step in a `for` Loop
This method reverses the elements of a one-dimensional array. Note the multiple variable declarations in the *initialization* and the multiple (comma-separated) expressions in the *step* part of the loop header:

```
public static void Reverse(Object[] arr) {
  for (int s=0, t=arr.Length-1; s<t; s++, t--) {
    Object tmp = arr[s]; arr[s] = arr[t]; arr[t] = tmp;
  }
}
```

**Example 106** Using `foreach` on an Array
This loop concatenates the strings in the array `arr`, inserting two copies of each string. The binding of an array element to local variable `s` in the `foreach` loop involves an explicit conversion to type String, so the example will compile and execute regardless whether the type of `arr` is String[] or Object[].

```
StringBuilder sb = new StringBuilder();
foreach (String s in arr)
  sb.Append(s).Append(s);
```

**Example 107** Explicitly Using an IEnumerator Instead of `foreach`
A `foreach` loop as in example 106 is syntactic sugar for a `while` loop using an enumerator (section 24.2). Note the explicit conversion to String; in the `foreach` statement it is invisible but nevertheless performed. Even if the loop body were to terminate abruptly by a `return` statement, the `finally` block would call the enumerator's `Dispose` method if it has one, so the enumerator can immediately free any resources that it holds on to. The IDisposable interface is described in section 13.10.

```
StringBuilder sb = new StringBuilder();
IEnumerator enm = arr.GetEnumerator();
try {
  while (enm.MoveNext()) {
    String s = (String)enm.Current;
    sb.Append(s).Append(s);
  }
} finally {
  Console.WriteLine("(now in finally block)");
  IDisposable disp = enm as System.IDisposable;
  if (disp != null)
    disp.Dispose();
}
```

### 13.6.3    The `while` Statement

A `while` statement has the form

```
while (condition)
    body
```

where the *condition* is an expression of type `bool`, and *body* is a statement but not a declaration statement or a labeled statement. The `while` statement is executed as follows:

1. The *condition* is evaluated. If it is false, the loop terminates.
2. If it is true, then

    (a) The *body* is executed
    (b) Execution continues at 1.

An infinite loop can be written   `while (true)` *body*   which may be clearer than the "forever" idiom `for (;;)` *body*   shown in section 13.6.1.

### 13.6.4    The `do-while` Statement

A `do-while` statement has the form

```
do
    body
while (condition);
```

where the *condition* is an expression of type `bool`, and *body* is a statement but not a declaration statement or a labeled statement. The `do-while` statement is executed as follows:

1. The *body* is executed.
2. The *condition* is evaluated. If it is false, the loop terminates.
3. If it is true, then execution continues at 1.

The *body* is always executed at least once because the *condition* is tested only after executing the *body*. This also means that the *condition* does not contribute to establishing a precondition that guarantees successful execution of the *body*. Usually it is safer and more appropriate to use a `while` loop or `for` loop, which do test the *condition* before executing the *body*.

**Example 108** Array Search Using a `while` Loop

This method converts a weekday (Thursday, say) into a day number (4, say), by searching an array of weekday names. Note that directly after the `while`-loop, the *negation* of the loop condition holds. Thus if `i < wdays.Length` holds after the loop, it must be the case that `wday == wdays[i]`:

```
static int WeekDayNo1(String wday) {
  int i=0;
  while (i < wdays.Length && wday != wdays[i])
    i++;
  // Now i >= wdays.Length or wday == wdays[i]
  if (i < wdays.Length) return i+1;
  else                  return -1;          // Here used to mean 'not found'
}
static readonly String[] wdays =
{ "Monday", "Tuesday", "Wednesday", "Thursday", "Friday", "Saturday", "Sunday" };
```

**Example 109** Searching for a Substring

The call `Substring1(q,t)` returns true if `q` appears as a substring somewhere in `t`. The outer loop considers all points in `t` where `q` could fit, and the inner loop compares the characters at such points to `q`.

```
static bool Substring1(String query, String target) {
  for (int j=0, n=target.Length-query.Length; j<=n; j++) {
    int k=0, m=query.Length;
    while (k<m && target[j+k] == query[k])
      k++;
    // Now k>=m (and target[j..]==query[0..m-1]) or target[j+k] != query[k]
    if (k>=m)
      return true;
  }
  return false;
}
```

**Example 110** Infinite Loop Because of Misplaced Semicolon

The misplaced semicolon (`;`) makes the loop body an empty statement. Since `i++` is not executed, the loop goes on forever.

```
int i=0;
while (i<10);
  i++;
```

**Example 111** Using `do-while`

Roll a die and compute sum of eyes until 5 or 6 comes up:

```
int sum = 0, eyes;
do {
  eyes = 1 + rnd.Next(6);
  sum += eyes;
} while (eyes < 5);
```

## 13.7   Returns, Labeled Statements, Exits, and Jumps

### 13.7.1   The `return` Statement

The simplest form of a return statement, without an expression argument, is this:

```
return;
```

This form of `return` statement may occur in the body of a method or anonymous delegate whose *returntype* is void, in the body of a constructor, or in a set-accessor of a property or indexer, but not in an operator nor in the get-accessor of a property or indexer. Execution of the `return` statement exits the method or constructor, and continues execution at the place from which it was called.

Alternatively, a `return` statement may have an expression argument:

```
return expression;
```

This form of `return` statement may occur inside the body of a method or anonymous delegate whose *returntype* is non-void, in the get-accessor of a property or indexer, or in an operator, but not in a constructor nor in the set-accessor of a property or indexer. The type of the *expression* must be implicitly convertible to the return type of the enclosing function. The `return` statement is executed as follows: First the *expression* is evaluated to some value v. Then it exits the method, and continues execution at the method call expression that called the method; the value of that expression will be v.

See section 13.8.2 for execution of a return statement inside a try statement with an associated finally block.

### 13.7.2   The `break` Statement

A break statement is legal only inside a switch or loop, and has the form

```
break;
```

Executing break exits the innermost enclosing switch or loop, and continues execution after that switch or loop. A break statement is not allowed to exit a finally block.

See section 13.8.2 for execution of a break statement inside a try statement with an associated finally block.

### 13.7.3   The `continue` Statement

A continue statement is legal only inside a loop, and has the form

```
continue;
```

Executing continue terminates the current iteration of the innermost enclosing loop, and continues the execution at the *step* (in for loops; see section 13.6.1), or with the next element (in foreach loops; see section 13.6.2) or the *condition* (in while and do-while loops; see sections 13.6.3 and 13.6.4).

A continue statement is not allowed to exit a finally block.

See section 13.8.2 for execution of a continue statement inside a try statement with an associated finally block.

**Example 112** Redundant `return` at End of `void` Method

There is an implicit argumentless `return` statement at the end of every `void` method and every constructor. Writing it explicitly does not change the program's behavior but is poor style.

```
public static void Print(String s) {
  Console.WriteLine(s);
  return;
}
```

**Example 113** Using `return` to Terminate a Loop Early

This method behaves the same as `WeekDayNo2` in example 108:

```
static int WeekDayNo3(String wday) {
  for (int i=0; i < wdays.Length; i++)
    if (wday.Equals(wdays[i]))
      return i+1;
  return -1;                              // Here used to mean 'not found'
}
```

**Example 114** Using `break` to Terminate a Loop Early

The `break` statement is used to exit the loop as soon as an empty string is found in the string array `arr`. However, using `break` in a loop often makes it difficult to understand and maintain.

```
static void SearchNonBlank1(String[] arr) {
  bool found = false;
  foreach (String s in arr)
    if (s == "") {
      found = true;
      break;
    }
  Console.WriteLine(found);
}
```

**Example 115** Using `continue` to Start a New Iteration

The `continue` statement terminates the current iteration of the `foreach`-loop when the string is empty, and goes on to the next string in the array. However, using `continue` in a loop often makes it difficult to understand and maintain.

```
static void PrintNonBlank3(String[] arr) {
  foreach (String s in arr) {
    if (s == "")
      continue;
    Console.WriteLine(s);
  }
}
```

### 13.7.4 The Labeled Statement

A labeled statement declares *label* as the name of a statement; it has the form

> *label* : *statement*

where *label* is an identifier. The scope of *label* is the entire block enclosing the labeled statement, including nested blocks. It is illegal to declare the same *label* twice in a block, including its nested blocks.

### 13.7.5 The goto Statement

A goto statement has one of the forms

```
goto label;
goto case constant;
goto default;
```

The goto case and goto default statements are only allowed inside a switch statement. A goto case *constant* can target only the cases of the innermost enclosing switch statement (whereas a plain goto may target labels outside it; see example 118). The *constant* must be a compile-time constant expression, implicitly convertible to the governing type of the innermost enclosing switch statement.

The effect of a goto statement is that execution continues at the statement labeled *label* or at the clause in the enclosing switch statement labeled case *constant* or default.

The goto *label* statement must be within the scope of the *label*. This permits goto to leave a block or loop or switch, but not to leave a method or constructor, or to enter a block or loop or switch.

A goto statement is not allowed to exit a finally block.

See section 13.8.2 for execution of a goto statement inside a try statement that has an associated finally block.

## 13.8 Throwing and Catching Exceptions

### 13.8.1 The throw Statement

A throw statement has one of the forms

```
throw expression;
throw;
```

where the type of *expression* must be implicitly convertible to class Exception (section 19). A throw statement of the form throw *expression*; is executed as follows: The *expression* is evaluated to obtain an exception object v. If it is null, then an instance of NullReferenceException is thrown; otherwise, the exception object v is thrown. Thus a thrown exception is never null. In any case, the enclosing block statement is terminated abruptly; see section 19. The thrown exception may be caught by a dynamically enclosing try-catch statement: one whose execution has begun and not yet completed (section 13.8.2). If the exception is not caught, then the entire program execution will be aborted, and information from the exception will be printed at the command prompt or shown in a dialog.

A throw statement of the form throw; is only permitted inside the body of a catch statement. Its effect is to rethrow the exception handled by the enclosing catch block.

Throwing an exception is slow, so exceptions should not be used for standard control flow.

**Example 116**  Using `goto` to Exit a Loop

This method uses `goto` to exit the inner `for`-loop by jumping to the end of the outer `for`-loop, thus skipping the first `return` statement. In more complex examples the use of `goto` can lead to very unclear code; the use of `while` as in the equivalent example 109 is often preferable.

```
static bool Substring1(String query, String target) {
  for (int j=0, n=target.Length-query.Length; j<=n; j++) {
    for (int k=0, m=query.Length; k<m; k++)
      if (target[j+k] != query[k])
        goto nextPos;
    return true;
  nextPos: { }            // Label on an empty statement
  }
  return false;
}
```

**Example 117**  Throwing an Exception to Indicate Failure

Instead of returning the error value -1 as in example 113, throw a WeekdayException (example 141).

```
static int WeekDayNo4(String wday) {
  for (int i=0; i < wdays.Length; i++)
    if (wday.Equals(wdays[i]))
      return i+1;
  throw new WeekdayException(wday);
}
```

**Example 118**  Implementing a Finite State Machine Using Labeled Statements, `goto` and `switch`

This method tests whether string `str` matches the regular expression $(a|b)*abb$: a sequence of $a$'s and $b$'s ending with *abb*. It is a finite state machine with initial state `state1` and success state `state4`.

```
public static bool Match(String str) {
  int stop = str.Length, i = 0;
  state1:
    if (i==stop) return false;
    switch (str[i++]) {
    case 'a': goto state2;
    case 'b': goto state1;
    default: return false;
    }
  state2: ...
  state3: ...
  state4:
    if (i==stop) return true;
    switch (str[i++]) {
    case 'a': goto state2;
    case 'b': goto state1;
    default: return false;
  } }
```

### 13.8.2 The `try-catch-finally` Statement

A `try-catch-finally` statement has this form and is used to catch certain exceptions thrown by *trybody*:

```
try
    trybody
catchclause₁
catchclause₂
...
finally
    finallybody
```

where *trybody* and *finallybody* are block statements. There may be zero or more `catch` clauses, and the `finally` clause may be absent, but at least one `catch` or `finally` clause must be present. No `return` or `break` or `continue` or `goto` can exit the *finallybody*. A *catchclause* must have one of these three forms:

```
catch (exceptiontype identifier)
    catchbody

catch (exceptiontype)
    catchbody

catch
    catchbody
```

where *exceptiontype* is Exception or a subclass (section 19) and *identifier* is a variable name. A *catchbody* is a block statement. A `catch` clause of the third form is equivalent to `catch (Exception)` and can occur only last. We say that clause `catch (E_i)` *catchbody* matches exception type E if E is $E_i$ or a subclass of $E_i$. Note that the third form `catch` *catchbody* matches all exception types.

The `try-catch-finally` statement is executed by executing the *trybody*. If the execution of *trybody* terminates normally, or exits by `return` (when inside a method or constructor) or `break` or `continue` (when inside a switch or loop) or by `goto`, then any `catch` clauses are ignored.

If *trybody* terminates abruptly by throwing exception e of class E and one or more `catch` clauses (with exception types $E_1$, $E_2$, ...) are present, then the `catch` clauses are examined in sequence until the first matching clause `catch (E_i)`, if any, is located. If an exception variable $x_i$ is declared in the found `catch` clause, then e is bound to variable $x_i$, and the corresponding *catchbody_i* is executed. The *catchbody* may terminate normally, or exit by executing `return` or `break` or `continue` or `goto` or by throwing an exception. If there is no `finally` clause this determines how the entire `try-catch-finally` statement terminates. A thrown exception e is never null (section 13.8.1), so $x_i$ cannot be null either. If there is no matching `catch` clause, then the entire `try-catch-finally` terminates abruptly with exception e.

If there is a `finally` clause, then the *finallybody* will be executed regardless of whether the execution of *trybody* terminated normally, whether *trybody* was exited by executing `return` or `break` or `continue` or `goto`, whether any exception thrown by *trybody* was caught by a `catch` clause, and whether the *catchbody* was exited by executing `return`, `break`, `continue` or `goto` or by throwing an exception.

If execution of *finallybody* terminates normally, then the entire `try-catch-finally` terminates as determined by *trybody* (or *catchbody_i*, if one was executed). If execution of the *finallybody* terminates abruptly by throwing an exception e2, then the entire `try-catch-finally` terminates with exception e2, and any exception e thrown by the *trybody* (or *catchbody_i*) will be lost. See example 142.

**Example 119** A try-catch Statement

This example calls the method WeekDayNo4 (example 117) inside a try-catch statement that catches exceptions of class WeekdayException (example 141) and its base class Exception. The second catch clause will be executed if the array access args[0] fails because there is no command line argument: this throws IndexOutOfRangeException which is a subclass of Exception. If an exception is caught, it is bound to the variable x, and printed by an implicit call (section 7) to the exception's ToString-method:

```
public static void Main(String[] args) {
  try {
    Console.WriteLine(args[0] + " is weekday number " + WeekDayNo4(args[0]));
  } catch (WeekdayException x) {
    Console.WriteLine("Weekday problem: " + x);
  } catch (Exception x) {
    Console.WriteLine("Other problem: " + x);
  }
}
```

**Example 120** A try-finally Statement

This method attempts to read three lines from a text file (see section 22.4), each containing a single floating-point number. Regardless whether anything goes wrong during reading (premature end of file, ill-formed number), the finally clause will close the reader before the method returns. It would do so even if the return statement were inside the try block. The same effect may be achieved with the using statement; see example 122.

```
static double[] ReadRecord(String filename) {
  TextReader reader = new StreamReader(filename);
  double[] res = new double[3];
  try {
    res[0] = double.Parse(reader.ReadLine());
    res[1] = double.Parse(reader.ReadLine());
    res[2] = double.Parse(reader.ReadLine());
  } finally {
    reader.Close();
  }
  return res;
}
```

## 13.9 The `checked` and `unchecked` Statements

An operation on integral numeric values may produce a result that is too large. In a *checked context*, run-time integer overflow will throw an OverflowException, and compile-time integer overflow will produce a compile-time error. In an *unchecked context*, both compile-time and run-time integer overflow will wrap around (discard the most significant bits), not throw any exception nor produce a compile-time error.

A checked statement creates a checked context for a *block-statement* and has the form

```
checked
    block-statement
```

An unchecked statement creates an unchecked context for a *block-statement* and has the form

```
unchecked
    block-statement
```

In both cases, only arithmetic operations textually inside the *block-statement* are affected. Thus arithmetic operations performed in methods called from the *block-statement* are not affected, whereas arithmetic operations in anonymous delegate expressions textually inside the *block-statement* are affected. Checked and unchecked statements are analogous to checked and unchecked expressions; see section 12.3.

## 13.10 The `using` Statement

The purpose of the using statement is to ensure that a resource, such as a file handle or database connection, is released as soon as possible after its use. The using statement may have the form

```
using (t x = initializer)
    body
```

This declares variable res to have type t which must be implicitly convertible to IDisposable, initializes res with the result of evaluating the *initializer* expression, and executes the *body*. Finally method Dispose() is called on res, regardless of whether *body* terminates normally, throws an exception, or exits by return or break or continue or goto. The *body* must be a statement but not a declaration statement or a labeled statement. Variable res is read-only; its scope is *body* where it cannot be assigned to, nor used as a ref or out argument. The using statement is equivalent to this block statement:

```
{
    t res = initializer;
    try     { body }
    finally { if (res != null) ((IDisposable)res).Dispose(); }
}
```

The IDisposable interface from namespace System describes a single method:

- void Dispose() is called to close or release resources, such as files, streams or database connections, held by an object. Calling this method multiple times must not throw an exception; all calls after the first one may just do nothing.

## 13.11 The `lock` Statement

The lock statement is described in section 20.2.

**Example 121** Checked and Unchecked Integer Operations

The checked and unchecked statements affect only the operations textually enclosed by the statements. Thus overflow that occurs in methods called from the statement is *not* affected by the explicit overflow checking context. For instance, the call int.Parse("9999999999") always throws OverflowException, regardless of checked or unchecked context.

In a checked context, an overflowing computation performed at compile-time will cause a compile-time error, not throw an exception at run-time.

```
checked {
  Console.WriteLine(int.MaxValue + 1);    // Compile-time error
  Console.WriteLine(int.MinValue - 1);    // Compile-time error
  Console.WriteLine((uint)(0-1));         // Compile-time error
  int i = int.Parse("9999999999");        // Throws OverflowException
}
unchecked {
  Console.WriteLine(int.MaxValue + 1);    // -2147483648 (wrap-around)
  Console.WriteLine(int.MinValue - 1);    // 2147483647  (wrap-around)
  Console.WriteLine((uint)(0-1));         // 4294967295  (wrap-around)
  int i = int.Parse("9999999999");        // Throws OverflowException
}
```

See also example 66.

**Example 122** The using Statement

In the using statement below we create a TextReader from a given text file and attempt to read three floating-point numbers from it. The using statement makes sure that regardless of whether the block terminates normally or by throwing an exception, the TextReader and the file get closed; this example behaves the same as example 120. Class TextReader implements interface IDisposable, so it can be used in the using statement.

```
static double[] ReadRecord(String filename) {
  using (TextReader reader = new StreamReader(filename)) {
    double[] res = new double[3];
    res[0] = double.Parse(reader.ReadLine());
    res[1] = double.Parse(reader.ReadLine());
    res[2] = double.Parse(reader.ReadLine());
    return res;
  }
}
```

## 13.12   The `yield` Statement and Iterators (C# 2.0)

The `yield` statement is used to define enumerators and enumerables (section 24.2) in a convenient way. The `yield` statement can be used only inside the body of a method or operator, or the get-accessor of a property or indexer, whose return type is IEnumerator, IEnumerable, IEnumerator<T>, or IEnumerable<T>. The body of this *iterator method* is then called an *iterator block*, and the *yield type* of the iterator block is Object or T, respectively. A `yield` statement cannot appear in an anonymous method.

A `yield` statement must have one of these two forms:

```
yield return expression;
yield break;
```

The type of the *expression* must be implicitly convertible to the yield type of the enclosing iterator block.

The statement `yield return` *expression* returns a value to a caller, just like a `return` statement, but it does not terminate the enclosing iterator block and does not execute any associated `finally`-clauses. Instead, the execution of the iterator block can be resumed just after the `yield` statement, possibly causing the iterator block to execute more `yield` statements. When the iterator block executes the statement `yield break`, or terminates normally by reaching the end of the iterator block, or throws an exception, it executes any associated `finally` clauses, and its execution cannot be resumed any more. Thus using the `yield` statement, an iterator block can produce a sequence of zero or more values.

An iterator method cannot have `ref` or `out` parameters, and cannot contain a `return` statement. A `yield return` *expression* statement cannot appear inside a `catch` clause or inside a `try` statement that has an associated `catch` clause. A `yield break` statement can appear anywhere in the iterator method except in a `finally` clause or an anonymous method.

The compiler turns the iterator block into an unnamed class that implements IEnumerator and IEnumerator<T>, so it has a property `Current` whose type is the yield type, and methods `MoveNext()` with return type `bool` and `Dispose()` with return type `void`. A call to the iterator method creates an instance of this class, called an enumerator object. It has four states: Before (the initial state), Running, Suspended, and After. The value of the `Current` property is defined only in the Suspended state. The effect of the `MoveNext` and `Dispose` methods is shown below, where State←*s* means that the state changes to *s*.

If the iterator method has return type IEnumerable or IEnumerable<T>, the compiler also creates another unnamed class that implements IEnumerable and IEnumerable<T>, so it has a `GetEnumerator()` method. Then a call to the iterator method creates an instance of this class, from which independent enumerator objects can be obtained by `foreach` statements.

| State | Call `MoveNext()` | `yield return e` | `yield break`, or end of block | Throw exn | Call `Dispose()` |
|---|---|---|---|---|---|
| Before | State←Running<br>Restore variables<br>Start executing block | N/A | N/A | N/A | State←After |
| Running | Unspecified. | State←Suspended<br>`Current`←e<br>Return `true` | State←After<br>Execute finally<br>Return `false` | State←After<br>Execute finally<br>Throw exn | Unspecified |
| Suspended | State←Running<br>Restore variables<br>Resume after last yield | N/A | N/A | N/A | State←Running<br>Execute finally<br>State←After |
| After | Return `false` | N/A | N/A | N/A | No effect |

**Example 123** An Iterator for Integer Sequences

The `yield` statement can be used to enumerate a sequence of integers (struct Seq from example 61) by declaring `GetEnumerator` as shown below. It has the same effect as a method that returns an object of the complicated class SeqEnumerator in example 57. In fact `GetEnumerator` below will be transformed into a class, similar to SeqEnumerator, that implements IEnumerator (section 24.2). The `GetEnumerator` method may be called implicitly in a `foreach` statement as in example 61, or explicitly as shown here.

```
struct Seq : IEnumerable {
  private readonly int b, k, n;              // Sequence b+k*[0..n-1]
  ...
  public IEnumerator GetEnumerator() {
    for (int i=0; i<n; i++) {
      yield return b + k * i;
    }
} }
```

**Example 124** Enumerating Solutions to the Eight Queens Problem

A solution to the *n*-queens problem is a placement of *n* queens on an *n*-by-*n* chessboard so that no queen can attack any other queen: there can be at most one queen on any row, column, or diagonal. For $n = 8$ we have the eight queens problem on an ordinary chessboard. The iterator method `Queens(w, n)` below enumerates partial *n*-queens solutions in which `w+1` queens have been placed in the first `w+1` columns of the board. It follows that `Queens(n-1, n)` enumerates all solutions to the *n*-queens problem.

```
public static IEnumerable<int[]> Queens(int w, int n) {
  if (w < 0)
    yield return new int[n];
  else
    foreach (int[] sol in Queens(w-1, n))
      for (int r=1; r<=n; r++) {
        for (int c=0; c<w; c++)
          if (sol[c] == r || sol[c]+(w-c) == r || sol[c]-(w-c) == r)
            goto fail;
        sol[w] = r;
        yield return sol;
        fail: { }
      }
}
...
foreach (int[] sol in Queens(n-1, n)) {
  foreach (int r in sol)
    Console.Write("{0} ", r);
  Console.WriteLine();
}
```

# 14    Struct Types

A struct value is an instance of a struct type. A struct type can contain fields, methods, type declarations and other members, just like a class, but a struct type is a value type. This means that a variable or array element of struct type directly contains an instance of the struct type (a struct value), whereas a variable or array element of class type contains only a reference to a class instance (an object). Also, the assignment of a struct value to a struct type variable is performed by *copying* the fields of the struct value to the fields of the struct value held in the variable; see example 64. By contrast, the assignment of an object to a variable of class type only copies a reference into the variable; see example 64. Similarly, passing a struct type argument by value or returning a struct type result from a method will copy the struct value; see example 86.

Struct types are well-suited for representing pairs, complex numbers, rational numbers, and other small, value-oriented or functional data structures: data structures that may be freely copied because their fields are never modified after creation. Such fields should be declared readonly.

A *struct-declaration* of struct type S has the form

*struct-modifiers* struct S *struct-interface-clause*
    *struct-body*

A declaration of struct type S introduces a new value type S (section 5.1). The *struct-modifiers* can be new and a class access modifier (section 10.12). It cannot be abstract or sealed. The *struct-interface-clause* may be left out; if it is present it has the form  : I1, I2,..., where I1, I2, ... is a non-empty comma-separated list of interface types that must be implemented by struct type S; see section 15.2.

A struct declaration may consist of one or more partial type declarations; see section 26.

The *struct-body* can have the same members as a *class-body* (section 10.1). A struct type is similar to a class, but there are some significant differences:

- A struct type implicitly inherits from System.ValueType which in turn inherits from Object (see section 5.2). A struct type can inherit from no other class or struct type, and no class or struct type can inherit from a struct type. As a consequence a struct type cannot be abstract or sealed, and a struct member cannot be protected or protected internal.

- A struct type can have no virtual methods, properties, or indexers, and all calls are non-virtual. The *method-modifiers* virtual, sealed and abstract are not permitted, and new and override can be used only on members inherited from Object or ValueType, such as ToString in example 125.

- A struct type is a value type and therefore a variable or field of struct type cannot be null. A struct type has a predefined argumentless constructor S() that initializes the struct's instance fields with their default initial values; this determines the struct type's default initial value. No argumentless constructor can be declared explicitly in a struct type.

- If sarr is an array whose element type is a struct type S, then each array element sarr[i] holds an entire struct value, not just a reference to one. Hence creating new S[3] will set aside space for 3 instances of struct type S; see example 64.

- Conversion between a struct type and type Object or interfaces is performed by boxing and unboxing (sections 5.3.3 and 14.1).

- Instance field declarations cannot have initializers: a field is always initialized with its default value.

**Example 125**  A Struct Type for Points
The SPoint struct type declaration is very similar to the Point class declaration in example 40. The difference is that assigning an SPoint value to a variable copies the SPoint value; see examples 64 and 86. (Thus struct types are most suitable for data structures whose fields are read-only as in example 128.)

```
public struct SPoint {
  internal int x, y;
  public SPoint(int x, int y) { this.x = x; this.y = y; }
  public SPoint Move(int dx, int dy) { x += dx; y += dy; return this; }
  public override String ToString() { return "(" + x + ", " + y + ")"; }
}
```

**Example 126**  Differences between Struct Values and Objects
An array of structs directly contains the struct values (not references to them), and element assignment copies the struct value. Assigning a struct value to a variable of type Object creates a boxed copy of the struct value on the heap, and assigns the variable a reference to that copy; see section 14.1.

```
SPoint p = new SPoint(11, 22);          // Create a struct value in p
SPoint[] arr = { p, p };                // Two more copies of p
arr[0].x = 33;
Console.WriteLine(arr[0] + " " + arr[1]);  // Prints (33, 22) (11, 22)
Object o = p;                           // Another copy of p, in heap
p.x = 44;
Console.WriteLine(p + " " + o);         // Prints (44, 22) (11, 22)
Console.WriteLine(o is SPoint);         // Prints True
Console.WriteLine(o is int);            // Prints False
```

**Example 127**  The this Reference in a Struct Type
In a struct type declaration, this is assignable like a ref parameter, so method Move inside struct type SPoint from example 125 can equivalently be written as shown in the first line below. Although this does not create a "new" struct value, it may be less efficient than direct field assignment.

Even when a struct method returns this, the method call chain p.Move(5,5).Move(6,6) may not have the expected effect. The expression p.Move(5,5) is a value, so the second call to Move works on a copy of struct p, not the struct held in variable p. Also, a readonly field of struct type is a value, so q.Move(5,5) works on a copy of q and therefore does not modify the field q; see section 14.3.

```
public SPoint Move(int dx, int dy) { return this = new SPoint(x+dx, y+dy); }
...
static readonly SPoint q = new SPoint(33, 44);
public static void Main(String[] args) {
  SPoint p = new SPoint(11, 22);      // Now p = (11, 22)
  p.Move(9,8);                        // Now p = (20, 30)
  p.Move(5,5).Move(6,6);              // Now p = (25, 35) not (31, 41)
  q.Move(5,5);                        // Now q = (33, 44) not (38, 49)
}
```

## 14.1 Boxing of Struct Values

When a value of a struct type is assigned to a variable of a reference type, the value is automatically *boxed*. That is, a copy of the struct is allocated on the heap, as in the picture below: variable o of type Object refers to a boxed struct on the heap. This is the state after executing the code in example 126:

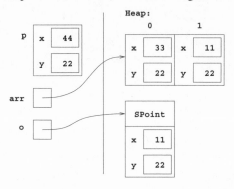

Similar boxing happens whenever a struct value, enum or simple value is bound to a variable, parameter or field of reference type, or is returned from a method whose return type is a reference type.

When a value gets boxed, its compile-time type is embedded in the box object, so it can subsequently be used in instance tests such as (o is SPoint).

## 14.2 The `this` Reference in a Struct

Inside a struct type declaration, this is a variable referring to an instance of the struct type. In methods, properties and indexers it can be read from and assigned to, as if it were a ref parameter; see example 127.

In the constructors of a struct declaration, the this reference can only be assigned to, not read from, as if it were an out parameter. However, unlike an out parameter in a method, it does not have to be definitely assigned in the constructors: the struct's fields are always initialized anyway.

## 14.3 Struct Expressions: Value or Variable

An instance method in a class is always invoked on an object reference, either explicitly as in o.M(...) or implicitly as in M(...) which means this.M(...). Therefore, if method M assigns to an instance field, then that will affect the field in the object referred to by expression o or this.

However, when invoking an instance method in a struct type by o.M(...), one must distinguish whether o is a *variable* or a *value*. The *variable* case is when o is a local variable or parameter x, this, a non-readonly field f, or an array element access a[i]. The *value* case is when o is any other expression, such as a boxing conversion, a read-only field, or a call to a method, delegate, property or indexer.

When o is a variable, an instance field assignment performed by M in a call o.M(...) will affect the field of the struct held in variable o. On the other hand, when o is a value, then a field assignment performed by M in a call o.M(...) will affect a field of an anonymous struct value that is not accessible in any other way. In particular, this happens in a call chain such as p.Move(5,5).Move(6,6) because p.Move(5,5) is a value, not a variable; see example 127. Moreover, it happens when o is a readonly field; then o.Move(5,5) has no effect on the field o.

**Example 128** A Struct Type for Rational Numbers

A rational number has the form n/d, where n and d are long integers, and can be represented as a struct of type Frac. The Frac type defines a constructor, overloaded arithmetic operators + and *, an implicit conversion from long, an explicit conversion to double, comparison operators == and !=, methods Equals and GetHashCode, and method CompareTo so it implements IComparable. Unfortunately the default argumentless constructor Frac() initializes n and d to zero, so the desirable invariant d $\neq$ 0 does not hold. Fortunately, computing with such ill-formed Frac values will throw DivideByZeroException (in auxiliary method Gcd).

```csharp
struct Frac : IComparable {
  public readonly long n, d;         // NB: Meaningful only if d!=0
  public Frac(long n, long d) {
    long f = Gcd(n, d); this.n = n/f; this.d = d/f;
  }
  public static Frac operator+(Frac r1, Frac r2) {
    return new Frac(r1.n*r2.d+r2.n*r1.d, r1.d*r2.d);
  }
  public static Frac operator*(Frac r1, Frac r2) {
    return new Frac(r1.n*r2.n, r1.d*r2.d);
  }
  public static Frac operator++(Frac r) { return r + 1; }
  public static bool operator==(Frac r1, Frac r2) {
    return r1.n==r2.n && r1.d==r2.d;
  }
  public static bool operator!=(Frac r1, Frac r2) { ... }
  public int CompareTo(Object that) { ... }
  public override bool Equals(Object that) { ... }
  public override int GetHashCode() { ... }
  public static implicit operator Frac(long n) {
    return new Frac(n, 1);
  }
  public static explicit operator double(Frac r) {
    return ((double)r.n)/r.d;
  }
  public override String ToString() { ... }
  private static long Gcd(long m, long n) { ... }
}
...
Frac r1 = new Frac(6, 2), r2 = new Frac(5, 2);
Console.WriteLine("r1={0} and r2={1}", r1, r2);
Console.WriteLine((double)r2);     // Explicit conversion to double
r2 = r2 * r2;                      // Overloaded multiplication
Console.WriteLine("{0} {1} {2} {3} {4}", r2, ++r2, r2, r2++, r2);
r2 = 0;                            // Implicit conversion from long
for (int i=1; i<=10; i++) {
  r2 += new Frac(1, i);            // Overloaded += derived from overloaded +
  Console.WriteLine(r2 + " " + (r2 == new Frac(11, 6)));
}
```

# 15   Interfaces

## 15.1   Interface Declarations

An *interface* describes methods, properties, indexers and events but does not implement them. An *interface-declaration* may contain method descriptions, property descriptions, indexer descriptions, and event descriptions. The descriptions in an interface may appear in any order:

```
interface-modifiers interface I base-interfaces {
    method-descriptions
    property-descriptions
    indexer-descriptions
    event-descriptions
}
```

An interface may be declared at top-level or inside a namespace or class or struct. At top-level or in a namespace, the *interface-modifiers* may be public or internal or absent (which means internal). Inside a class or struct, the *interface-modifiers* may be one of the member access modifiers (section 10.3). In a class it may also be new to hide an interface inherited from a base class.

An interface declaration may consist of one or more partial type declarations; see section 26.

The *base-interfaces* clause may be absent. Otherwise the interface declaration has the form

```
interface-modifiers interface I : I1, I2, ... { ... }
```

where I1, I2, ... is a non-empty list of interfaces. If the *base-interfaces* clause is present, then interface I describes all those members described by I1, I2, ..., and interface I is a *subinterface* of I1, I2, .... Interface I can describe additional methods, properties, indexers and events not described by the base interfaces I1, I2, ..., and it may hide inherited member descriptions by describing new members.

A *method-description* for method M must have the form:

```
description-modifier returntype M(formal-list);
```

where the *description-modifier* should be new if the description hides a member description inherited from a base interface such as I1 (otherwise a compiler warning is given). No access modifiers can be given; all interface members are implicitly public. A *property-description* for a property P must have the form

```
description-modifier returntype P {
    get;
    set;
}
```

where one of get and set may be left out. An *indexer-description* must have the form

```
description-modifier returntype this[formal-list] {
    get;
    set;
}
```

where one of get and set may be left out. An *event-description* for an event E must have the form

```
description-modifier event delegate-type E;
```

**Example 129** Three Interface Declarations
The Colored interface describes property GetColor, interface Drawable describes method Draw, and ColoredDrawable describes both. The methods are implicitly public.

```
using System.Drawing;            // Color, Graphics, SolidBrush, Pen, ...
interface IColored { Color GetColor { get; } }
interface IDrawable { void Draw(Graphics g); }
interface IColoredDrawable : IColored, IDrawable {}
```

**Example 130** Classes Implementing Interfaces
Property GetColor and method Draw must be public as in the above interfaces.

```
class ColoredPoint : Point, IColored {
  protected Color c;
  public ColoredPoint(int x, int y, Color c) : base(x, y) { this.c = c; }
  public Color GetColor { get { return c; } }
}
class ColoredDrawablePoint : ColoredPoint, IColoredDrawable {
  public ColoredDrawablePoint(int x, int y, Color c) : base(x, y, c) { }
  public void Draw(Graphics g) {
    g.FillRectangle(new SolidBrush(c), x, y, 2, 2);
  }
}
class ColoredRectangle : IColoredDrawable {
  private int x1, x2, y1, y2;   // (x1, y1) upper left, (x2, y2) lower right
  protected Color c;
  public ColoredRectangle(int x1, int y1, int x2, int y2, Color c)
  { this.x1 = x1; this.y1 = y1; this.x2 = x2; this.y2 = y2; this.c = c; }
  public Color GetColor { get { return c; } }
  public void Draw(Graphics g) { g.DrawRectangle(new Pen(c), x1, y1, x2, y2); }
}
```

**Example 131** An Interface Is a Type
A Colored value has a GetColor property; a ColoredDrawable value in addition has a Draw method:

```
static void PrintColors(IColored[] cs) {
  for (int i=0; i<cs.Length; i++)
    Console.WriteLine(cs[i].GetColor);
}

static void Draw(Graphics g, IColoredDrawable[] cs) {
  for (int i=0; i<cs.Length; i++) {
    Console.WriteLine(cs[i].GetColor);
    cs[i].Draw(g);
  }
}
```

## 15.2    Classes and Struct Types Implementing Interfaces

A class C (section 10.1) may be declared to implement one or more interfaces by a *class-base-clause*. Similarly, a struct type S (section 14) may be declared to implement one or more interfaces by a *struct-interface-clause*. Both have the form

```
: I1, I2, ...
```

If this is applied to the declaration of a class C, it means that a reference of class C is implicitly convertible to type I1, I2, and so on by a reference conversion (section 5.3.2). If applied to the declaration of a struct type S, it means that a value of type S is implicitly convertible to type I1, I2, and so on by a boxing conversion (section 14.1). The interfaces I1, I2, and so on are called the *base interfaces* of the class or struct type.

The compiler will check that C declares — or inherits from a superclass — every function member described by I1, I2, ..., with exactly the prescribed signature, including ref and out modifiers, and the prescribed return type. Only public instance methods, properties, indexers and events in a class or struct can implement a member described by an interface; a static or non-public member cannot.

A class or struct may implement any number of interfaces.

## 15.3    Explicit Interface Member Implementations

When a class C implements an interface I, the class may declare an *explicit interface member implementation* of any method, property, indexer or event described by interface I. Such implementations have these forms:

```
returntype I.M(formal-list) method-body
returntype I.P { get get-body  set set-body }
returntype I.this[formal-list] { get get-body  set set-body }
event delegate-type I.E { add add-body  remove remove-body }
```

An explicit interface member implementation cannot have access modifiers, but is implicitly public. Also, it cannot include any of the modifiers abstract, virtual, override, new or static. A member cannot explicitly implement more than one interface.

A member declared by an explicit interface member implementation is an instance member and must be accessed as o.M(...) or o.P or o[...] where o is an expression of interface type, possibly obtained by an explicit cast as in example 133.

Explicit interface implementation is particularly useful when a class must implement both a generic interface such as IEnumerator<T> and a legacy non-generic interface such as IEnumerator; see section 24.2. Each of these interfaces describes a read-only property Current, but with different types: T and Object, respectively. Using explicit interface member implementation one can declare them as follows, thereby implementing both interface IEnumerator<T> and interface IEnumerator:

```
T IEnumerator<T>.Current { get { ... } }
Object IEnumerator.Current { get { ... } }
```

**Example 132** Interface Properties and Indexers

The ISeq interface is a subinterface of IEnumerable (a sequence can be enumerated) and describes a read-only property Count giving the length of a sequence, as well as two indexers that return sequence members. Struct Seq from example 61 implements ISeq when the property and indexers have been added.

```
interface ISeq : IEnumerable {
  int Count { get; }
  int this[int i] { get; }
  int[] this[params int[] ii] { get; }
}
struct Seq : ISeq {
  ...
  public int Count { get { return n; } }
  public int this[int i] { get { return b + k * i; } }
  public int[] this[params int[] ii] { get { ... this[ii[h]] ... } }
}
```

**Example 133** Explicit Interface Member Implementation

Explicit interface member implementations allow class C to implement method M0 specified by I1 as well as M0 specified by I2 although the latter hides the former. It also allows class C to implement the method signature M1() despite interfaces I2 and I3 having different return types for it. A subclass D of C inherits C's explicit interface member implementations.

```
interface I1 { void M0(); }
interface I2 : I1 {
  new void M0();
  int M1();
}
interface I3 : I1 {
  void M1();
  int P { get; }
  int this[int i] { get; }
}
class C : I1, I2, I3 {
  public void M0() { Console.Write("C.M0 "); }
  void I1.M0() { Console.Write("C:I1.M0 "); }
  void I2.M0() { Console.Write("C:I2.M0 "); }
  int  I2.M1() { Console.Write("C:I2.M1 "); return 1; }
  void I3.M1() { Console.Write("C:I3.M1 "); }
  int I3.P { get { return 11; } }
  int I3.this[int i] { get { return i+((I3)this).P; } }
  // void I3.M0() { }                  // Illegal: M0 not explicitly in I3
}
class D : C { }
...
C c = new C();
// C.M0    C:I1.M0       C:I2.M0       C:I2.M1       C:I3.M1
   c.M0(); ((I1)c).M0(); ((I2)c).M0(); ((I2)c).M1(); ((I3)c).M1();
```

# 16   Enum Types

An enum type is an integer type t and zero or more compile-time constants of that type.

An *enum-type-declaration* has the form:

```
enum-modifiers enum t base-clause {
    enum-member-list
}
```

where *enum-member-list* is a (possibly empty) comma-separated list of enum member declarations, each having one of these forms:

```
enum-member
enum-member = constant-expression
```

The *enum-modifiers* control the accessibility of the enum type and follow the same rules as class access modifiers (section 10.12). The modifiers abstract and sealed cannot be used. The *base-clause* determines the underlying *representation type* of the enum type. If the *base-clause* is present, it must have the form  : *type*  where *type* is one of byte, sbyte, short, ushort, int, or uint. If the *base-clause* is absent, then the underlying representation type is int.

The representation value of an *enum-member* is the value of the *constant-expression* if the *enum-member* has one. Otherwise, if the *enum-member* is the first one in the list, then the value is zero. Otherwise, it is the value of the preceding *enum-member*, plus one. The *constant-expression* must be compile-time constant, and may refer to (unqualified) *enum-members* from the same enum type, but it is a compile-time error for *enum-members* to be recursively defined. Distinct enum members may have the same underlying representation value. It is a compile-time error for the *constant-expression* to evaluate to a value not representable in the underlying representation type.

Outside an enum declaration, an *enum-member* must be written in its fully qualified form, such as Month.Jan.

An enum member has the type t of the enclosing enum type declaration. An enum member can be explicitly cast to the underlying representation type; there are no implicit conversions. The value 0 may be implicitly cast to the enum type; other values of the underlying representation type must be explicitly cast to the enum type. In either case the resulting enum value need not correspond to any declared enum member; this is not considered an error.

The following 14 operators can be applied to enum members:

```
==  !=  <  >  <=  >=  +  -  ^  &  |  ~  ++  --
```

The comparison operators must be applied to two arguments of the same enum type t; the result has type bool. The operators + and - can be used only to add an integer to an enum value of type t or subtract an integer from an enum value of type t; the result has type t. The bitwise operators (^, &, and |) must be applied to two arguments of the same enum type t; the result has type t.

Arithmetics on enum members may produce results in the underlying representation type that do not correspond to any declared enum member; this is not an error.

An enum type is a subclass of System.Enum, whose ToString method converts an enum value to a string as follows: If the enum value corresponds to one or more declared enum members, it will be formatted as a symbol, such as "Jan"; if it does not, it will be formatted as an integer, such as "7".

**Example 134** Representing Weekdays and Months Using Enum Types

When specifying a date it is desirable to use numbers for years (2003), dates (31) and ISO week numbers (22), but symbolic values for weekdays (Sat) and months (May). In calendrical calculations it is useful to assign numbers 0–6 to the weekdays (Mon–Sun) and numbers 1–12 to the months (Jan–Dec). This is done in the enum types Day and Month below; note the `Jan=1` in Month. Method `FromDaynumber` uses `m++` to increment a month number (an enum value), method `Weekday` computes the weekday by casting the remainder modulo 7 to enum type Day, and method `ToString` casts a month (an enum value) to `int`.

```
public enum Day { Mon, Tue, Wed, Thu, Fri, Sat, Sun }
public enum Month { Jan=1, Feb, Mar, Apr, May, Jun, Jul, Aug, Sep, Oct, Nov, Dec }
public class Date {
  readonly int yy /* 0-9999 */, dd /* 1-31 */;
  readonly Month mm;
  public Date(int yy, Month mm, int dd) { ... }
  ...
  public static int MonthDays(int y, Month m) {
    switch (m) {
    case Month.Apr: case Month.Jun: case Month.Sep: case Month.Nov:
      return 30;
    case Month.Feb:
      return LeapYear(y) ? 29 : 28;
    default:
      return 31;
  } }
  public static Date FromDaynumber(int n) {
    ...
    Month m = Month.Jan;
    int mdays;
    while ((mdays = MonthDays(y, m)) < d) {
      d -= mdays;
      m++;
    }
    return new Date(y, m, d);
  }
  public static Day Weekday(int y, Month m, int d) {
    return (Day)((ToDaynumber(y, m, d)+6) % 7);
  }
  public override String ToString() {   // ISO format such as 2003-05-31
    return String.Format("{0:D4}-{1:D2}-{2:D2}",  yy, (int)mm, dd);
  }
}
```

**Example 135** Naming Constants Using an Enum Type

Enum types can be used also to name constants whose values reflect some external representation.

```
public enum Color : uint
{ Red = 0xFF0000, Green = 0x00FF00, Blue = 0x0000FF }
```

## 17   Delegate Types

A declaration of a *delegate type* introduces a new distinct type D, useful for creating a closure (a function-type value) from a static or instance method regardless of its declaring class. A *delegate-type-declaration* has the form:

> *delegate-modifiers* delegate *returntype* D(*formal-list*);

The *delegate-modifiers* control the accessibility of the delegate type D and follow the same rules as class access modifiers (section 10.12). The modifiers abstract and sealed cannot be used. A delegate type is a reference type (section 5.2) and is derived from System.Delegate. Note that a delegate type declaration must be followed by a semicolon (;) whereas class, interface, struct type and enum type declarations must not.

Operations on delegates:

- To create a delegate dlg of type D, evaluate an expression new D(M) where M is a static or instance method, or new D(o.M) where M is an instance method. In both cases, the method must be compatible with delegate type D. The *invocation list* of the resulting delegate contains method M only.

  If M is an instance method in a reference type, then a reference (the value of this or o) is included with the method. If M is an instance method in a value type, then a boxing conversion (section 5.3.3) occurs and a reference to a boxed copy of the value is included with the method.

- To call a delegate object dlg, evaluate the delegate call expression dlg(*actual-list*) where *actual-list* must be as for a call to a method M (section 12.15) in the delegate's invocation list. A call to the delegate will call all methods in its invocation list, in order. If the invocation list is empty, then the call throws NullReferenceException. If the *returntype* is non-void, the result of the delegate is the result of the last method called. If the delegate has a ref parameter, that parameter is threaded through all the method calls. If the delegate has an out parameter, that parameter is set by the last method called. If a method in the invocation list throws an exception, then no more methods in the list are called, and the delegate call throws the same exception.

- Delegates can be combined using the operators + and +=. The invocation list of delegate dlg1+dlg2 consists of the invocation list of dlg1 followed by the invocation list of dlg2. A method can appear multiple times on the invocation list.

- Methods can be removed from a delegate using the operators - and -=. The invocation list of delegate dlg1-dlg2 consists of the invocation list of dlg1, except that methods appearing in the invocation list of dlg2 are removed one by one from the end of dlg1. That is, if a method appears multiple times in dlg1, the last occurrence in dlg1's invocation list is removed first.

A method is *compatible* with a delegate type if the method has the same *returntype* and the same signature (*formal-list*) as the delegate type; even ref and out specifiers must match.

**Example 136** Quicksort Using a Delegate To Compare Elements

Method Qsort sorts an array of objects using the delegate cmp of delegate type DComparer to compare elements. A comparer for strings may be a delegate created from the StringReverseCompare method, or a compatible anonymous method (section 12.20), with no need for a pre-existing method.

```
public delegate int DComparer(Object v1, Object v2);
private static void Qsort(Object[] arr, DComparer cmp, int a, int b) {
  if (a < b) {
    int i = a, j = b;
    Object x = arr[(i+j) / 2];
    do {
      while (cmp(arr[i], x) < 0) i++;       // Call delegate cmp
      while (cmp(x, arr[j]) < 0) j--;       // Call delegate cmp
      if (i <= j) {
        Object tmp = arr[i]; arr[i] = arr[j]; arr[j] = tmp;
        i++; j--;
      }
    } while (i <= j);
    Qsort(arr, cmp, a, j);
    Qsort(arr, cmp, i, b);
  }
}
static int StringReverseCompare(Object v1, Object v2)
{ return String.Compare((String)v2, (String)v1); }
...
String[] sa = { "New York", "Rome", "Dublin", "Riyadh", "Tokyo" };
Qsort(sa, new DComparer(StringReverseCompare), 0, sa.Length-1);
Qsort(sa, delegate(Object v1, Object v2) { return String.Compare((String)v2, (String)v1); },
      0, sa.Length-1);
```

**Example 137** Combining Delegates

Initially the invocation list of dlg3 has two methods: o.M1 and M2. After adding dlg3 to itself, its invocation list is o.M1, M2, o.M1, and M2, so calling dlg3 makes four method calls. Each method increments the parameter y which is passed by reference. Subtracting a delegate with invocation list o.M1 removes the last copy of o.M1 from dlg3. Subtracting o1.M1 has no effect if instances o1 and o are different.

```
public static void Main(String[] args) {
  TestDelegate o = new TestDelegate();
  D dlg1 = new D(o.M1), dlg2 = new D(M2), dlg3 = dlg1 + dlg2;
  dlg3 += dlg3;
  int y = 0;
  Console.WriteLine(dlg3(ref y));      // Prints: M1/1 M2/2 M1/3 M2/4 4
  dlg3 -= new D(o.M1);
  Console.WriteLine(dlg3(ref y));      // Prints: M1/5 M2/6 M2/7 7
}
public delegate int D(ref int x);
int M1(ref int x) { x++; Console.Write("M1/{0} ", x); return x; }
static int M2(ref int x) { x++; Console.Write("M2/{0} ", x); return x; }
```

# 18   Nullable Types over Value Types (C# 2.0)

A *nullable type* t? is used to represent possibly missing values of type t, where t is a value type such as int, a struct type, or a type parameter that has a struct constraint. A value of type t? either is non-null and contains a proper value of type t, or is the unique null value. The default value of a nullable type is null. The nullable type t? is an alias for System.Nullable<t> and is itself a value type. The types t? and t?? and t??? and so on are identical; making a nullable type nullable does not change it.

A nullable type such as int? is useful because the custom of using null to represent a missing value of reference type does not carry over to value types: null is not a legal value of the plain value type int.

Values v1 and v2 of nullable type support the following operations:

- Read-only property v1.HasValue of type bool returns true if v1 is non-null; false if it is null.
- Read-only property v1.Value of type t returns a copy of the proper value in v1 if v1 is non-null and has type t?; it throws InvalidOperationException if v1 is null.
- Standard implicit conversions: The implicit conversion from v of type t to t? gives a non-null value containing a copy of v. The implicit coercion from null to t? gives the null value.
- Standard explicit conversions: (t)v1 coerces from t? to t and is equivalent to v1.Value.
- Lifted conversions: Whenever there is an implicit (or explicit) coercion from value type ts to value type tt, there is an implicit (or explicit) coercion from ts? to tt?.
- Lifted unary operators  + ++ - -- ! ~ : If argument type and result type of an existing operator are non-nullable value types, then an additional lifted operator is automatically defined for the corresponding nullable types. If the argument is null, the result is null; otherwise the underlying operator is applied to the proper value in the argument.
- Lifted binary operators  + - * / % & | ^ << >> : If the argument types and the result type of an existing operator are non-nullable value types, then an additional lifted operator is automatically defined for the corresponding nullable types. If any argument is null, the result is null; otherwise the underlying operator is applied to the proper values in the arguments. The corresponding compound assignment operator, such as +=, is automatically defined for nullable types also.
- Equality comparisons: v1==v2 is true if both v1 and v2 are null or both are non-null and contain the same value, false otherwise; v1!=v2 is the negation of v1==v2. Unless other definitions are applicable, v1!=null means v1.HasValue and v1==null means !v1.HasValue,
- Ordering comparisons: v1<v2 and v1<=v2 and v1>v2 and v1>=v2 have type bool. A comparison evaluates to false if v1 or v2 is null; otherwise it compares the proper values in v1 and v2.
- The *null-coalescing* operator v1 ?? v2 evaluates to the proper value in v1 if it has one; otherwise evaluates v2. It can be used on reference types also, and then is equivalent to v1!=null ? v1 : v2.

The nullable type bool? has values null, false and true as in the three-valued logic of the SQL query language. In if, for, while, do-while and the ?: operator, a null value of type bool? means false. The operators & and | have special definitions that compute a proper truth value when possible:

| x&y | null | false | true |
|-------|-------|-------|-------|
| null | null | false | null |
| false | false | false | false |
| true | null | false | true |

| x\|y | null | false | true |
|-------|-------|-------|-------|
| null | null | null | true |
| false | null | false | true |
| true | true | true | true |

**Example 138** Partial Function with Nullable Return Type
Instead of throwing an exception, a computation that fails may return the null value of a nullable type.

```
public static int? Sqrt(int? x) {
  if (x.HasValue && x.Value >= 0)
    return (int)(Math.Sqrt(x.Value));
  else
    return null;
}
...
Console.WriteLine(":{0}:{1}:{2}:", Sqrt(5), Sqrt(null), Sqrt(-5));  // Prints :2:::
```

**Example 139** Computing with Nullable Integers
Arithmetic operators such as + and += are automatically lifted to nullable numbers. Ordering comparisons such as > are false if any argument is null; the equality comparisons are not. The null-coalescing operator ?? gets the proper value or provides a default: note that variable sum has plain type int.

```
int? i1 = 11, i2 = 22, i3 = null, i4 = i1+i2, i5 = i1+i3;
// Values: 11 22 null 33 null
int i6 = (int)i1;                    // Legal
// int i7 = (int)i5;                 // Legal but fails at run-time
// int i8 = i1;                      // Illegal
int?[] iarr = { i1, i2, i3, i4, i5 };
i2 += i1;
i2 += i4;
Console.WriteLine("i2 = {0}", i2);   // 66 = 11+22+33
int sum = 0;
for (int i=0; i<iarr.Length; i++)
  sum += iarr[i] ?? 0;
Console.WriteLine("sum = {0}", sum); // 66 = 11+22+33
for (int i=0; i<iarr.Length; i++)
  if (iarr[i] > 11)
    Console.Write("[{0}] ", iarr[i]); // 22 33
for (int i=0; i<iarr.Length; i++)
  if (iarr[i] != i1)
    Console.Write("[{0}] ", iarr[i]); // 22 null 33 null
```

**Example 140** The Nullable Bool Type
Like other lifted operators, the bool? operators ! and ^ return null when an argument is null. The operators & and | are special and can produce a non-null result although one argument is null.

```
bool? b1 = null, b2 = false, b3 = true;
bool? b4 = b1^b2, b5 = b1&b2, b6 = b1|b2;              // null false null
bool? b7 = b1^b3, b8 = b1&b3, b9 = b1|b3;              // null null true
Console.WriteLine(b1 ? "null is true" : "null is false");    // null is false
Console.WriteLine(!b1 ? "!null is true" : "!null is false"); // !null is false
```

# 19   Exceptions

An *exception* is an object of an exception type: a subclass of class Exception. An exception is used to signal and describe an abnormal situation during program execution. The evaluation of an expression or the execution of a statement may terminate abruptly by throwing an exception, either by executing a `throw` statement (section 13.8.1) or by executing a primitive operation, such as assignment to an array element, that may throw an exception.

A thrown exception may be caught in a dynamically enclosing `try-catch` statement (section 13.8.2). A caught exception may be re-thrown by a `throw` statement. If the exception is not caught, then the entire program execution will be aborted, and information from the exception is reported to the user (for example, in the command prompt console). What is printed on the console is determined by the exception's `ToString` method.

In an exception, the `Message` property is the message carried by the exception, and the `StackTrace` property is the stacktrace at the point where the exception was thrown. Both have type String.

Below is part of the exception class hierarchy, and for each exception the namespace in which it is declared. Predefined exceptions are subclasses of SystemException; user-defined exceptions should be made subclasses of ApplicationException:

| Exception Class | Namespace |
|---|---|
| Exception | System |
|   ApplicationException | System |
|   SystemException | System |
|     ArgumentException | System |
|       ArgumentNullException | System |
|       ArgumentOutOfRangeException | System |
|     ArrayTypeMismatchException | System |
|     DivideByZeroException | System |
|     FormatException | System |
|     IndexOutOfRangeException | System |
|     InvalidCastException | System |
|     InvalidOperationException | System |
|       ObjectDisposedException | System |
|     InvalidProgramException | System |
|     NotImplementedException | System |
|     NotSupportedException | System |
|     NullReferenceException | System |
|     OverflowException | System |
|     RankException | System |
|     StackOverflowException | System |
|     SynchronizationLockException | System.Threading |
|     ThreadInterruptedException | System.Threading |
|     ThreadStateException | System.Threading |
|     TypeInitializationException | System |
|     TypeLoadException | System |
|     IOException | System.IO |
|       DirectoryNotFoundException | System.IO |
|       EndOfStreamException | System.IO |
|       FileNotFoundException | System.IO |
|       InternalBufferOverflowException | System.IO |
|       PathTooLongException | System.IO |

**Example 141** Declaring an Application Exception Class
This is the class of exceptions thrown by method WeekDayNo4 (example 117). The string passed to the constructor of the base class ApplicationException is the string that will be returned by the Message property of the exception.

```
class WeekdayException : ApplicationException {
  public WeekdayException(String wday) : base("Illegal weekday: " + wday) {
  }
}
```

**Example 142** All Paths through a `try-catch-finally` Statement
To exercise all 12 paths through the `try-catch-finally` statement (section 13.8.2) in method M below, run the program with each of these command-line arguments: 101 102 201 202 301 302 411 412 421 422 431 432. The try clause terminates normally on arguments $1yz$, exits by return on $2yz$, and throws an exception on $3yz$ and $4yz$. However, when $z$ is 2, the finally clause takes over; see below. The catch clause ignores exceptions thrown on $3yz$ but catches those thrown on $4yz$. The catch clause terminates normally on 411, exits by return on 421, and throws an exception on 431 and 432. The finally clause terminates normally on $xy1$ and so lets the try or catch clause determine whether to terminate normally, by return, or by throwing an exception. The finally clause throws an exception on $xy2$. This is the (only) exception thrown if the try and catch clauses did not throw an uncaught exception, but if they did throw an uncaught exception then finally's exception will be thrown in addition.

Exits by break and continue statements are handled similarly to return; a more involved example could be constructed to illustrate their interaction.

```
class TryCatchFinally {
  public static void Main(String[] args)
  { Console.WriteLine(M(int.Parse(args[0]))); }

  static String M(int a) {
    try {
      Console.Write("try ... ");
      if (a/100 == 2) return "returned from try";
      if (a/100 == 3) throw new Exception("thrown by try");
      if (a/100 == 4) throw new ApplicationException("thrown by try");
    } catch (ApplicationException) {
      Console.Write("catch ... ");
      if (a/10%10 == 2) return "returned from catch";
      if (a/10%10 == 3) throw new Exception("thrown by catch");
    } finally {
      Console.WriteLine("finally");
      if (a%10 == 2) throw new Exception("thrown by finally");
    }
    return "terminated normally with " + a;
  }
}
```

# 20   Threads, Concurrent Execution, and Synchronization

## 20.1   Threads and Concurrent Execution

In sequential program execution, expressions are evaluated and statements are executed one after the other, in a single thread of execution: a *thread* is an independent sequential activity. A C# program may execute several threads concurrently, that is, potentially overlapping in time. For instance, one part of a program may continue computing while another part is blocked waiting for input; see example 143.

A thread is created and controlled using an object of the sealed class Thread found in the namespace System.Threading. A thread object is created from a delegate of type void ThreadStart(), also from System.Threading. When started, the new thread executes the body of that delegate. To every thread (independent sequential activity) there is a unique controlling Thread object, so the two are often identified.

To create and run a thread, declare an argumentless void method such as void Run(), create a ThreadStart delegate from Run, and create a thread object from the delegate:

```
Thread u = new Thread(new ThreadStart(Run))
```

Call u.Start() to allow the thread to execute Run concurrently with other threads. See example 143.

Threads can communicate with each other via shared state, by using and assigning static fields, instance fields, and array elements; see example 146. Two threads can communicate via a local variable or parameter only if both are created from anonymous delegates within the same method activation.

### States and State Transitions of a Thread

A thread is alive if it has been started and has not died. A thread dies by exiting the delegate from which it was created, either by returning or by throwing an exception. A live thread is in one of the states Enabled (ready to run), Running (actually executing), Sleeping (waiting for a timeout), Joining (waiting for another thread to die), Locking (trying to obtain the lock on object o), or Waiting (for notification on object o). The state transitions of a thread can be summarized by this table and the figure opposite:

| From State | To State | Reason for Transition |
|---|---|---|
| Enabled | Running | the system schedules the thread for execution |
| Running | Enabled | the system preempts the thread and schedules another one |
|  | Waiting | the thread executes Monitor.Wait(o), thus releasing the lock on o |
|  | Locking | the thread attempts to execute lock (o) { ... } |
|  | Sleeping | the thread executes Thread.Sleep() |
|  | Joining | the thread executes u.Join() |
|  | Dead | the thread exited its delegate by returning or by throwing an exception |
| Sleeping | Enabled | the sleeping period expired |
|  | Enabled | the thread was interrupted; throws ThreadInterruptedException when run |
| Joining | Enabled | the thread u being joined died, or the join timed out |
|  | Enabled | the thread was interrupted; throws ThreadInterruptedException when run |
| Waiting | Locking | another thread executed Monitor.Pulse(o) or Monitor.PulseAll(o) |
|  | Locking | the wait for the lock on o timed out |
|  | Locking | the thread was interrupted; throws ThreadInterruptedException when run |
| Locking | Enabled | the lock on o became available and was given to this thread |

**Example 143** Multiple Threads

The main program creates a new thread, binds it to u, and starts it. Now two threads are executing concurrently: one executes Main, and another executes Run. While the Main method is blocked waiting for keyboard input, the new thread keeps incrementing i. The new thread executes Sleep(0) to make sure that the other thread is allowed to run (when not blocked waiting for keyboard input).

```
using System; using System.Threading;
class ThreadDemo {
  private static int i;
  public static void Main() {
    Thread u = new Thread(new ThreadStart(Run));
    u.Start();
    Console.WriteLine("Repeatedly press Enter to get the current value of i:");
    for (;;) {
      Console.ReadLine();                      // Wait for keyboard input
      Console.WriteLine(i);
  } }
  private static void Run() {
    for (;;) {                                 // Forever
      i++;                                     //   increment i
      Thread.Sleep(0);                         //   yield to other thread
} } }
```

## The States and State Transitions of a Thread

A thread's transition from one state to another may be caused by a method call performed by the thread itself (shown in the typewriter font), by a method call possibly performed by another thread (shown in the *slanted* font); and by timeouts and other actions (shown in the default font). In the figure, u denotes another thread and o denotes an object used for locking.

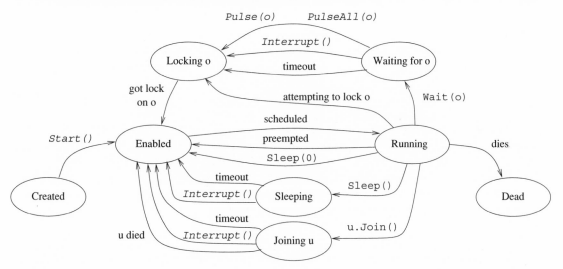

## 20.2   Locks and the `lock` Statement

Concurrent threads are executed independently. Therefore, when multiple concurrent threads access the same fields or array elements, there is danger of creating an inconsistent state; see example 145. To avoid this, threads may synchronize the access to shared state, such as objects and arrays. A single *lock* is associated with every object, array, and class. A lock can be held by at most one thread at a time. A thread may explicitly request a lock by executing a lock statement, which has this form:

```
lock (expression)
    block-statement
```

The *expression* must have reference type. The *expression* must evaluate to a non-`null` reference o; otherwise a NullReferenceException is thrown. After the evaluation of the *expression*, the thread becomes Locking on object o; see the figure on page 119. When the thread obtains the lock on object o (if ever), the thread becomes Enabled, and may become Running so the *block-statement* is executed. When the *block-statement* terminates or is exited by `return` or `break` or `continue` or `goto` or by throwing an exception, then the lock on o is released.

That is, the thread will execute the *block-statement* only when it has obtained the lock on the current object. It will hold the lock until it leaves the *block-statement*, and release it at that time. Moreover, it may temporarily release the lock by calling `Monitor.Wait(o)`; see below and in section 20.3.

When one or more static methods of a class C must ensure exclusive access to static fields, they can lock on the unique object of class Type that represents class C in the run-time system. This object is obtained by evaluating `typeof(C)`. Hence the critical sections may be enclosed in a `lock` statement such as this:

```
lock (typeof(C))
    block-statement
```

That is, the thread will execute the method body only when it has obtained the lock on the object returned by `typeof(C)`, which is the unique object of class Type associated with the class C; see section 12.19.

Mutual exclusion is ensured only if *all* threads accessing a shared object make sure to lock it before use. For instance, if we add an unsynchronized method RogueTransfer to a bank object (example 145), we can no longer be sure that a thread calling the synchronized method Transfer has exclusive access to the bank object: any number of threads could be executing RogueTransfer at the same time.

A *monitor* is an object whose fields are private and are manipulated only after obtaining object's lock, so that all field access is subject to synchronization; see example 146.

If a thread u needs to wait for some condition to become true, or for a resource to become available, it may temporarily release its lock on object o by calling `Monitor.Wait(o)`. The thread must hold the lock on object o, otherwise exception SynchronizationLockException is thrown. The thread u will be added to the *wait set* of o, that is, the set of threads waiting for notification on object o. This notification must come from another thread which has obtained the lock on o and which executes `Monitor.Pulse(o)` or `Monitor.PulseAll(o)`. The notifying thread does not release its lock on o. After being notified, u must obtain the lock on o again before it can proceed. Thus when the call to `Monitor.Wait` returns, thread u will hold the lock on o just as before the call; see example 146.

**Example 144** Mutual Exclusion

A Printer thread forever prints a (-) followed by a (/). If we create and run two concurrent printer threads by executing new Thread(new ThreadStart(Printer.Run)).Start() twice, then only one of them can hold the lock on object mutex at a time, so no other symbols can be printed between (-) and (/) in one iteration of the for loop, and the program must print -/-/-/-/-/ and so on. If the lock-statement is removed, it may print --//--/-/-//--// and so on. The call Util.Pause(100,300) pauses between 100 and 300 ms to emphasize the inherent non-determinacy of unsynchronized concurrency.

```
class Printer {
  static readonly Object mutex = new Object();
  public static void Run() {
    for (;;) {
      lock (mutex) {
        Console.Write("-");
        Util.Pause(100,300);
        Console.Write("/");
      }
      Util.Pause(200);
} } }
```

**Example 145** Synchronized Methods in an Object

The bank object below has two accounts. Money is repeatedly being transferred from one account to the other by clerks. The total amount of money should remain constant at 30. This holds when the Transfer method locks the accounts, because only one clerk can access them at a time. If the lock-statement is removed, one clerk can overwrite the other's deposits and withdrawals, and the sum may differ from 30.

```
class Bank {
  private int account1 = 10, account2 = 20;
  public void Transfer(int amount) {
    lock (this) {
      int new1 = account1 - amount;
      Util.Pause(10);
      account1 = new1; account2 = account2 + amount;
      Console.WriteLine("Sum is " + (account1+account2));
} } }
class Clerk {
  private Bank bank;
  public Clerk(Bank bank) { this.bank = bank; }
  public void Run() {
    for (;;) {                                // Forever
      bank.Transfer(Util.Random(-10, 10));    //   transfer money
      Util.Pause(200, 300);                   //   then take a break
} } }
... Bank bank = new Bank();
... Clerk clerk1 = new Clerk(bank), clerk2 = new Clerk(bank);
... new Thread(new ThreadStart(clerk1.Run)).Start();
... new Thread(new ThreadStart(clerk2.Run)).Start();
```

## 20.3   Operations on Threads

The current thread, whose state is Running, may call these methods among others. More Thread methods are described in the .Net Framework Class Library.

- `Thread.Sleep(n)` sleeps for n milliseconds: the current thread becomes Sleeping, and after n milliseconds becomes Enabled. If n is 0 then it becomes Enabled immediately, but by going from Running to Enabled it allows the system to schedule another Enabled thread, if any. May throw ThreadInterruptedException if the thread is interrupted while sleeping.
- `Thread.CurrentThread()` returns the current thread object.

Let u be an object of class Thread. Then

- `u.Start()` changes the state of u to Enabled, so that the delegate from which it was created will be called when a processor becomes available.
- `u.Interrupt()` interrupts the thread u: if u is Running or Enabled or Locking, then its interrupted status is set to true. If u is Sleeping or Joining it will become Enabled, and if it is Waiting it will become Locking; in these cases u will throw ThreadInterruptedException when and if it becomes Running (and then the interrupted status is set to false).
- `u.Join()` waits for thread u to die; may throw ThreadInterruptedException if the current thread is interrupted while waiting.
- `u.Join(n)` works as `u.Join()` but times out and returns after at most n milliseconds. There is no indication whether the call returned because of a timeout or because u died.

## 20.4   Operations on Locked Objects

A thread which holds the lock on an object o may call the following methods from the Monitor class in the System.Threading namespace. The methods throw ArgumentNullException if o is null, and SynchronizationLockException if the calling thread does not hold the lock on o.

- `Monitor.Wait(o)` releases the lock on o, changes its own state to Waiting, and adds itself to the set of threads waiting for notification on o. When notified by `Pulse` or `PulseAll` (if ever), the thread must obtain the lock on o, so when the call to `Wait` returns, it again holds the lock on o. May throw ThreadInterruptedException if the thread is interrupted while waiting.
- `Monitor.Wait(o, n)` works as `Monitor.Wait(o)` except that the thread will change state to Locking after n milliseconds, regardless of whether there has been a notification on o or not. There is no indication whether the state change was caused by a timeout or because of a notification.
- `Monitor.Pulse(o)` chooses an arbitrary thread among the threads waiting for notification on o (if any), and changes the state of that thread to Locking. The chosen thread cannot actually obtain the lock on o until the current thread has released it.
- `Monitor.PulseAll(o)` works as `Monitor.Pulse(o)`, except that it changes the state to Locking for *all* threads waiting for notification on o.

**Example 146** Producers and Consumers Communicating via a Monitor

A Buffer has room for one integer, and has a method `Put` for storing into the buffer (if empty) and a method `Get` for reading from the buffer (if non-empty); it is a monitor (page 120). A thread calling `Get` must obtain the lock on the buffer. If it finds that the buffer is empty, it calls `Wait` to release the lock and wait until something has been put into the buffer. If another thread calls `Put` and thus `Pulse`, then the getting thread will start competing for the buffer lock again, and if it gets it, will continue executing.

```
class Buffer {
  private int contents;
  private bool empty = true;
  public int Get() {
    lock (this) {
      while (empty) Monitor.Wait(this);
      empty = true;
      Monitor.Pulse(this);
      return contents;
  } }
  public void Put(int v) {
    lock (this) {
      while (!empty) Monitor.Wait(this);
      empty = false; contents = v;
      Monitor.Pulse(this);
} } }
```

**Example 147** Deadlock

Careless locking of more than one object can cause deadlock. Assume that we have one left shoe and one right shoe (two objects), and that two people (threads) want to use them. We can let first one person, then the other, use both shoes. But if we create two threads by `new Person("groucho", left, right)` and `new Person("harpo", right, left)`, then the first person may lock the left shoe, and the second person may lock the right one, and then both will wait forever for the other shoe. This is called deadlock. It can be avoided by always locking the objects in the same fixed order (for instance, left before right).

```
class Person {
  String name, fst, snd;
  public Person(String name, String fst, String snd) {
    this.name = name; this.fst = fst; this.snd = snd;
    new Thread(new ThreadStart(Run)).Start();
  }
  public void Run() {
    lock (fst) {
      Console.WriteLine(name + " got " + fst);
      Thread.Sleep(0);          // yield to other threads
      lock (snd) { Console.WriteLine(name + " got " + snd); }
      Console.WriteLine(name + " released " + snd);
    }
    Console.WriteLine(name + " released " + fst);
} }
```

# 21   Mathematical Functions

Class Math provides static methods to compute standard mathematical functions. Floating-point numbers (double and float) according to IEEE754, include positive and negative infinities as well as non-numbers, called NaN. There is also a distinction between positive zero and negative zero, ignored here.

These methods return non-numbers (NaN) when applied to illegal arguments, including NaNs, and return infinities in case of overflow; they do not throw exceptions. They behave sensibly when applied to positive or negative infinities: they return the limit if it exists, or else NaN. Angles are given and returned in radians, not degrees. The rounding methods will round to the nearest even integer in case of a tie. The methods Abs and Sign are overloaded also on arguments of type decimal, float, int, long, sbyte, and short; and the methods Min and Max are overloaded also on the unsigned simple types.

- static double E is the constant $e \approx 2.71828$, the base of the natural logarithm.
- static double PI is the constant $\pi \approx 3.14159$, the circumference of a circle with diameter 1.
- static double Abs(double x) is the absolute value: x if x>=0, and -x if x<0.
- static double Acos(double x) is the arc cosine of x, in the range $[0, \pi]$, for -1<=x<=1.
- static double Asin(double x) is the arc sine of x, in the range $[-\pi/2, \pi/2]$, for -1<=x<=1.
- static double Atan(double x) is the arc tangent of x, in the range $[-\pi/2, \pi/2]$.
- static double Atan2(double y, double x) is the arc tangent of y/x in the quadrant of the point (x, y), in the range $]-\pi, \pi]$. When x is 0, the result is $\pi/2$ with the same sign as y.
- static double Ceiling(double x) is the smallest integral double value >=x.
- static double Cos(double x) is the cosine of x, in the range $[-1, 1]$.
- static double Exp(double x) is the exponential of x, that is, $e$ to the power x.
- static double Floor(double x) is the largest integral double value <=x.
- static double IEEERemainder(double x, double y) is the remainder of x/y, that is, x-y*$n$, where $n$ is the mathematical integer closest to x/y. May be negative even when x and y are positive.
- static double Log(double x) is the base $e$ logarithm or natural logarithm of x, for x>=0.
- static double Log10(double x) is the base 10 logarithm of x, for x>=0.
- static double Max(double x, double y) is the greatest of x and y.
- static double Min(double x, double y) is the smallest of x and y.
- static double Pow(double x, double y) is x to the power y, that is, $x^y$. If y is 1, then the result is x. If y is 0, then the result is 1.0. If x<0 and y is not integral, then the result is NaN.
- static double Round(double x) is the whole number that is closest to x.
- static double Round(double x, int d) is the number closest to x, rounded to d $\leq$ 15 digits.
- static double Sin(double x) is the sine of x radians.
- static int Sign(double x) returns +1 or 0 or −1 according as x>0, or x==0, or x<0.
- static double Sqrt(double x) is the positive square root of x, for x>=0.
- static double Tan(double x) is the tangent of x radians.

**Example 148** Floating-point Factorial

This method computes the factorial function $n! = 1 \cdot 2 \cdot 3 \cdots (n-1) \cdot n$ using logarithms.

```
static double Fact(int n) {
  double res = 0.0;
  for (int i=1; i<=n; i++)
    res += Math.Log(i);
  return Math.Exp(res);
}
```

**Example 149** Generating Gaussian Pseudo-random Numbers

This example uses the Box-Muller transformation to generate N Gaussian, or normally distributed, random numbers with mean 0 and standard deviation 1.

```
Random rnd = new Random();
for (int i=0; i<n; i+=2) {
  double x1 = rnd.NextDouble(), x2 = rnd.NextDouble();
  Print(Math.Sqrt(-2 * Math.Log(x1)) * Math.Cos(2 * Math.PI * x2));
  Print(Math.Sqrt(-2 * Math.Log(x1)) * Math.Sin(2 * Math.PI * x2));
}
```

**Example 150** Mathematical Functions: Infinities, NaNs, and Special Cases

```
Print("Illegal arguments, NaN results:");
Print(Math.Sqrt(-1));               // NaN
Print(Math.Log(-1));                // NaN
Print(Math.Pow(-1, 2.5));           // NaN
Print(Math.Acos(1.1));              // NaN
Print("Infinite results:");
Print(Math.Log(0));                 // -Infinity
Print(Math.Pow(0, -1));             // Infinity
Print(Math.Exp(1000.0));            // Infinity (overflow)
Print("Infinite arguments:");
double infinity = Double.PositiveInfinity;
Print(Math.Sqrt(infinity));         // Infinity
Print(Math.Log(infinity));          // Infinity
Print(Math.Exp(-infinity));         // 0
Print(Math.Pow(infinity, 0.5));     // Infinity
Print(Math.Pow(0.5, infinity));     // 0
Print(Math.Pow(0.5, -infinity));    // Infinity
Print(Math.Pow(2, infinity));       // Infinity
Print("Special cases:");
Print(Math.Pow(0, 0));              // 1.0
Print(Math.Pow(infinity, 0));       // 1.0
Print(Math.Pow(-infinity, 0));      // 1.0
Print(Math.Pow(-infinity, 0.5));    // Infinity
Print(Math.Pow(1, infinity));       // NaN
Print(Math.Pow(1, -infinity));      // NaN
```

## 22 Input and Output

Sequential input and output uses objects called *streams*. There are two kinds of streams: *character streams* and *byte streams*, also called text streams and binary streams. Character streams are used for input from text files and human-readable output to text files, printers, and so on, using 16-bit Unicode characters. Byte streams are used for compact and efficient input and output of simple data (int, double, ...) as well as objects and arrays, in machine-readable form.

There are separate classes for handling character streams and byte streams. The classes for character input and output are called Readers and Writers. The classes for byte input and output are called Streams. This section describes input and output using the System.IO namespace.

One can create subclasses of the stream classes, overriding inherited methods to obtain specialized stream classes. We shall not further discuss how to do that here.

The stream class hierarchies are shown in the following table, with related input and output classes shown on the same line. The table shows, for instance, that BufferedStream and FileStream are subclasses of Stream, and that StringReader is a subclass of TextReader. Abstract classes are shown in *italics*.

|  | Input Streams | Output Streams |
|---|---|---|
| **Char.** | *TextReader* | *TextWriter* |
|  | StringReader | StringWriter |
|  | StreamReader | StreamWriter |
| **Byte** | BinaryReader | BinaryWriter |
|  | *Stream* | |
|  | FileStream | |
|  | BufferedStream | |
|  | CryptoStream | |
|  | MemoryStream | |
|  | NetworkStream | |

### 22.1 Creating Streams

An input stream or reader has an underlying source of data to read from, and an output stream or writer has an underlying sink of data to write to. A stream may either be created outright (e.g., a StreamReader may be created and associated with a named file on disk, for reading from that file) or it may be created from an existing stream to provide additional features (e.g., a BufferedStream may be created from a Stream for more efficient input). The figure opposite shows how streams may be created from existing streams, or from other data.

The stream classes are divided along two lines: character streams (top) versus byte streams (bottom), and input streams (left) versus output streams (right). For byte streams there is no distinction between the classes for input and output streams. The arrows show what streams can be created from other streams (solid arrow heads), and what stream classes are base classes of other stream classes (open arrow heads). For instance, the arrow from Stream to BinaryReader shows that one can create a BinaryReader from a Stream, and the arrow from MemoryStream to Stream shows that MemoryStream is a (subclass of) Stream. Hence one can create a BinaryReader from a MemoryStream.

**Example 151**  A Complete Input-Output Example

```
using System;
using System.IO;

class BasicIOExample {
  public static void Main() {
    TextReader r = Console.In;
    int count = 0;
    String s = r.ReadLine();
    while (s != null && !s.Equals("")) {
      count++;
      s = r.ReadLine();
    }
    Console.WriteLine("You entered " + count + " nonempty lines");
  }
}
```

**Creating Streams from Other Streams**    An arrow A → B shows that a B object can be created from an A object (solid arrow heads) or that an A object is a B object, that is, class B is the base class of class A (open arrow heads).

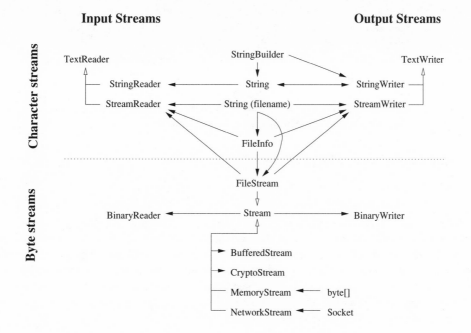

## 22.2 Overview of Input and Output Methods

The following table summarizes the naming conventions for methods of the input and output classes as well as their main characteristics, such as their end-of-stream behavior.

| Method Name | Effect |
| --- | --- |
| Read | Inputs characters from a TextReader (section 22.4) or inputs bytes from a Stream (section 22.7) or inputs one character from a BinaryReader (section 22.6). It *blocks*, that is, does not return, until some input is available. Returns $-1$ on end-of-stream, except for the Read(byte[], ...) overloads which return 0. |
| Read*t* | Inputs a value of type *t* from a BinaryReader (section 22.6). Blocks until some input is available; throws EndOfStreamException on end-of-stream. |
| Peek | Returns the next character from a TextReader (section 22.4) without advancing the stream. Blocks until some input is available; returns $-1$ on end-of-stream. |
| PeekChar | Returns the next character from a BinaryReader (section 22.6) without advancing the stream. Blocks until some input is available; returns $-1$ on end-of-stream. |
| Write | Outputs the textual representation of a value (of type char, int, double, ..., String, Object) to a TextWriter (section 22.5); or outputs bytes to a Stream (section 22.7); or outputs the binary representation of a value to a BinaryWriter (section 22.6). |
| WriteLine | Same as Write from TextWriter, but outputs a newline after each call. |
| Flush | Writes any buffered data to the underlying stream. The purpose is to make sure that all data have been written to the file system or the network. |
| Close | Flushes and closes the stream, and releases resources held by the stream. Further operations on the stream, except Close, may throw an ObjectDisposedException. Writers and output streams should be explicitly closed to make sure that all data have been written to disk or network; otherwise output may be lost. |
| Deserialize | Deserializes objects from a Stream (examples 152 and 207). Defined in classes System.Runtime.Serialization.Binary.BinaryFormatter and System.Runtime.Serialization.Soap.SoapFormatter. |
| Serialize | Serializes objects to a Stream (examples 152 and 207). Defined in classes System.Runtime.Serialization.Binary.BinaryFormatter and System.Runtime.Serialization.Soap.SoapFormatter. |

## 22.3 Using Declarations, Exceptions, Thread Safety

A program using the input and output classes must contain the declaration

```
using System.IO;
```

Most input and output operations can throw an exception of class IOException or one of its subclasses (section 19). Hence a method doing input or output should do so in a try-catch block (section 13.8.2).

The standard implementation of input-output is not thread-safe: multiple concurrent threads (section 20) cannot safely read from or write to the same stream without corrupting it, so one should not use the same stream from multiple threads. Classes TextReader and TextWriter have a static method Synchronized for creating threadsafe readers and writers.

**Example 152** Input and Output: Eleven Examples in One
This example illustrates output to a human-readable text file; input and output of simple values with binary files; input and output of arrays and objects with binary files; input and output of simple values with random access binary files; input and output using strings and string builders; output to standard output and standard error; and input from standard input.

```
// Write numbers and words on file "f.txt" in human-readable form:
TextWriter twr = new StreamWriter(new FileStream("f.txt", FileMode.Create));
twr.Write(4711); twr.Write(' '); twr.Write("cool"); twr.Close();
// Write simple type values to a binary file "p.dat":
BinaryWriter bwr = new BinaryWriter(new FileStream("p.dat", FileMode.Create));
bwr.Write(4711); bwr.Write(' '); bwr.Write("cool"); bwr.Close();
// Read simple type values from binary file "p.dat":
BinaryReader brd = new BinaryReader(new FileStream("p.dat", FileMode.Open));
Console.WriteLine(brd.ReadInt32() + "|" + brd.ReadChar() + "|" + brd.ReadString());
// Write an object or array to binary file "o.dat":
FileStream fs1 = new FileStream("o.dat", FileMode.Create);
BinaryFormatter bf = new BinaryFormatter();
bf.Serialize(fs1, new int[] { 2, 3, 5, 7, 11 }); fs1.Close();
// Read objects or arrays from binary file "o.dat":
FileStream fs2 = new FileStream("o.dat", FileMode.Open);
int[] ia = (int[]) bf.Deserialize(fs2);
Console.WriteLine("{0} {1} {2} {3} {4}", ia[0], ia[1], ia[2], ia[3], ia[4]); fs2.Close();
// Read and write parts of file "raf.dat" in arbitrary order:
FileStream fs = new FileStream("raf.dat", FileMode.OpenOrCreate, FileAccess.ReadWrite);
BinaryWriter bw = new BinaryWriter(fs);
bw.Write(3.1415); bw.Write(42);
fs.Seek(0, SeekOrigin.Begin);
BinaryReader br = new BinaryReader(fs);
Console.WriteLine("{0} {1}", br.ReadDouble(), br.ReadInt32());
// Read from a String as if it were a text file:
TextReader tr = new StringReader("abc");
Console.WriteLine("abc: " + (char)tr.Read() + (char)tr.Read() + (char)tr.Read());
// Write to a StringBuilder as if it were a text file:
TextWriter tw = new StringWriter();
tw.Write('d'); tw.Write('e'); tw.Write('f');
Console.WriteLine(tw.ToString());
// Write characters to standard output and standard error:
Console.Out.WriteLine("std output"); Console.Error.WriteLine("std error");
// Read characters from standard input (the keyboard):
Console.WriteLine("Type some characters and press Enter: ");
TextReader intext = Console.In;
String response = intext.ReadLine();
Console.WriteLine("You typed: '{0}'", response);
// Read a character from standard input (the keyboard):
Console.Write("Type one character and press Enter: ");
char c = (char)Console.In.Read();
Console.WriteLine("First character of your input is: " + c);
```

## 22.4 Sequential Character Input: TextReaders

The abstract class TextReader and its subclasses StringReader and StreamReader are used for character-oriented sequential input. In addition to the classes shown here, see the corresponding Writer classes (section 22.5). The standard input stream Console.In is a TextReader; see example 151. The TextReader class has the following methods:

- int Read() reads the next character from the stream and returns it. Returns −1 on end-of-stream.
- int Read(char[] b, int i, int n) reads at most n characters into into b[i..(i+n-1)] and returns the number of characters read. Returns immediately if n is 0. Returns 0 on end-of-stream. Throws ArgumentOutOfRangeException if i<0 or n<0, ArgumentException if i+n>b.Length, and ArgumentNullException if b is null.
- int ReadBlock(char[] buf, int i, int n) works as above but blocks until either n characters are read or end-of-stream is reached.
- String ReadLine() returns the next line from the stream. Returns null at end-of-stream.
- String ReadToEnd() returns the characters from the current position to the end of stream.
- int Peek() returns the next character without advancing the stream. Returns −1 on end-of-stream.
- void Close() closes the reader and any underlying stream. Any subsequent operation, except Close, will throw ObjectDisposedException.

### 22.4.1 Sequential Character Input from a Byte Stream or File: StreamReader

A StreamReader is a character input stream that reads characters from a byte stream or from a file. The StreamReader converts bytes from the underlying stream or file into characters using a character encoding. The input operations are buffered for efficiency. It has the same members as TextReader (section 22.4), and also these constructors and property:

- StreamReader(Stream s) creates a character input stream (a reader) from byte stream s, using UTF-8 character encoding.
- StreamReader(Stream s, Encoding enc) works as above, but with enc as character encoding.
- StreamReader(String filename) creates a character input stream associated with the named file on the file system, using UTF-8 character encoding. Throws FileNotFoundException if the named file cannot be found, DirectoryNotFoundException if the directory cannot be found, Argument-NullException if filename is null, ArgumentException if it is the empty string, and IOException if it contains invalid path or file name syntax.
- StreamReader(String filename, Encoding enc) works as above, but uses character encoding enc.
- Read-only property CurrentEncoding.EncodingName of type String is the name of the character encoding used by this StreamReader, for instance "Unicode (UTF-8)".

Examples 120, 122 and 191, and the examples opposite, present various ways to use StreamReader and TextReader.

**Example 153** Reading Numbers from a File

This example reads one number from each line of a text file and computes the sum of the numbers. Method double.Parse is culture sensitive, so one must use culture en-US or similar to parse a number whose decimal point is a period (.); see the full example source code. To parse more numbers from each line, one may use the Split method from section 7.1.

```
double sum = 0.0;
TextReader rd = new StreamReader("foo");
String line;
while (null != (line = rd.ReadLine()))
  sum += double.Parse(line);
rd.Close();
Console.WriteLine("The sum is {0}", sum);
```

**Example 154** Scanning Tokens from a Text Reader

Language processors, such as compilers, usually convert the raw stream of characters read from a file into a stream of tokens, where a token is a numeral, an identifier, an operator, a separator such as a left or right parenthesis, and so on. This example shows how this conversion can be performed: given a TextReader it prints a sequence of tokens. A token is an object of abstract class Token with derived classes Int, Id, Op, and Sep. An exercise for the reader: Using the yield statement from section 13.12, modify the method to return an IEnumerable<Token>.

```
public static void Tokenize(TextReader rd) {
  while (rd.Peek() != -1) {
    if (Char.IsWhiteSpace((char)rd.Peek()))           // Whitespace, skip
      rd.Read();
    else if (Char.IsDigit((char)rd.Peek())) {         // Number
      int val = rd.Read() - '0';
      while (Char.IsDigit((char)rd.Peek()))
        val = 10 * val + rd.Read() - '0';
      Console.WriteLine(new Int(val));
    } else if (Char.IsLetter((char)rd.Peek())) {      // Identifier
      StringBuilder id = new StringBuilder().Append((char)rd.Read());
      while (Char.IsLetterOrDigit((char)rd.Peek()))
        id.Append((char)rd.Read());
      Console.WriteLine(new Id(id.ToString()));
    } else
      switch (rd.Peek()) {
      case '+': case '-': case '*': case '/':         // Operator
        Console.WriteLine(new Op((char)rd.Read())); break;
      case '(': case ')':                             // Separator
        Console.WriteLine(new Sep((char)rd.Read())); break;
      default:                                        // Illegal token
        throw new ApplicationException("Illegal character '"+(char)rd.Peek()+"'");
      }
  }
}
```

## 22.5    Sequential Character Output: TextWriters

The abstract class TextWriter and its subclasses StreamWriter and StringWriter are used for character-oriented sequential output. For instance, the standard output stream `Console.Out` and standard error stream `Console.Error` are TextWriters. A call to `Console.Write` is really a call to `Console.Out.Write`, and similarly for `Console.WriteLine`. Class TextWriter has the following methods:

- `void Write(char[] b)` writes the contents of character array b to the stream.
- `void Write(char[] b, int i, int n)` writes n characters from b starting at position i; throws ArgumentNullException if b is null, ArgumentOutOfRangeException if `i<0` or `n<0`, and ArgumentException if `i+n>b.Length`.
- `void Write(char c)` writes the character c to the stream.
- `void Write(int i)` writes the text representation of i to the stream; and similarly for `bool`, `long`, `uint`, `ulong`, `float`, `double`, `decimal`, and `String`.
- `void Write(Object o)` writes `o.ToString()` to the stream if o is non-null; otherwise nothing.
- `void Write(String s, Object o1, ..., Object on)` writes `String.Format(s,o1,...,on)` to the stream; see section 7.2.
- `void WriteLine()` writes a line terminator to the stream.
- `String Encoding.EncodingName` is the name of the character encoding, e.g. `"Unicode (UTF-8)"`.
- `void Flush()` writes all data to the underlying stream (or string builder), and then clears all buffers.
- `void Close()` flushes and closes the stream.

For each `Write` method there is a `WriteLine` method with the same signature that writes a line terminator (`\r\n` by default; see section 7 for string escape codes). All methods may throw IOException on error.

### 22.5.1    Sequential Character Output to a Byte Stream or File: StreamWriter

A StreamWriter is a character output stream that writes to an associated byte stream or file, converting characters to bytes using a character encoding. The output operations are buffered for efficiency. A StreamWriter has the same members as a TextWriter (section 22.5), and in addition these constructors:

- `StreamWriter(Stream s)` creates a writer that writes to s using UTF-8 character encoding.
- `StreamWriter(s, Encoding enc)` works as above, but uses character encoding enc.
- `StreamWriter(String filename)` creates a character output stream and associates it with the named file. If the file exists, then it overwrites the file; otherwise it creates a new empty file. Throws ArgumentNullException if filename is null, ArgumentException if it is the empty string, DirectoryNotFoundException if the directory is not found, UnauthorizedAccessException if access to the file or directory is denied, and SecurityException if the caller does not have required permissions.
- `StreamWriter(String filename, bool append)` works as above, but if append is true, it does not overwrite the file. Instead, output will be appended to the existing file contents.
- `StreamWriter(filename, append, Encoding enc)` uses character encoding enc.
- `StreamWriter(filename, append, enc, int n)` works as above, but sets the buffer size to n.

**Example 155** Writing Numbers to a Text File

Simulate 1,000 rolls of a die and print the outcome to the text file `dice.txt`, 20 numbers to a line. It is important to close the text writer after writing; otherwise some or all of the output may be lost.

```
using System;
using System.IO;                    // StreamWriter, Textwriter

public class TextWriterExample {
  public static void Main() {
    TextWriter tw = new StreamWriter("dice.txt");
    Random rnd = new Random();
    for (int i=1; i<=1000; i++) {
      int die = (int)(1 + 6 * rnd.NextDouble());
      tw.Write(die); tw.Write(' ');
      if (i % 20 == 0) tw.WriteLine();
    }
    tw.Close();                     // Without this, the output file may be empty
  }
}
```

**Example 156** Printing an HTML Table

This example generates a temperature conversion table in HTML. The Fahrenheit temperature $f$ corresponds to the Celsius temperature $c = 5 \cdot (f - 32)/9$. The number of fractional digits is controlled by format specifications $\{0:\#0\}$ and $\{1:0.0\}$ (see section 7.2). The HTML TABLE tag is used to control the alignment of numbers into columns.

```
TextWriter tw = new StreamWriter(new FileStream("temperature.html", FileMode.Create));
tw.WriteLine("<TABLE BORDER><TR><TH>Fahrenheit<TH>Celsius</TR>");
for (double f=100; f<=400; f+=10) {
  double c = 5 * (f - 32) / 9;
  tw.WriteLine("<TR ALIGN=RIGHT><TD>{0:#0}<TD>{1:0.0}", f, c);
}
tw.WriteLine("</TABLE>");
tw.Close();                    // Without this, the output file may be empty
```

**Example 157** Printing a Text Table

To write a conversion table in text format in a fixed-pitch font, replace the format specifications in example 156 by $\{0,10:\#0\}$ and $\{1,10:0.0\}$ and delete the HTML tags. See section 7.2 for more formatting codes.

## 22.6    Binary Input and Output: BinaryReader and BinaryWriter

A BinaryReader reads values of simple type or String from a binary-format stream. Conversely, a BinaryWriter writes such values to a binary-format stream. The classes have the following constructors:

- `BinaryReader(Stream s)` creates a reader that reads from input stream s in UTF-8 encoding.
- `BinaryReader(Stream s, Encoding enc)` creates a reader that reads from s in encoding enc.
- `BinaryWriter(Stream s)` creates a writer that writes to s using the UTF-8 encoding.
- `BinaryWriter(Stream s, Encoding enc)` creates a writer that uses encoding enc.

They throw ArgumentException if s is closed or does not support reading (resp. writing), and ArgumentNullException if s or enc is null.

The BinaryReader class has the following methods:

- `int Read()` reads one character and returns its integer value. Returns −1 on end-of-stream.
- `int Read(byte[] b, int i, int n)` and `int Read(char[] b, int i, int n)` read n bytes (characters) from the stream into `b[i...i+n-1]` and returns the number of bytes (characters) read. Throws ArgumentOutOfRangeException if i<0 or n<0, ArgumentException if i+n>b.Length, and ArgumentNullException if b is null. Returns 0 on end-of-stream.
- `ReadBoolean()`, `ReadByte()`, `ReadSByte()`, `ReadChar()`, `ReadInt16()`, `ReadUInt16()`, `ReadInt32()`, `ReadUInt32()`, `ReadInt64()`, `ReadUInt64()`, `ReadSingle()`, `ReadDouble()`, and `ReadDecimal()` read bytes from the underlying stream and return a value of type bool, byte, sbyte, char, short, ushort, int, uint, long, ulong, float, double, or decimal. The methods throw EndOfStreamException on end-of-stream.
- `byte[] ReadBytes(int i)` and `char[] ReadChars(int i)` read i bytes (or characters) from the stream into a new byte array (or character array) and returns the array.
- `String ReadString()` reads bytes and converts them to a string using the encoding.
- `char PeekChar()` returns the next character from the stream without advancing the stream.

BinaryWriter has these methods and property; they throw IOException if the underlying stream is closed:

- Read-only property `BaseStream` of type Stream is the BinaryWriter's underlying stream.
- `Write(byte[] b, int i, int n)` and `Write(char[] b, int i, int n)` writes n bytes or characters from `b[i...i+n-1]`. Throws ArgumentOutOfRangeException if i<0 or n<0, ArgumentException if i+n>b.Length, and ArgumentNullException if b is null.
- `Write(bool v)` and similar overloads on byte, sbyte, char, short, ushort, int, uint, long, ulong, float, double, and decimal, write value v to in binary format to the underlying stream.
- `Write(String s)` converts string s to bytes using the encoding and writes them to the stream.
- `Write(byte[] b)` and `Write(char[] b)` write the bytes or characters from the array.
- `Seek(int i, SeekOrigin so)` sets the position to i bytes relative to so and returns the new position of the stream; so can be `SeekOrigin.Begin`, `SeekOrigin.Current` or `SeekOrigin.End`.
- `Flush()` writes all data in buffers to the underlying stream or file, and then clears all buffers.
- `Close()` flushes and closes the writer.

**Example 158** Binary Input and Output of Simple Type Data

Method `WriteData` demonstrates writing simple data to a BinaryWriter, and method `ReadData` demonstrates all ways to read simple values from a BinaryReader. The methods complement each other, so after writing a stream with `WriteData`, one can read it using `ReadData`. Namely, an integer written using BinaryWriter's method `Write(int)` can be read using BinaryReader's method `ReadInt32()`.

```
public static void Main() {
  BinaryWriter bw = new BinaryWriter(new FileStream("tmp1.dat", FileMode.Create));
  WriteData(bw); bw.Close();
  BinaryReader br = new BinaryReader(new FileStream("tmp1.dat", FileMode.Open));
  ReadData(br);
}

static void WriteData(BinaryWriter bw) {
  bw.Write(true);                            // Write 1 byte
  bw.Write((byte)120);                       // Write 1 byte
  bw.Write('A');                             // Write 1 byte (UTF-8)
  bw.Write("foo");                           // Write 1+3 bytes (UTF-8)
  bw.Write("Rhône");                         // Write 1+6 bytes (UTF-8)
  bw.Write(300.1);                           // Write 8 bytes
  bw.Write(300.2F);                          // Write 4 bytes
  bw.Write(1234);                            // Write 4 bytes
  bw.Write(12345L);                          // Write 8 bytes
  bw.Write((short)32000);                    // Write 2 bytes
  bw.Write((sbyte)-1);                       // Write 1 byte
  bw.Write((short)-1);                       // Write 2 bytes
}

static void ReadData(BinaryReader br) {
  Console.Write(      br.ReadBoolean());     // Read 1 byte
  Console.Write(" " + br.ReadByte());        // Read 1 byte
  Console.Write(" " + br.ReadChar());        // Read 1 byte
  Console.Write(" " + br.ReadString());      // Read 1+3 bytes
  Console.Write(" " + br.ReadString());      // Read 1+6 bytes
  Console.Write(" " + br.ReadDouble());      // Read 8 bytes
  Console.Write(" " + br.ReadSingle());      // Read 4 bytes
  Console.Write(" " + br.ReadInt32());       // Read 4 bytes
  Console.Write(" " + br.ReadInt64());       // Read 8 bytes
  Console.Write(" " + br.ReadInt16());       // Read 2 bytes
  Console.Write(" " + br.ReadSByte());       // Read 1 byte
  Console.Write(" " + br.ReadUInt16());      // Read 2 bytes
  Console.WriteLine();
}
```

**Example 159** Binary input/output to random access file

See examples 160 and 161.

## 22.7　Byte Input and Output: Stream

The abstract class Stream and its subclasses (all of whose names end in Stream) are used for byte-oriented input and output. A stream is associated with some resource to read from or write to, typically a file or an area of memory. A stream may support either reading, seeking, or writing, or a combination of these. A stream has a current position, indicating which byte to read from or write to next. If s is a variable of type Stream, then

- Read-only property s.CanRead is true if the stream is not closed and supports reading; else false.
- Read-only property s.CanSeek is true if the stream is not closed and supports seeking; else false.
- Read-only property s.CanWrite is true if the stream is not closed and supports writing; else false.
- Read-only property s.Length of type long is the number of bytes in the stream, if the stream supports seeking; otherwise throws NotSupportedException.
- Read-write property s.Position of type long returns the current position of the stream. Setting s.Position to v sets the current position of the stream to v.

Variables of class Stream (and any subtype) have the following methods:

- int ReadByte() reads one byte $(0 \ldots 255)$ and returns it as an int, blocking until input is available; returns $-1$ on end-of-stream.
- int Read(byte[] b, int i, int n) reads at most n bytes from the stream and copies the bytes read into b[i..i+n-1], and returns the number of bytes actually read as an int and advances the position of the stream by the number of bytes read. Returns 0 on end-of-stream. Throws ArgumentOutOfRangeException if i<0 or n<0, ArgumentException if i+n>b.Length, ArgumentNullException if b evaluates to null, NotSupportedException if the stream does not support reading, and ObjectDisposedException if the stream has been closed.
- void Seek(long v, SeekOrigin so) sets the current position of the stream to so+v, where so must be SeekOrigin.Begin, SeekOrigin.Current or SeekOrigin.End. Throws NotSupportedException if s does not support seeking.
- void WriteByte(byte v) writes v to the stream and advances the current position by one byte. Throws NotSupportedException if the stream does not support writing, ObjectDisposedException if the stream has been closed.
- void Write(byte[] b, int i, int n) writes n bytes from b[i..i+n-1] to s and advances the current position by n bytes. Throws ArgumentOutOfRangeException if i<0 or n<0, ArgumentException if i+n>b.Length, ArgumentNullException if b evaluates to null, NotSupportedException if the stream does not support writing, ObjectDisposedException if the stream has been closed.
- void SetLength(long v) sets the length the stream s to v. If v<s.Length the stream is truncated. If v>s.Length the stream is expanded. Throws NotSupportedException if the stream does not support both seeking and writing.
- void Flush() writes all data in buffers to the underlying resource and clears all buffers.
- void Close() flushes and closes the stream and releases any underlying resources such as files or network connections.

**Example 160** Organizing a String Array File for Random Access
This example shows a way to implement random access to large numbers of texts, such as millions of cached Web pages or millions of DNA sequences. We define a string array file to have three parts: (1) a sequence of Strings, each of which is in UTF-8 format; (2) a sequence of long integers, representing the start offsets of the strings; and (3) an integer, which is the number of strings in the file.

We put the number of strings and the string offset table at the end of the file, so we do not need to know the number of strings or the length of each string before writing the file. The strings can be written to the file incrementally, and the only structure we need to keep in memory is the table (ArrayList) of string lengths. Using a List<long> (section 24.6) for the table would give even better performance.

```
static void WriteStrings(String filename, String[] dna) {
  FileStream raf = new FileStream(filename, FileMode.Create);
  BinaryWriter sw = new BinaryWriter(raf);
  raf.SetLength(0);                               // Truncate the file
  ArrayList offsettable = new ArrayList();        // Contains longs
  foreach (String s in dna) {
    offsettable.Add(raf.Position);                // Store string offset
    sw.Write(s);                                  // Write string
  }
  foreach (long v in offsettable) {               // Write string offsets
    Console.WriteLine(v);
    sw.Write(v);
  }
  sw.Write(offsettable.Count);                    // Write string count
  sw.Close();
}
```

**Example 161** Random Access Reads from a String Array File
The method call ReadOneString(f, i) reads string number i from a string array file f (example 160) in three stages, using three calls to Seek. First, it reads the offset table length N from the last 4 bytes of the file. Second, since an int takes 4 bytes and a long takes 8 bytes (section 5.1), the string offset table must begin at position Length-4-8*N, and so the offset si of string number i can be read from position Length-4-8*N+8*i. Third, the string itself is read from offset si.

```
static String ReadOneString(String filename, int i) {
  const int IntSize = 4, LongSize = 8;
  FileStream raf = new FileStream(filename, FileMode.Open);
  raf.Seek(raf.Length - IntSize, SeekOrigin.Begin);
  BinaryReader br = new BinaryReader(raf);
  int N = br.ReadInt32();
  raf.Seek(raf.Length - IntSize - LongSize * N + LongSize * i, SeekOrigin.Begin);
  long si = br.ReadInt64();
  raf.Seek(si, SeekOrigin.Begin);
  String s = br.ReadString();
  br.Close();
  return s;
}
```

### 22.7.1    Byte Input and Output from and to a File: FileStream

A FileStream is a Stream that can read from and write to a file on the file system. It has the same members as Stream (section 22.7), and these constructors:

- `FileStream(String name, FileMode fm)` creates a byte input stream and associates it with file name in the file system. The FileMode parameter `fm` determines how the files is opened:

  - `FileMode.Append`: open file if it exists and seek to the end of the file; else create a new file.
  - `FileMode.Create`: overwrite the file if it exists; else create a new file.
  - `FileMode.CreateNew`: create a new file; throw IOException if the file exists.
  - `FileMode.Open`: open existing file; throw FileNotFoundException if the file does not exist.
  - `FileMode.OpenOrCreate`: open the file if it exists; else create a new file.
  - `FileMode.Truncate`: open the file and set the file size to 0 bytes; throws FileNotFound-Exception if the file does not exist.

  Throws ArgumentException if `name` is an empty string, ArgumentNullException if `name` is `null`,

- `FileStream(String name, FileMode fm, FileAccess fa)` works like the preceding, but `fa` determines how `name` may be accessed by the FileStream and can have one of the following values `FileAccess.Read`, `FileAccess.Write`, or `FileAccess.ReadWrite` depending on whether the file may be read from, written to, or both.

- `FileStream(String name, FileMode fm, FileAccess fa, FileShare fs)` works like the preceding, but `fs` determines how different FileStreams share the file.

- `FileStream(name, fm, fa, fs, int bs)` works like the preceding, but sets the buffer size to `bs`.

- `FileStream(name, fm, fa, fs, int bs, bool asynch)` works like the preceding, but uses asynchronous input and output if `asynch` is true.

Class FileStream also adds the following methods to those inherited from class Stream:

- `void Lock(long i, long n)` locks the file from position `i` to position `i+n-1`. This prevents other processes from changing that section of the file, but they may still read it.

- `void Unlock(long i, long n)` unlocks the file from position `i` to position `i+n-1`, thus permitting other processes to modify the file (if they have the necessary permissions).

Both methods throw ArgumentOutOfRangeException if `i<0` or `n<0`.

### 22.7.2   Byte Input and Output from and to a Byte Array: MemoryStream

A MemoryStream is a Stream that reads from and or writes to a byte array in memory. A memory stream has a capacity indicating the maximum number of bytes in the stream, and a length indicating the current number of bytes in the stream. The capacity is set at the creation of the stream, and cannot be changed unless the stream is resizable. Class MemoryStream has these constructors:

- `MemoryStream()` creates a new resizable MemoryStream with capacity 0 that supports reading, writing, and seeking.

- `MemoryStream(int n)` creates a new resizable MemoryStream with capacity n that supports reading, writing, and seeking. Throws ArgumentOutOfRangeException if n<0.

- `MemoryStream(byte[] b)` creates a new non-resizable MemoryStream with capacity b.Length that supports reading, writing, and seeking. Throws ArgumentNullException if b is null.

- `MemoryStream(byte[] b, bool wr)` works as above, but supports writing only if wr is true.

- `MemoryStream(byte[] b, int i, int n)` creates a new non-resizable MemoryStream based on b[i..i+n-1] with capacity n that supports reading, writing, and seeking. Throws Argument-NullException if b is null, ArgumentOutOfRangeException if i<0 or n<0, and ArgumentException if i+n>b.Length.

- `MemoryStream(byte[] b, int i, int n, bool wr)` works as the preceding, but does not support writing unless wr is true.

Class MemoryStream has the same members as class Stream (section 22.7) and in addition, if ms is a variable of type MemoryStream, then:

- `ms.SetLength(n)` where n has type long sets the length of ms to n. If n<ms.Length the stream is truncated and the current position is set to that after the last byte of the stream. If n>ms.Capacity and ms is resizable, the capacity of ms is increased and the new bytes in the stream are initialized to 0. If ms is non-resizable and n>ms.Capacity or ms does not support writing, NotSupportedException is thrown. If n<0 ArgumentOutOfRangeException is thrown.

- Read-write property `ms.Capacity` of type int is the current capacity of the stream. Setting the capacity to n throws NotSupportedException if ms is non-expandable or closed, and throws ArgumentOutOfRangeException if n<ms.Length.

- `ms.ToArray()` of type byte[] writes the stream contents to a new byte array, regardless of the current position of the stream.

- `ms.WriteTo(st)`, where st is an expression of type Stream, writes the stream contents to the stream st. Throws ArgumentNullException if st is null, and ObjectDisposedException if ms or st is closed.

## 22.8    Directories

Classes Directory and DirectoryInfo implement methods for manipulating directories. Class Directory provides static methods and class DirectoryInfo provides similar instance methods. Every call to a Directory method incurs a security check, whereas a DirectoryInfo instance may be able to save some checks.

- `Directory.GetCurrentDirectory()` of type String returns the string representation of the current working directory.
- `DirectoryInfo(String path)` creates a new DirectoryInfo object with the associated directory path name. Throws DirectoryNotFoundException if the directory does not exist.

If d is a variable of type DirectoryInfo, then:

- `d.Name` of type String is the name of d.
- `d.Parent` of type DirectoryInfo is the parent directory of d; or `null` if d is a root directory.
- `d.GetDirectories()` of type `DirectoryInfo[]` returns the subdirectories of d.
- `d.GetFiles()` of type `FileInfo[]` returns the files in d.

## 22.9    Files

An object of class FileInfo represents a file name, that is, a file path in the file system. The file name may denote a file or nothing at all (if there is no file or path of that name). Even if the file name does denote a file, a given program may lack the permission to read or write to that file, or to read a directory on the path to the file. These are a few of the constructors and methods in class FileInfo:

- `FileInfo(String name)` creates a file name corresponding to the path name, which may be relative or absolute. Throws ArgumentException if name is an empty string or has an invalid format, ArgumentNullException if name is null, PathTooLongException if the given name or the corresponding full path are too long, or UnauthorizedAccessException or SecurityException if the caller does not have required permissions.
- Read-only property `Exists` is true if a file denoted by this file name exists; otherwise false.
- Read-only properties `Name` and `FullName` of type String are the file's simple name and its full path.
- Read-only property `Extension` of type String is the file name's last extension including its leading period (`.`); or the empty string if there is no extension.
- Read-only property `Length` of type `long` is the length of the file in bytes.
- `FileStream Create()` creates a new file and returns a FileStream associated with it.
- `void Delete()` deletes the file if it exists; otherwise does not nothing.
- `FileStream OpenRead()` creates a FileStream associated with the file for reading.
- `FileStream OpenWrite()` creates a FileStream associated with the file for writing.
- `StreamReader OpenText()` creates a StreamReader associated with the file for reading.
- `StreamWriter AppendText()` creates a StreamWriter for appending text to the file.
- `StreamWriter CreateText()` creates a new file and returns a StreamWriter for writing to it.

**Example 162** Reading and Printing a Directory Hierarchy
The call ShowDir(0, dir) will print the name of directory dir, call itself recursively to print all sub-directories of dir, and then print the names of all files in dir. Because indent is increased for every recursive call, the layout reflects the directory structure.

```
using System.IO;          // Directory, DirectoryInfo, FileInfo
public class DirectoryHierarchyExample {
  public static void ShowDir(int indent, DirectoryInfo dir) {
    Indent(indent); Console.WriteLine(dir.Name);
    DirectoryInfo[] subdirs = dir.GetDirectories();
    foreach (DirectoryInfo d in subdirs)
      ShowDir(indent+4, d);
    FileInfo[] files = dir.GetFiles();
    foreach (FileInfo file in files) {
      Indent(indent); Console.WriteLine(file.Name);
    }
  }
  public static void Indent(int indent) { ... }
  public static void Main() {
    DirectoryInfo dir = new DirectoryInfo(Directory.GetCurrentDirectory());
    ShowDir(0, dir);
  }
}
```

**Example 163** File Names, Paths and File Information
Paths may be given as relative or absolute. Regardless of the host operating system a file path may be given in Windows format (with backslashes as directory separators) or in Unix format (with forward slashes as directory separators).

```
FileInfo fi1 = new FileInfo("example3\\Prog.cs.old" ); // Windows, Relative
Console.WriteLine(fi1.Extension);                      // Extension is ".old"
FileInfo fi2 = new FileInfo("c:tmp\\foo");             // Windows, Volume+relative
Console.WriteLine(fi2.Extension);                      // Extension is ""
FileInfo fi3 = new FileInfo("c:\\tmp\\foo");           // Windows, Volume+absolute
FileInfo fi4 = new FileInfo("example3/Prog.cs");       // Unix, Relative
Console.WriteLine(fi4.Name);                           // Prog.cs
Console.WriteLine(fi4.FullName);                       // C:\tmp\example3\Prog.cs
FileInfo fi5 = new FileInfo("/etc/passwd");            // Unix, Absolute
Console.WriteLine("--- Printing contents of {0} ---", fi4.Name);
StreamReader sr = fi4.OpenText();
String line;
while ((line = sr.ReadLine()) != null)
  Console.WriteLine(line);
sr.Close();
```

## 22.10   Network Communication

A pair of distinct processes may communicate through *sockets*. The processes may be on the same machine, or on different machines connected by a network.

Sockets are often used in client/server architectures, where the server process creates a *server socket* that listens for connections from clients. When a client connects to the server socket, a fresh socket is created on the server side and is connected to the socket that the client used when connecting to the server. The socket connection is used for bidirectional communication between client and server; both ends can obtain a stream from the socket, that can be written to and read from.

Here are a constructor and some methods from the Socket class in namespace System.Net.Sockets:

- `Socket(AddressFamily af, SocketType st, ProtocolType pt)` creates a server socket of the specified kind.

- `void Listen(int queue)` transfers the socket to listening mode.

- `Socket Accept()` listens for a connection, blocking until a connection is made. Creates and returns a new Socket when a connection is made. Throws SocketException if the socket is not in listening mode.

- `void Bind(EndPoint ep)` binds the socket to a given end point ep (network address and port number) which may be an IPEndPoint expression as in example 164.

- `void Close()` closes the socket.

- Read-only property `EndPoint RemoteEndPoint` returns the remote end point to which this socket is connected.

- `int Send(byte[] b)` and `int Receive(byte[] b)` are used to send data to and receive data from the socket.

Although it is possible to communicate using only Sockets, it is usually preferable to wrap a Socket in a NetworkStream and communicate through that in either binary or character format.

Class NetworkStream (from namespace System.Net.Sockets) is a subclass of abstract class Stream (section 22.7), and in addition contains the following constructor and property:

- `NetworkStream(Socket s)` creates a new stream associated with socket s.

- Read-only property `bool DataAvailable` indicates whether data are available to read from the stream.

**Example 164** Socket Communication Between Processes

This example program runs as a server process or as a client process, depending on the first command line argument. The server and client may run on the same machine, or on machines communicating via a network. Several clients may connect to the same server. The server creates a server socket that accepts connections on port 2357. When a client connects, a new socket is created and an integer is received on that socket. If the integer is a prime, the server replies true on that socket, otherwise false. Each client process asks the server about the primality of the numbers 1 through 99 and prints those that are primes. For simplicity the client creates a new socket for every request to the server, but this is inefficient.

```
using System.IO;           // BinaryReader, BinaryWriter
using System.Net;          // AddressFamily, Dns, IPAddress, ProtocolType, ...
using System.Net.Sockets;  // NetworkStream, Socket, SocketType,
class SocketTest {
  const int PortNo = 2357;
  public static void Main(String[] args) {
    bool server = (args.Length == 1 && args[0] == "server");
    bool client = (args.Length == 2 && args[0] == "client");
    if (server) {              // Server: accept questions about primality
      Socket serversocket =
        new Socket(AddressFamily.InterNetwork, SocketType.Stream, ProtocolType.Tcp);
      serversocket.Bind(new IPEndPoint(IPAddress.Any, PortNo));
      serversocket.Listen(10);  // Max queue = 10 connections.
      for (;;) {               // For ever, accept connections
        NetworkStream s = new NetworkStream(serversocket.Accept());
        BinaryReader input  = new BinaryReader(s);
        BinaryWriter output = new BinaryWriter(s);
        int number = input.ReadInt32();
        output.Write(IsPrime(number));
        input.Close(); output.Close();
      }
    } else if (client) {       // Client: ask questions about primality
      IPAddress ipa = Dns.Resolve(args[1]).AddressList[0];
      for (int i=1; i<100; i++) {
        Socket clientsocket =
          new Socket(AddressFamily.InterNetwork, SocketType.Stream, ProtocolType.Tcp);
        clientsocket.Connect(new IPEndPoint(ipa, PortNo));
        NetworkStream n = new NetworkStream(clientsocket);
        BinaryWriter output = new BinaryWriter(n);
        BinaryReader input = new BinaryReader(n);
        output.Write(i);
        if (input.ReadBoolean())
          Console.Write(i + " ");
        output.Close(); input.Close();
      }
    } else { ... }             // Neither server nor client
  }
  static bool IsPrime(int p) { ... }
}
```

# 23   Generic Types and Methods (C# 2.0)

Generic types and methods provide a way to strengthen type checking at compile-time, to avoid some type checks and casts at run-time, and to improve run-time data representation, while at the same time making programs more expressive, reusable and readable. The ability to have generic types and methods is also known as parametric polymorphism.

## 23.1   Generics: Safety, Generality and Efficiency

The original C# (and Java) language did not support generic types and methods. Therefore a library for manipulating arbitrary kinds of values would have to cast those values to type Object. For instance, we might use an ArrayList `cool` to hold Person objects, but the `Add` method and the indexer of the `cool` arraylist would have to accept and return values of type Object. This works, but has several negative consequences that can be avoided by using generic types; see examples 165 and 166.

## 23.2   Generic Types, Type Parameters, and Constructed Types

A *generic class* declaration `class C<T1,...,Tn> { ... }` has one or more *type parameters* `T1,...,Tn`. The body of the declaration is an ordinary class body (section 10.1) in which the type parameters `Ti` can be used almost as if they were ordinary types; see section 23.6. A generic class is also called a parametrized class.

A generic class `C<T1>` is not itself a class. Rather, it is a mechanism or template from which classes such as `C<int>` or `C<String>` or even `C<C<String>>`, and so on, can be generated, by replacing the type parameter `T1` by a type expression `t1`, such as `int` or `String` or `C<String>`. The resulting classes are called *constructed types*. The type `t1` used to replace the type parameter `T1` can be any type expression: a class, an array type, a struct type, a simple type, an interface, a delegate type, or it can itself be a constructed type. However, it cannot be the pseudo-type `void` (which can be used only to indicate that a method has no return value).

Generic interfaces (section 23.5), generic delegate types (section 23.8) and generic struct types (section 23.10) can be declared also, and constructed types can be created from them. Again, a generic interface is not an interface and a generic struct type is not a struct type, but interfaces and struct types can be constructed from generic interfaces and generic struct types.

Generic methods (section 23.7) can be declared by specifying type parameters on the method declaration in addition to any type parameters specified on the enclosing class or interface or struct type.

The declaration of a property, indexer, operator, event or constructor may use the type parameters of the enclosing class or interface or struct type (see example 168), but cannot have additional type parameters of its own.

Section 23.11 compares the implementation of C# generic types and methods with C++ templates and Java 1.5 generic types and methods.

**Example 165** Using Non-generic ArrayList: Run-Time Type Checks and Wrapping of Values
The System.Collections.ArrayList cool should hold only Person objects, but without generic types, the compiler cannot check that only Person objects are added to cool. Hence at run-time the program must check and cast objects when extracting them from the list. These checks take time, and may fail:

```
ArrayList cool = new ArrayList();
cool.Add(new Person("Kristen"));
cool.Add(new Person("Bjarne"));
cool.Add(new Exception("Larry"));        // Wrong, but no compile-time check
cool.Add(new Person("Anders"));
Person p = (Person)cool[2];              // Compiles OK, but fails at run-time
```

**Example 166** Using Generic ArrayList: Compile-Time Type Checks, No Wrapping of Values
With generic types, cool can be declared to have type System.Collections.Generic.List<Person>, the compiler can check that only Person objects are passed to the cool.Add method, and therefore the array list cool can contain only Person objects. At run-time there is no need to check and cast objects when extracting from the list. Thus generic types improve execution speed as well as our trust in the program.

```
List<Person> cool = new List<Person>();
cool.Add(new Person("Kristen"));
cool.Add(new Person("Bjarne"));
cool.Add(new Exception("Larry"));        // Wrong, detected at compile-time
cool.Add(new Person("Anders"));
Person p = cool[2];                      // No run-time check needed
```

**Example 167** A Generic Class for Logging
Generic class Log<T> is similar to class Log in example 59, but can log any type T of object, not just strings. Note the use of default(T) instead of null in the Last property; null is not a legal result of Last when T is instantiated with a value type.

```
public class Log<T> {
  private static int instanceCount = 0;
  private int count = 0;
  private T[] log = new T[SIZE];
  public Log() { instanceCount++; }
  public static int InstanceCount { get { return instanceCount; } }
  public void Add(T msg) { log[count++ % SIZE] = msg; }
  public int Count { get { return count; } }
  public T Last {
    get { return count==0 ? default(T) : log[(count-1)%SIZE]; }
    set { ... }
  }
  public T[] All { ... }
}
...
Log<DateTime> log2 = new Log<DateTime>();
log2.Add(DateTime.Now);
```

## 23.3    Generic Classes

A declaration of a *generic class* C<T1,...,Tn> may have this form:

> *class-modifiers* class C<T1,...,Tn> *class-base-clause*
>    *class-body*

The T1,...,Tn are *type parameters*. The *class-modifiers*, *class-body* and *class-base-clause* are as for a non-generic class declaration (section 10.1). In addition, a generic class can have type parameter constraints; see section 23.4.

Inside *class-base-clause* and *class-body* the type parameters T1,...,Tn may be used wherever a type is expected, and so may the type parameters of any enclosing generic class or generic struct type. See section 23.6 for details.

A generic class C<T1,...,Tn> in itself is not a class. However, each *constructed type* C<t1,...,tn> is a class, just like a class declared by replacing each type parameter Ti with the corresponding type ti in the *class-body*. A type ti that is substituted for a type parameter Ti in a constructed type can be any type: a class, a struct type (for instance, int or bool), an interface, a delegate type, or it can itself be a constructed type. However, it cannot be the pseudo-type void; the void pseudo-type can be used only to indicate that a method has no return value.

Each type constructed from a generic class C<T1,...,Tn> is a distinct class and has a distinct copy of the static fields (if any) declared in the *class-body*. For instance, in example 167, there will be an instanceCount static field for each type constructed from Log<T>: one for Log<String>, one for Log<int>, and so on.

A constructed type C<t1,...,tn> is accessible when all its parts are accessible. Thus if the generic class C<T1,...,Tn> or any of the type arguments t1,...,tn is private, then the constructed type is private also.

A scope can have several classes, generic or not, with the same name C, if they have different numbers of type parameters. Only the number of type parameters is used to distinguish the classes, not the parameter names nor the parameter constraints, if any.

A generic class declaration is illegal if there exist types t1,...,tn such that the constructed type C<t1,...,tn> would contain two or more method declarations with the same signature.

An overloaded operator declared in a generic class C<T1,...,Tn> must have at least one argument whose type is the same as that of the enclosing type C<T1,...,Tn>, as explained in section 10.15.

The usual conversion rules hold for generic classes and generic interfaces. When generic class C<T1> is declared to be a subclass of generic class B<T1> or is declared to implement interface I<T1>, then the constructed type C<t1> can be implicitly converted to the constructed types B<t1> and I<t1>: an expression of type C<t1> can be used wherever a value of type B<t1> or I<t1> is expected.

However, generic classes are invariant in their type parameters. Hence even if t11 is implicitly convertible to t12, the constructed type C<t11> is not implicitly convertible to the constructed type C<t12>. For instance, LinkedList<String> is not implicitly convertible to LinkedList<Object>. If it were, one could create a LinkedList<String>, cast it to LinkedList<Object>, store an Object into it, and rather unexpectedly get an Object back out of the original LinkedList<String>.

**Example 168** Declaration of a Generic Class
An object of generic class LinkedList<T> is a linked list whose elements have type T; it implements interface IMyList<T> (example 173). The generic class declaration has a nested class, an indexer with result type T, methods that take arguments of type T, an `Equals` method that checks that its argument can be cast to IMyList<T>, a method that returns an IEnumerator<T>, an explicit conversion from array of T to LinkedList<T>, and an overloaded operator (+) that performs list concatenation. See also example 177.

```
public class LinkedList<T> : IMyList<T> {
  protected int size;                // Number of elements in the list
  protected Node first, last;        // Invariant: first==null iff last==null
  protected class Node {
    public Node prev, next;
    public T item;
    ...
  }
  public LinkedList() { first = last = null; size = 0; }
  public LinkedList(params T[] elems) : this() { ... }
  public int Count { get { return size; } }
  public T this[int i] { get { ... }   set { ... } }
  public void Add(T item) { Insert(size, item); }
  public void Insert(int i, T item) { ... }
  public void RemoveAt(int i) { ... }
  public override bool Equals(Object that) {
    if (that is IMyList<T> && this.size == ((IMyList<T>)that).Count) ...
  }
  public override int GetHashCode() { ... }
  public static explicit operator LinkedList<T>(T[] arr) { ... }
  public static LinkedList<T> operator +(LinkedList<T> xs1, LinkedList<T> xs2) { ... }
}
```

**Example 169** Subclass Relations between Generic Classes and Interfaces
The constructed type Point<String> is implicitly convertible to IMovable, and both ColorPoint<String,uint> and ColorPoint<String,Color> are implicitly convertible to Point<String> and IMovable.

```
interface IMovable { void Move(int dx, int dy); }
class Point<Label> : IMovable {
  protected internal int x, y;
  private Label lab;
  public Point(int x, int y, Label lab) { this.x = x; this.y = y; this.lab = lab; }
  public void Move(int dx, int dy) { x += dx; y += dy; }
}
class ColorPoint<Label, Color> : Point<Label> {
  private Color c;
  public ColorPoint(int x, int y, Label lab, Color c) : base(x, y, lab) { ... }
}
```

## 23.4    Constraints on Type Parameters

A declaration of a generic class C<T1,...,Tn> may have type parameter constraints:

> *class-modifiers* class C<T1,...,Tn> *subtype-clause  parameter-constraints*
>     *class-body*

The *parameter-constraints* is a list of *constraint-clauses*, each of this form:

> where T : $c_1$, $c_2$, ..., $c_m$

In the constraint clause, T is one of the type parameters T1,...,Tn and each $c_i$ is a *constraint*. A given type parameter Ti can have at most one constraint clause; that clause may involve one or more constraints $c_1$, $c_2$, ..., $c_m$. The order of the constraint clauses for T1,...,Tn does not matter.

A *constraint* c must have one of these four forms:

- c is a type expression: a non-sealed class or an interface or a type parameter. The type expression may be a constructed type and involve the type parameters T1,...,Tn and type parameters of enclosing generic classes and struct types. An array type, or a type parameter that has a struct constraint, cannot be used as a constraint. Nor can the classes Object, System.ValueType, System.Delegate, System.Array, or System.Enum. At most one of the constraints on a type parameter can be a class, and that constraint must appear first. There can be any number of constraints that are interfaces or type parameters.

- c is the special class constraint. This means that the type parameter must be instantiated by a reference type. The special class constraint can appear only first in a constraint list.

- c is the special struct constraint. This means that the type parameter must be instantiated by a value type: a simple type such as int, or a struct type. The struct constraint can appear only first in a constraint list. It follows that a type parameter cannot have both a class constraint and a struct constraint.

- c is the special new() constraint. This means that the type parameter must be instantiated by a type that has an argumentless constructor. If a type parameter has a struct constraint it is thereby guaranteed to have an argumentless constructor; in that case the new() constraint is redundant and illegal. Example 174 illustrates the use of the new() constraint.

It is illegal for constraints to be circular as in class C<T,U> where T : U where U : T { ... }.

The types t1,...,tn used when constructing a type must satisfy the *parameter-constraints*: if type parameter Ti is replaced by type ti throughout in the *parameter-constraints*, then for each resulting constraint t : c where c is a type expression, it must hold that t is convertible to c by an implicit reference conversion or a boxing conversion.

An override method or explicit interface implementation method gets its constraints from the base class method or the interface method, and cannot have explicit constraints of its own. A generic method that implements a method described by a base interface must have the same constraints as the interface method.

**Example 170** Type Parameter Constraints

Interface IPrintable describes a method `Print` that will print an object on a TextWriter. The generic PrintableLinkedList<T> can implement IPrintable provided the list elements (of type T) do.

```
class PrintableLinkedList<T> : LinkedList<T>, IPrintable where T : IPrintable {
  public void Print(TextWriter fs) {
    foreach (T x in this)
      x.Print(fs);
  }
}
interface IPrintable { void Print(TextWriter fs); }
```

**Example 171** Constraints Involving Type Parameters. Multiple Constraints

The elements of a type T are mutually comparable if any T-value x can be compared to any T-value y using x.CompareTo(y). This is the case if type T implements IComparable<T>; see section 24.3. The requirement that T implements IComparable<T> is expressible by the constraint `T : IComparable<T>`.

Type ComparablePair<T,U> is a type of ordered pairs of (T,U)-values. For (T,U)-pairs to support comparison, both T and U must support comparison, so constraints are required on both T and U.

```
struct ComparablePair<T,U> : IComparable<ComparablePair<T,U>>
  where T : IComparable<T>
  where U : IComparable<U>
{
  public readonly T Fst;
  public readonly U Snd;
  public int CompareTo(ComparablePair<T,U> that) {     // Lexicographic ordering
    int firstCmp = this.Fst.CompareTo(that.Fst);
    return firstCmp != 0 ? firstCmp : this.Snd.CompareTo(that.Snd);
  }
  public bool Equals(ComparablePair<T,U> that) {
    return this.Fst.Equals(that.Fst) && this.Snd.Equals(that.Snd);
  }
  ...
}
```

**Example 172** The `class` and `struct` Constraints

Without the `class` constraint, type parameter T in `C1` might be instantiated with a value type, and then `null` would not be a legal value of field `f`. Conversely, without the `struct` constraint, type parameter U in `D1` might be instantiated with a reference type, and then the nullable type U? is rejected by the compiler. Thus either class declaration would be rejected by the compiler if its constraint was left out.

```
class C1<T> where T : class {
  T f = null;                          // Legal: T is a reference type
}
class D1<U> where U : struct {
  U? f;                                // Legal: U is a value type
}
```

## 23.5   Generic Interfaces

A declaration of a *generic interface* I<T1,...,Tn> has one of these forms:

> *interface-modifiers* interface I<T1,...,Tn> *extends-clause*
>    *interface-body*

> *interface-modifiers* interface I<T1,...,Tn> *extends-clause parameter-constraints*
>    *interface-body*

In both cases, the T1,...,Tn are type parameters as for generic classes (section 23.3), and the *interface-modifiers*, *extends-clause* and *interface-body* are as for non-generic interfaces (section 15.1). If present, the *parameter-constraints* are as for generic classes; see section 23.4.

A type constructed from the generic interface has form I<t1,...,tn> where the t1,...,tn are types. The types t1,...,tn must satisfy the *parameter-constraints*, if any, on the generic interface I<T1,...,Tn> as described in section 23.4.

## 23.6   How Can Type Parameters Be Used?

Within the body { ... } of a generic class class C<T1,...,Tn> { ... } or generic interface or struct, a type parameter Ti may be used almost as if it were a public type.

- One can use type parameter Ti in the return type or parameter types of methods, operators, properties, anonymous delegates, and indexers; in the type of fields, variables and parameters; and in member classes, interfaces, struct types and delegate types.

- One can use new Ti[10] to create an array whose element type is Ti; one can use (o is Ti) to test whether o is an instance of Ti; one can use (o as Ti) to test and cast to type Ti; one can use (Ti)e for type casts; one can use Ti when constructing a type C1<Ti> from a generic type; and one can use Ti in a typeof expression such as typeof(Ti) or typeof(C<Ti>).

- One can use the expression default(Ti) to obtain the default value for type Ti. This is the null reference when Ti is instantiated with a reference type, and an appropriate value (0, 0.0, false, a zero enum member, a struct with default value fields) when Ti is instantiated with a value type.

- One can use new Ti() to create an instance of Ti only if there is a parameter constraint of the form Ti : new() on Ti. See section 23.4 and example 174.

- One cannot call static methods on a type parameter Ti, as in Ti.M().

**Example 173** A Generic List Interface

The generic interface IMyList<T> extends the IEnumerable<T> interface (section 24.2) with methods to add and remove list elements, an indexer to get and set the element at a particular position, and a generic method Map<U> that takes as argument a delegate of generic type Mapper<T,U> (example 180) and builds a list of type IMyList<U>. Note that the generic method Map<U> has an additional type parameter U.

```
public interface IMyList<T> : IEnumerable<T> {
  int Count { get; }                    // Number of elements
  T this[int i] { get; set; }           // Get or set element at index i
  void Add(T item);                     // Add element at end
  void Insert(int i, T item);           // Insert element at index i
  void RemoveAt(int i);                 // Remove element at index i
  IMyList<U> Map<U>(Mapper<T,U> f);     // Map f over all elements
}
```

**Example 174** A Generic Polynomial Type, Implementing Generic Interface Twice

A value of type AddMul<A,R> supports addition and multiplication with values of type A, giving results of type R. A value of type Polynomial<E> is a polynomial with coefficients of type E; for this to make sense, values of type E must support addition and multiplication with values of type E, and type E must have an argumentless constructor E() that creates a zero element of E.

In return, polynomials over E support addition and multiplication with values of type E (thus implementing interface AddMul<E,Polynomial<E>>) and support addition and multiplication with themselves (thus implementing interface AddMul<Polynomial<E>,Polynomial<E>>).

```
interface AddMul<A,R> {
  R Add(A e);               // Addition with A, giving R
  R Mul(A e);               // Multiplication with A, giving R
}

class Polynomial<E> : AddMul<E,Polynomial<E>>,
                      AddMul<Polynomial<E>,Polynomial<E>>
  where E : AddMul<E,E>, new() {
  private readonly E[] cs;
  public Polynomial() { this.cs = new E[0]; }
  public Polynomial<E> Add(Polynomial<E> that) { ... }
  public Polynomial<E> Mul(Polynomial<E> that) {
    ...
    for (int i=0; i<newlen; i++) {
      E sum = new E();                  // Permitted by constraint E : new()
      ...
  }
  public Polynomial<E> Add(E that) { ... }
  public Polynomial<E> Mul(E that) { ... }
}
```

## 23.7    Generic Methods

A generic method is a method that takes one or more type parameters. A generic method may be declared inside a generic or non-generic class, struct type or interface.

A declaration of a generic method M<T1,...,Tn> has one of the forms:

*method-modifiers  returntype* M<T1,...,Tn>(*formal-list*)
   *method-body*

*method-modifiers  returntype* M<T1,...,Tn>(*formal-list*)
   *parameter-constraints*
   *method-body*

The *method-modifiers*, *returntype*, and *formal-list* are as for non-generic methods (section 10.7). If present, the *parameter-constraints* are as for generic classes (section 23.4).

The type parameters T1,...,Tn may be used as types in the *returntype*, *formal-list* and *method-body*; as may the type parameters of any enclosing generic class or struct type or interface. A type parameter Ti of a generic method may have the same name as a type parameter of an enclosing generic class or interface or struct type, but this produces a compiler warning.

A scope can have several methods, generic or not, with the same signature M(*formal-list*), if they have different numbers of type parameters. Only the number of type parameters is used to distinguish the methods, not the parameter names or the parameter constraints, if any.

When a generic method is declared inside a generic type (class or struct type or interface) declaration, it is a compile-time error if there is an instantiation of the type parameters of the enclosing generic type and the generic method that causes two method declarations to have the same signature.

If a generic method overrides a generic virtual method declared in a base class or implements a generic method described in an interface, then it must have same *parameter-constraints* as those methods. The names of the type parameters are not significant, only their ordinal positions in the type parameter list T1,...,Tn.

An application of a generic method can either be written M<t1,...,tn>(...) with generic type arguments t1,...,tn for the method's type parameters T1,...,Tn, or without them M(...). In the latter case, the compiler will attempt to infer the appropriate type arguments t1,...,tn automatically. Type parameter constraints are not taken into account during such inference, but must be satisfied by the resulting type arguments t1,...,tn. When inference is successful, the inferred type arguments are used to determine the method's signature for use in subsequent overloading resolution; see section 12.15.4.

In those cases where the inference is unsuccessful, the generic method will not take part in subsequent overloading resolution. If no other method exists with an appropriate signature, then overloading resolution fails, and one must write the method application in the first format M<t1,...,tn>(...), giving the type arguments explicitly.

**Example 175** A Generic Quicksort Method Using a Comparer Object
This method sorts an array of type T[] where T is a type parameter. A parameter of type IComparer<T>
determines the element ordering; see section 24.3 and example 190.

```
private static void Qsort<T>(T[] arr, IComparer<T> cmp, int a, int b) {
  if (a < b) {
    int i = a, j = b;
    T x = arr[(i+j) / 2];
    do {
      while (cmp.Compare(arr[i], x) < 0) i++;
      while (cmp.Compare(x, arr[j]) < 0) j--;
      if (i <= j) {
        T tmp = arr[i]; arr[i] = arr[j]; arr[j] = tmp;
        i++; j--;
      }
    } while (i <= j);
    Qsort<T>(arr, cmp, a, j);
    Qsort<T>(arr, cmp, i, b);
  }
}
```

**Example 176** A Generic Quicksort Method for Comparable Values
This method sorts an array of type T[] whose elements of type T must be comparable to themselves. This
is expressed by the method's parameter constraint as in example 171.

```
private static void Qsort<T>(T[] arr, int a, int b)
  where T : IComparable<T> {
  ...
    while (arr[i].CompareTo(x) < 0) i++;
    while (x.CompareTo(arr[j]) < 0) j--;
  ...
}
```

**Example 177** A Generic Method in a Generic Class
The generic class LinkedList<T> in example 168 can be equipped with a generic method Map<U> that
takes an additional type parameter U and returns a new list of type LinkedList<U>. The generic interface
IMyList<T> is from example 173 and the generic delegate type Mapper<T,U> is from example 180.

```
public class LinkedList<T> : IMyList<T> {
  ...
  public IMyList<U> Map<U>(Mapper<T,U> f) {      // Map f over all elements
    LinkedList<U> res = new LinkedList<U>();
    foreach (T x in this)
      res.Add(f(x));
    return res;
  }
}
```

## 23.8    Generic Delegate Types

A declaration of a *generic delegate type* D<T1, . . . , Tn> has one of these forms:

> *delegate-modifiers returntype* delegate D<T1, . . . ,Tn>(*formal-list*);

> *delegate-modifiers returntype* delegate D<T1, . . . ,Tn>(*formal-list*)
>    where *parameter-constraints*;

The *delegate-modifiers*, *returntype* and *formal-list* are as for non-generic delegates (section 17), except that the type parameters T1, . . . ,Tn may be used in the *returntype* and *formal-list*.

The *parameter-constraints* are as for generic classes (section 23.4).

## 23.9    Abbreviations for Constructed Types

With the using directive one can introduce abbreviations for constructed types, which may otherwise become very verbose. The relevant form of the using directive (section 25.1) is this one:

```
using T = t;
```

where T is a type name. The right hand side t is a type, possibly involving types constructed from generic types. A using directive can appear only at top-level immediately at the beginning of a compilation unit or a namespace declaration (section 25), not inside classes, interfaces, or struct types.

A using directive does not affect other using directives in the same namespace. Thus although a using directive can make types in method headers and declarations more readable, the using directives themselves can become rather unwieldy.

For instance, assume we want to introduce a type alias IntSet for the constructed type Set<int> and a type alias IntSet2Int for the type IDictionary<Set<int>,int> in this program:

```
using System.Collections.Generic;              // Open namespace
class Nfa {
  static IList<int> Rename(IDictionary<Set<int>,int> renamer,
                       IList<Set<int>> states) { ... }
}
```

Then the right-hand sides of using directives must use the full type paths, like this:

```
using IntSet = Set<int>;                       // Type abbreviation
using IntSet2Int = System.Collections.Generic.IDictionary<Set<int>,int>;
class Nfa {
  static List<int> Rename(IntSet2Int renamer, List<IntSet> states) { ... }
}
```

In particular, in the definition of IntSet2Int, the System.Collections.Generic prefix is needed, and Set<int> cannot be replaced by IntSet. One solution to this problem would be to artificially introduce nested namespace declarations: a using directive in an outer namespace does affect using directives in inner namespaces. But this is not recommended.

**Example 178** A Generic Comparer As a Delegate

The generic delegate type DComparer<T> describes a method that takes two arguments of type T and compares them, just like method Compare in an object of type IComparer<T> (section 24.3). Note that the method String.Compare (section 7) is compatible with the constructed delegate type DComparer<String>, and that the type casts of method StringReverseCompare of example 136 are avoided.

```
public delegate int DComparer<T>(T v1, T v2);
...
DComparer<String> strCmp = new DComparer<String>(String.Compare);
```

**Example 179** Generic Quicksort Method Using a Delegate to Compare Elements

This generic method is a faster and more typesafe version of the delegate-based sorting method in example 136. It sorts an array of type T[] where T is a type parameter, just as in example 175, but the element ordering is determined by a delegate of type DComparer<T> from example 178. Note that all type casts, boxing and unboxing can be avoided, even when sorting values of simple type such as integers.

```
private static void Qsort<T>(T[] arr, DComparer<T> cmp, int a, int b) {
  ...
  while (cmp(arr[i], x) < 0) i++;
  while (cmp(x, arr[j]) < 0) j--;
  ...
}
```

**Example 180** Generic Delegate Type Describing a Function

A delegate of the generic delegate type Mapper<A,R> is a method that takes an argument of type A and produces a result of type R; this is the same as a function of type A → R. For instance, method Math.Sign (section 21) is compatible with the constructed delegate type Mapper<double,int>.

```
public delegate R Mapper<A,R>(A x);
```

**Example 181** Mapping a Method and an Anonymous Method Over a Linked List

The generic LinkedList<T> method Map<U>(...) in example 177 takes an argument of generic delegate type Mapper<T,U> defined in example 180. A delegate of that type may be created from an existing method such as Math.Sign, or it may be an anonymous method expression (section 12.20).

The anonymous method passed as argument to method Map<String>(...) below is compatible with the constructed delegate type Mapper<double, String>.

```
LinkedList<double> dLst = ...;
IMyList<int> iLst = dLst.Map<int>(new Mapper<double, int>(Math.Sign));
IMyList<String> sLst = dLst.Map<String>(delegate(double d) { return "s" + d; });
```

## 23.10  Generic Struct Types

A declaration of a *generic struct type* S<T1,...,Tn> is very similar to the declaration of a generic class. It has one of these forms:

> *struct-modifiers* struct S<T1,...,Tn> *struct-interfaces*
>   *struct-body*

> *struct-modifiers* struct I<T1,...,Tn> *struct-interfaces parameter-constraints*
>   *struct-body*

In both cases, the T1,...,Tn are type parameters as for generic classes (section 23.3), and the *struct-modifiers* and *struct-body* are as for non-generic struct types (section 14). The *parameter-constraints* are as for generic classes; see section 23.4.

A type constructed from the generic struct type has form S<t1,...,tn> where the t1,...,tn are types. The types t1,...,tn must satisfy the *parameter-constraints* on the generic struct, if any, as described in section 23.4.

Generic struct types are used in the generic collection library, for instance to represent key/value pairs in dictionaries; see section 24.8 and example 187.

## 23.11  The Implementation of Generic Types and Methods

Generic types and methods in C# resemble C++ type templates and function templates, and resemble generic types and methods in Java 1.5. However, the design and implementation of C# generics provide better type safety and less code duplication than C++ templates, and provides better performance and more features than Java 1.5 generic types and methods.

In C#, a generic type declaration or generic method declaration can be fully type-checked before any constructed type is created for given type arguments, and then the type-check is valid for all possible type arguments. Hence type errors are discovered as early as possible. In C++, a class template or function template cannot be type-checked before a type instance is created for given type parameters, and the type check must be performed separately for every set of given type parameters.

In C#, each constructed type, such as Pair<double, int>, where Pair is from example 182, in principle gives rise to a new type (in the run-time system) with its own field layout; this permits unboxed storage of fields. To save space and code duplication, every combination of type arguments that are reference types will share the same field layout: all references have the same size regardless of type. Thus the two constructed types Pair<DateTime, String> and Pair<String, String> have the same field layouts. On the other hand, different combinations of type arguments that are value types may require different field layouts at run-time, because values of different value types take up different amounts of memory. For instance, the constructed struct types Pair<double, int> and Pair<int, int> have different field layouts.

This implementation technique for C# has the considerable advantage that it permits generic types and generic methods to handle value types unboxed, which reduces memory usage and increases speed. By contrast, the Java 1.5 implementation of generics uses boxed representation of all values of type parameters, which requires costly boxing, heap references, and unboxing when accessing the values.

On the other hand, the C# implementation has the disadvantage that it may cause some code duplication (at run-time), but this problem is much less pronounced than for C++ templates.

**Example 182** A Generic Struct Type for Pairs

A pair of two values of type T and U can be represented by a generic struct type Pair<T,U> like this. The generic struct type has read-only fields for holding the components, and a constructor for creating pairs.

```
public struct Pair<T,U> {
  public readonly T Fst;
  public readonly U Snd;
  public Pair(T fst, U snd) {
    this.Fst = fst;
    this.Snd = snd;
} }
```

**Example 183** Logging Pairs

The constructed type Pair<DateTime, String> is the type of pairs of a DateTime struct and a String object. A log (example 167) of such pairs can be created and used as follows. Note that an element of array allMsgs is known to be a Pair<DateTime, String>, not just an Object.

```
Log<Pair<DateTime,String>> log = new Log<Pair<DateTime,String>>();
log.Add(new Pair<DateTime,String>(DateTime.Now, "Tea leaves"));
log.Add(new Pair<DateTime,String>(DateTime.Now.AddMinutes(2), "Hot water"));
log.Add(new Pair<DateTime,String>(DateTime.Now.AddMinutes(7), "Ready"));
Pair<DateTime,String>[] allMsgs = log.All;
foreach (Pair<DateTime,String> p in allMsgs)
   ... p.Fst ... p.Snd ...
```

**Example 184** A Generic Struct Type to Represent Possibly Missing Values

Struct type Option<T> can represent a value of type T that may be missing. Sometimes the null reference is used to mean "missing", but this is impossible for plain value types. The predefined generic struct type System.Nullable<T> serves a similar purpose but can be used only for argument types T that are value types; see section 18. Note that the default value of the HasValue field below is false, so the struct type's argumentless constructor Option<T>() constructs a new missing value.

```
public struct Option<T> {
  public readonly bool HasValue;
  private readonly T value;
  public Option(T value) { this.HasValue = true; this.value = value; }
  public T Value {
    get { if (HasValue) return value;
          else throw new InvalidOperationException("No value");
  } }
  public static implicit operator Option<T>(T value) { return new Option<T>(value); }
  public static explicit operator T(Option<T> option) { return option.Value; }
  public override String ToString() { return HasValue ? value.ToString() : "[No value]"; }
}
...
public static Option<double> Sqrt(double x) {
  return x >= 0.0 ? new Option<double>(Math.Sqrt(x)) : new Option<double>();
}
```

# 24   Generic Collections: Lists and Dictionaries (C# 2.0)

Namespace System.Collections.Generic provides efficient, convenient and typesafe data structures for representing collections of related data. These data structures include lists, stacks, queues, and dictionaries (also called maps). A list is an ordered sequence where elements can be added and removed at any position; a stack is an ordered sequence where elements can be added and removed only at one end; a queue is an ordered sequence where elements can be added at one end and removed at the other end; and a dictionary associates values with keys. The collection classes are not thread-safe; using the same collection instance from two concurrent threads produces unpredictable results.

The most important generic collection interfaces and classes are related as follows:

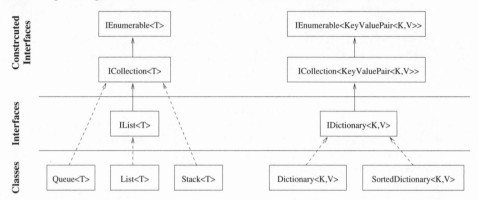

## 24.1   The ICollection<T> Interface

The generic interface ICollection<T> extends IEnumerable<T>, so its elements can be enumerated. In addition, it describes the following members:

- Read-only property int Count returns the number of elements in the collection.

- Read-only property bool IsReadOnly returns true if the collection is read-only and cannot be modified; otherwise false.

- void Add(T x) adds element x to the collection. Throws NotSupportedException if the collection is read-only.

- void Clear() removes all elements from the collection. Throws NotSupportedException if the collection is read-only.

- bool Contains(T x) returns true if element x is in the collection; false otherwise.

- void CopyTo(T[] arr, int i) copies the collection's members to array arr, starting at array index i. Throws ArgumentOutOfRangeException if i<0, and throws ArgumentException if i+Count>arr.Length. Throws InvalidCastException if some collection element is not convertible to the array's element type.

- bool Remove(T x) removes an occurrence of element x from the collection. Returns true if an element was removed, else false. Throws NotSupportedException if the collection is read-only.

**Example 185** Using Generic Collections

The `Print` methods are defined in examples 186 and 187.

```
using System.Collections.Generic;  // IList, IDictionary, List, Dictionary, ...
...
IList<bool> list1 = new List<bool>();
list1.Add(true); list1.Add(false); list1.Add(true); list1.Add(false);
Print(list1);                      // Must print: true false true false
bool b1 = list1[3];                // false
IDictionary<String, int> dict1 = new Dictionary<String, int>();
dict1.Add("Sweden", 46); dict1.Add("Germany", 49); dict1.Add("Japan", 81);
Print(dict1.Keys);                 // May print:  Japan Sweden Germany
Print(dict1.Values);               // May print:  81 46 49
int i1 = dict1["Japan"];           // 81
Print(dict1);                      // Print key/value pairs in some order
IDictionary<String, int> dict2 = new SortedDictionary<String, int>();
dict2.Add("Sweden", 46); dict2.Add("Germany", 49); dict2.Add("Japan", 81);
Print(dict2.Keys);                 // Must print: Germany Japan Sweden
Print(dict2.Values);               // Must print: 49 81 46
Print(dict2);                      // Print key/value pairs in sorted key order
```

**Choosing an Appropriate Collection Class**   The running time or time complexity of an operation on a collection is usually given in $O$ notation, as a function of the size $n$ of the collection. Thus $O(1)$ means *constant time*, $O(\log n)$ means *logarithmic time* (time at most proportional to the logarithm of $n$), and $O(n)$ means *linear time* (time at most proportional to $n$). For accessing, adding, or removing an element, these roughly correspond to *very fast*, *fast*, and *slow*.

In the table, $n$ is the number of elements in the collection and $i$ is an integer index. Thus adding or removing an element of a List is fast only near the end of the list, where $n-i$ is small. The subscript $a$ indicates *amortized complexity*: over a long sequence of operations, the average time per operation is $O(1)$, although any single operation could take time $O(n)$.

| Operation | List | Dictionary | SortedDictionary | Queue | Stack | Operation |
|---|---|---|---|---|---|---|
| Add(o) | $O(1)_a$ | | | $O(1)_a$ | $O(1)_a$ | Enqueue(o), Push(o) |
| Insert(i,o) | $O(n-i)_a$ | | | | | |
| Add(k, v) | | $O(1)_a$ | $O(n)$ | | | |
| Remove(o) | $O(n)$ | $O(1)$ | $O(n)$ | $O(1)$ | $O(1)$ | Dequeue(), Pop() |
| RemoveAt(i) | $O(n-i)$ | $O(1)$ | | | | |
| Contains(o) | $O(n)$ | | | $O(n)$ | $O(n)$ | Contains(o) |
| ContainsKey(o) | | $O(1)$ | $O(\log n)$ | | | |
| ContainsValue(o) | | $O(n)$ | $O(n)$ | | | |
| IndexOf(o) | $O(n)$ | | | | | |
| IndexOfKey(i) | | | $O(\log n)$ | | | |
| IndexOfValue(i) | | | $O(n)$ | | | |
| this[i] | $O(1)$ | | | | | |
| this[k] | | $O(1)$ | $O(\log n)$ | | | |

## 24.2    Enumerators and Enumerables

### 24.2.1    The IEnumerator and IEnumerator<T> Interfaces

An enumerator is an object that enumerates (produces) a stream of elements, such as the elements of a collection. A class or struct type that has a method `GetEnumerator` with return type IEnumerator or IEnumerator<T> can be used in a `foreach` statement (section 13.6.2).

Interface System.Collections.IEnumerator describes these members:

- Read-only property `Object Current` returns the enumerator's current value, or throws Invalid-OperationException if the enumerator has not reached the first element or is beyond the last element.

- `bool MoveNext()` advances the enumerator to the next (or first) element, if possible; returns true if it succeeded so that `Current` is valid; false otherwise. Throws InvalidOperationException if the underlying collection has been modified since the enumerator was created.

- `void Reset()` resets the enumerator so that the next call to `MoveNext` will advance it to the first element, if any.

The generic interface System.Collections.Generic.IEnumerator<T> describes one property and two methods, one of them because IEnumerator<T> extends interface IDisposable (section 13.10):

- Read-only property `T Current` returns the enumerator's current value, or throws InvalidOperationException if the enumerator has not reached the first element or is beyond the last element.

- `bool MoveNext()` is just as for IEnumerator above.

- `void Dispose()` is called by the consumer (for instance, a `foreach` statement) when the enumerator is no longer needed. It should release the resources held by the enumerator. Subsequent uses of `Current` should throw InvalidOperationException, and subsequent calls to `MoveNext` should return false.

### 24.2.2    The IEnumerable and IEnumerable<T> Interfaces

An enumerable type is one that implements interface IEnumerable or IEnumerable<T>. This means that it has a method `GetEnumerator` that can produce an enumerator; see examples 132 and 173.

Interface System.Collections.IEnumerable describes this method:

- `IEnumerator GetEnumerator()` returns an enumerator.

The generic interface System.Collections.Generic.IEnumerable<T> describes this method:

- `IEnumerator<T> GetEnumerator()` returns an enumerator.

All collection types with element type T implement IEnumerable<T> and IEnumerable. Type Array (section 9.3) and all array types implement IEnumerable. For a given type t, array type t[] also implements IList<t> and therefore IEnumerable<t>. If a user type needs to implement both IEnumerable<T> and IEnumerable, it must declare the `GetEnumerator` method twice, using explicit interface member implementations with different return types; see section 15.3.

**Example 186** Traversing a Collection

The prototypical traversal of a collection coll (which implements IEnumerable<T>) uses a foreach statement:

```
public static void Print<T>(ICollection<T> coll) {
  foreach (T x in coll)
    Console.Write("{0} ", x);
  Console.WriteLine();
}
```

**Example 187** Traversing a Dictionary

A dictionary dict implements IEnumerable<KeyValuePair<K,V>> so its key/value pairs (see section 24.8) can be printed like this:

```
public static void Print<K,V>(IDictionary<K,V> dict) {
  foreach (KeyValuePair<K,V> entry in dict)
    Console.WriteLine("{0} --> {1}", entry.Key, entry.Value);
  Console.WriteLine();
}
```

**Example 188** An Enumerator Class for LinkedList<T>

Class LinkedListEnumerator is a member class of and implements an enumerator for class LinkedList<T> from example 168. The Dispose method releases any data and list nodes reachable through the current element. The yield statement (section 13.12) provides an alternative simpler way to define enumerators.

```
private class LinkedListEnumerator : IEnumerator<T> {
  T curr;                    // The enumerator's current element
  bool valid;                // Is the current element valid?
  Node next;                 // Node holding the next element, or null
  public LinkedListEnumerator(LinkedList<T> lst) {
    next = lst.first; valid = false;
  }
  public T Current {
    get { if (valid) return curr; else throw new InvalidOperationException(); }
  }
  public bool MoveNext() {
    if (next != null)  {
      curr = next.item; next = next.next; valid = true;
    } else
      valid = false;
    return valid;
  }
  public void Dispose() { curr = default(T); next = null; valid = false; }
}
```

## 24.3    Ordered Values: Comparables and Comparers

Some values can be compared to each other: they are ordered. The types of such values may implement an interface that describes comparison methods. In general a comparison method returns a negative number to indicate less-than, zero to indicate equality, and a positive number to indicate greater-than.

The comparisons must define a *partial ordering*, that is, they must be reflexive, anti-symmetric, and transitive. Let us define that negative is the opposite sign of positive and vice versa, and that zero is the opposite sign of zero. Then the requirements on a comparison method such as `CompareTo` are:

- `x.CompareTo(x)` must be zero.
- `x.CompareTo(y)` and `y.CompareTo(x)` must be have opposite signs.
- If `x.CompareTo(y)` and `y.CompareTo(z)` have the same sign, then `x.CompareTo(z)` must have that sign also.

### 24.3.1    The IComparable and IComparable<T> Interfaces

The non-generic interface System.IComparable describes a single method. Note that this interface is in the System namespace, not in the System.Collections namespace.

- `int CompareTo(Object that)` must return a negative number when the current object (`this`) is less than `that`, zero when they are equal, and a positive number when `this` is greater than `that`.

The numeric types `int`, `double`, ..., the String class (section 7) and all enum types (section 16) implement IComparable.

The generic interface System.IComparable<T> describes these methods:

- `int CompareTo(T that)` must return a negative number when the current object (`this`) is less than `that`, zero when they are equal, and a positive number when `this` is greater than `that`.
- `bool Equals(T that)` must return true if the current object (`this`) is equal to `that`, else false. Must be equal to `this.CompareTo(that)==0`, but can often be implemented more efficiently.

Type `int` implements IComparable<int>, type `double` implements IComparable<double>, and similarly for all the other numeric types, for the String class (section 7), and for enum types.

### 24.3.2    The IComparer and IComparer<T> Interfaces

The non-generic interface System.Collections.IComparer describes this method:

- `int Compare(Object o1, Object o2)` must return a negative number when `o1` is less than `o2`, zero when they are equal, and a positive number when `o1` is greater than `o2`.

The generic interface System.Collections.Generic.IComparer<T> describes these methods:

- `int Compare(T v1, T v2)` must return a negative number when `v1` is less than `v2`, zero when they are equal, and a positive number when `v2` is greater than `v1`.
- `bool Equals(T v1, T v2)` must return true if `v1` is equal to `v2`, else false.
- `int GetHashCode(T v)` must return a hashcode for `v`; see section 5.2.

**Example 189** A Class of Comparable Points in Time

A Time object represents the time of day 00:00–23:59. The method call `t1.CompareTo(t2)` returns a negative number if `t1` is before `t2`, a positive number if `t1` is after `t2`, and zero if they are the same time. By defining two overloads of `CompareTo`, the class implements both the non-generic IComparable interface and the constructed interface IComparable<Time>.

```
using System;                            // IComparable
using System.Collections.Generic;        // IComparable<T>
public class Time : IComparable, IComparable<Time> {
  private readonly int hh, mm;           // 24-hour clock
  public Time(int hh, int mm) { this.hh = hh; this.mm = mm; }
  public int CompareTo(Object that) {
    return CompareTo((Time)that);
  }
  public int CompareTo(Time that) {
    return hh != that.hh ? hh - that.hh : mm - that.mm;
  }
  public bool Equals(Time that) {
    return hh == that.hh && mm == that.mm;
  }
  public override String ToString() { return String.Format("{0:00}:{1:00}", hh, mm); }
}
```

**Example 190** A Comparer for Integer Pairs

Integer pairs are ordered lexicographically by this comparer, which has features from examples 73 and 189.

```
using System.Collections;                // IComparer
using System.Collections.Generic;        // IComparer<T>
public struct IntPair {
  public readonly int fst, snd;
  public IntPair(int fst, int snd) { this.fst = fst; this.snd = snd; }
}
public class IntPairComparer : IComparer, IComparer<IntPair> {
  public int Compare(Object o1, Object o2) {
    return Compare((IntPair)o1, (IntPair)o2);
  }
  public int Compare(IntPair v1, IntPair v2) {
    return v1.Fst<v2.Fst ? -1 : v1.Fst>v2.Fst ? +1
         : v1.Snd<v2.Snd ? -1 : v1.Snd>v2.Snd ? +1 : 0;
  }
  public bool Equals(IntPair v1, IntPair v2) {
    return v1.Fst==v2.Fst && v1.Snd==v2.Snd;
  }
  public int GetHashCode(IntPair v) {
    return v.Fst ^ v.Snd;
  }
}
```

## 24.4    The IList<T> Interface

The generic interface IList<T> extends ICollection<T> and describes lists with elements of type T. It has the following members in addition to those of ICollection<T>:

- Read-write indexer `T this[int i]` returns or sets list element number i, counting from 0. Throws ArgumentOutOfRangeException if i<0 or i>=Count. Throws NotSupportedException if used to set an element on a read-only list.

- `void Add(T x)` adds element x at the end of the list.

- `int IndexOf(T x)` returns the least position whose element equals x, if any; otherwise −1.

- `void Insert(int i, T x)` inserts x at position i. Existing elements at position i and higher have their position incremented by one. Throws ArgumentOutOfRangeException if i<0 or i>Count. Throws NotSupportedException if the list is read-only.

- `bool Remove(T x)` removes the first element of the list that equals x, if any. Returns true if an element was removed. All elements at higher positions have their position decremented by one. Throws NotSupportedException if the list is read-only.

- `void RemoveAt(int i)` removes the element at index i. All elements at higher positions have their position decremented by one. Throws ArgumentOutOfRangeException if i<0 or i>=Count. Throws NotSupportedException if the list is read-only.

Interface IList<T> is implemented by class List<T> which represents a list using an array; see section 24.6. The current collection library also includes a class LinkedList<T> of linked lists, but it does not implement IList<T>, and the details may change, so class LinkedList<T> is not further described here.

## 24.5    The IDictionary<K,V> Interface

The generic interface IDictionary<K,V> extends ICollection<KeyValuePair<K,V>>, so it can be seen as a collection of key/value pairs (entries), where the keys have type K and the values have type V. Since a dictionary implements also IEnumerable<KeyValuePair<K,V>>, the key/value pairs can be enumerated.

There can be no two entries with the same key, and a key of reference type cannot be null.

The interface describes these members in addition to those of ICollection<KeyValuePair<K,V>>:

- Read-only property `ICollection<K> Keys` returns a collection of the keys in the dictionary.

- Read-only property `ICollection<V> Values` returns a collection of the values in the dictionary.

- Read-write indexer `V this[K k]` gets or sets the value at dictionary key k. Throws ArgumentException when getting (but not when setting) if key k is not in the dictionary. Throws NotSupportedException if used to set an element in a read-only dictionary.

- `void Add(K k, V v)` inserts value v at key k in the dictionary. Throws ArgumentException if key k is already in the dictionary. Throws NotSupportedException if the dictionary is read-only .

- `bool ContainsKey(K k)` returns true if the dictionary contains an entry for key k, else false.

- `bool Remove(K k)` removes the entry for key k, if any. Returns true if a key was removed.

**Example 191** Building a Text File Index
This example uses generic Dictionary and List collections to build a list of all words in a given text file, and the line numbers on which they occur. The file is read using a StreamReader (section 22.4).

```
static IDictionary<String, List<int>> IndexFile(String filename) {
  IDictionary<String, List<int>> index = new Dictionary<String, List<int>>();
  Regex delim = new Regex("[^a-zA-Z0-9]+");
  TextReader rd = new StreamReader(filename);
  int lineno = 0;
  String line;
  while (null != (line = rd.ReadLine())) {
    String[] res = delim.Split(line);
    lineno++;
    foreach (String s in res)
      if (s != "") {
        if (!index.ContainsKey(s))
          index[s] = new List<int>();
        index[s].Add(lineno);
      }
  }
  rd.Close();
  return index;
}
```

**Example 192** Using a Dictionary to Represent a Set
There is no predefined type for representing a set: an unordered collection of elements with no duplicates. However, a set of elements of type T can be represented by generic class Set<T> below. The implementation uses a dictionary with keys of type T; the dictionary's values (here of type bool) are unused. A Set<T> is a collection and hence enumerable. This class is used in examples 197 and 198.

```
class Set<T> : ICollection<T> {
  private Dictionary<T,bool> dict;
  public Set() { dict = new Dictionary<T,bool>(); }
  public bool Contains(T x) { return dict.ContainsKey(x); }
  public void Add(T x) {
    if (!Contains(x))
      dict.Add(x, false);
  }
  public IEnumerator<T> GetEnumerator() { return dict.Keys.GetEnumerator(); }
  public Set<T> Intersection(Set<T> that) {
    Set<T> res = new Set<T>();
    foreach (T x in this)
      if (that.Contains(x))
        res.Add(x);
    return res;
  }
  ...
}
```

## 24.6   The List<T> Class

The generic class List<T> implements IList<T> and IList. The elements are stored in an array that grows as needed when elements are added. Element access by index is fast, but insertion and deletion are slow except at the list's end. Class List<T> has the members described by IList<T> and these, among others:

- Constructor List<T>() creates an empty list.
- Constructor List<T>(int capacity) creates an empty list with a given initial capacity.
- Constructor List<T>(IEnumerable<T> enm) creates a list containing enm's elements.
- Read-write property int Capacity gets or sets the current capacity of the list. Throws ArgumentOutOfRangeException if setting the capacity less than the number of elements.
- void AddRange(IEnumerable<T> enm) adds enm's elements at the end of the list.
- IList<T> AsReadOnly() returns a read-only list that is a wrapper around the given list.
- int BinarySearch(T x) searches the list for x using binary search. Returns an index i>=0 for which a[i].CompareTo(k) == 0, if any; otherwise returns i<0 such that ~i would be the proper position for k. The list must be sorted, as by Sort(), or else the result is undefined.
- int BinarySearch(T x, IComparer<T> cmp) works as above, but compares elements using cmp.Compare. The list must be sorted, as by Sort(cmp), or else the result is undefined.
- int BinarySearch(int i, int n, T x, IComparer<T> cmp) works as above, but searches the list segment with indexes i..(i+n-1) only.
- void CopyTo(int src, T[] arr, int dst, int n) copies n list elements starting at list position src to the array arr, starting at array position dst. Throws ArgumentOutOfRangeException if src<0 or dst<0 or n<0. Throws ArgumentException if src+n>Count or dst+n>arr.Length.
- int IndexOf(T x, int i) returns the least index greater than or equal to i at which an element equals x, if any; otherwise returns −1. Throws ArgumentOutOfRangeException if i<0 or i>Count.
- int IndexOf(T x, int i, int n) returns the least index greater than or equal to i and smaller than i+n at which an element equals x, if any; otherwise returns −1.
- void InsertRange(int i, IEnumerable<T> enm) inserts enm's elements at index i. Existing elements at position i and higher have their position incremented.
- int LastIndexOf(T x) and two other overloads are similar to IndexOf, but returns the greatest index rather than the least index at which an element equals x.
- void RemoveRange(int i, int n) removes the elements in index range i..(i+n-1).
- void Reverse() reverses the order of the list elements.
- void Reverse(int i, int n) reverses the list elements in index range i..(i+n-1).
- void Sort() sorts the list using quicksort, comparing elements using their CompareTo method. The list elements must implement IComparable<T>. The sort is not stable.
- void Sort(IComparer<T> cmp) sorts the list, comparing elements using cmp.Compare.
- void Sort(int i, int n, IComparer<T> cmp) sorts the segment with indexes i..(i+n-1).
- T[] ToArray() returns a new array containing the elements of the list.
- void TrimToSize() shrinks the list's capacity to the actual number of elements.

**Example 193** Simple List Operations

By running this example you can see the difference between fast element addition at the end of an array-based list, and slow element insertion at the head of the list. The two operations take time $O(1)_a$ and $O(n)$ respectively; see the table on page 159. For some other List operations, see examples 185 and 194.

```
List<int> lst = new List<int>();
lst.Add(7); lst.Add(9); lst.Add(13); lst.Add(7);
Print(lst);                        // 7 9 13 7
int i1 = lst[2];                   // 13
int i2 = lst.IndexOf(7);           // 0
int i3 = lst.IndexOf(12);          // -1
lst.Remove(8); Print(lst);         // 7 9 13 7
lst.Remove(7); Print(lst);         // 9 13 7
lst.Insert(3, 88); Print(lst);     // 9 13 7 88
int count = 100000;
Console.WriteLine("Adding elements at end of list (fast) ...");
for (int i=0; i<count; i++)
  lst.Add(i);
lst.Clear();
Console.WriteLine("Adding elements at head of list (slow) ...");
for (int i=0; i<count; i++)
  lst.Insert(0, i);
```

**Example 194** Collecting Database Query Results in a List and Returning Them in an Array

Sometimes a method must return an array of results, where the number of results is not known in advance. In that case, the results could be produced in a List and transferred to an array when the method returns. This method performs a database query, reads each record resulting from the query and puts it into a List<Record>, then copies the records to an array and returns that. The full example source code shows also how to open the database connection.

```
using System.Data.Odbc;          // OdbcConnection OdbcCommand OdbcDataReader
using System.Collections.Generic; // List<T>
struct Record {
  public readonly String name, msg;
  ...
}
...
static Record[] GetMessages(OdbcConnection conn) {
  String query = "SELECT name, msg, severity FROM Message ORDER BY name";
  OdbcCommand cmd = new OdbcCommand(query, conn);
  OdbcDataReader r = cmd.ExecuteReader();
  List<Record> results = new List<Record>();
  while (r.Read())
    results.Add(new Record(r.GetString(0), r.GetString(1), r.GetInt32(2)));
  r.Close();
  return results.ToArray();
}
```

## 24.7    The Dictionary<K,V> Class

The generic class Dictionary<K,V> implements IDictionary<K,V> and is used to represent dictionaries or maps with keys of type K and associated values of type V. A dictionary is implemented as a hash table, so the keys should have a good GetHashCode method but need not be ordered. In an unordered dictionary any key can be looked up, inserted, updated, or deleted in amortized constant time.

Objects used as dictionary keys should be treated as immutable, or else subtle errors may be encountered. If an object is used as key in a dictionary, and the object is subsequently modified so that its hashcode changes, then the key and its entry may be lost in the dictionary.

Class Dictionary<K,V> has the members described by IDictionary<K,V> as well as these:

- Constructor Dictionary() creates an empty dictionary.
- Constructor Dictionary(int capacity) creates an empty dictionary with given initial capacity.
- Constructor Dictionary(int capacity, IComparer<K> cmp) creates an empty dictionary with the given initial capacity using the Equals and GetHashCode methods from cmp.
- Constructor Dictionary(IDictionary<K,V> dict) creates a new dictionary that contains dict's key/value pairs.
- Constructor Dictionary(IDictionary<K,V> dict, IComparer<K> cmp) creates a new dictionary from dict's key/value pairs, using the Equals and GetHashCode methods from cmp.
- bool ContainsValue(V v) returns true if the dictionary contains an entry with value v. In contrast to ContainsKey(k), this is slow: it requires a linear search of all key/value pairs.
- bool TryGetValue(K k, out V v) binds v to the value associated with key k and returns true if the dictionary contains an entry for k; otherwise binds v to default(V) and returns false.

## 24.8    The KeyValuePair<K,V> Struct Type

A struct of generic struct type KeyValuePair<K,V> is used to hold a key/value pair, or entry, from a dictionary (sections 24.5 and 24.7). See example 187. Note that key/value pairs obtained by enumeration of a dictionary are *copies* of key/value pairs in the dictionary, so setting the key or value in such a pair does not affect the dictionary. The KeyValuePair<K,V> struct type has the following members:

- Constructor KeyValuePair(K k, V v) creates a pair of key k and value v.
- Field K Key holds the key in the key/value pair.
- Field V Value holds the value in the key/value pair.

## 24.9    The SortedDictionary<K,V> Class

Generic class SortedDictionary<K,V> implements IDictionary<K,V> and represents a dictionary with ordered keys of type K and associated values of type V. However, the current (August 2004) implementation is array-based and should be used only for dictionaries that are *guaranteed* to be small. Adding or removing an element takes time proportional to the size of the dictionary, so adding or removing a sequence of $m$ elements can take *quadratic time*, that is, time proportional to $m^2$, which is very slow. A sorted-dictionary implementation based on balanced binary trees scales much better; such an implementation should be available in the .Net Framework when released.

**Example 195** Simple Dictionary Operations

The indexer dict[k] throws ArgumentException when used to get the value of a key k not in the dictionary. When used to set the value of a key, as in dict[k]=v, it succeeds whether or not the key is in the dictionary already.

```
Dictionary<String, int> dict = new Dictionary<String, int>();
dict.Add("Sweden", 46); dict.Add("Germany", 49);
dict["Japan"] = 81;                       // New entry, no exception thrown
Print(dict.Keys);                         // Japan Sweden Germany
Console.WriteLine(dict.Count);            // 3
// Console.WriteLine(dict["Greece"]);     // ArgumentException
// dict.Add("Germany", 49);              // ArgumentException
bool b1 = dict.Remove("Greece");          // False (but no exception)
bool b2 = dict.Remove("Japan");           // True
Print(dict.Keys);                         // Sweden Germany
bool b3 = dict.ContainsKey("Germany");    // True
dict["Sweden"] = 45;                      // No exception
Console.WriteLine(dict["Sweden"]);        // 45
```

**Example 196** Fast Set Membership Test: Use a Dictionary or Binary Search?

Imagine that we want to exclude C# keywords (section 2) from the file index in example 191. So we need a fast way to recognize such names. Method IsKeyword1 uses a Dictionary built from a 77-element array of C# keywords, and method IsKeyword2 uses binary search in the sorted array. The Dictionary is ten times faster than the binary search in this case.

```
static readonly String[] keywordarray =
  { "abstract", "as", "base", "bool", "break", "byte", ..., "while" };
static readonly IDictionary<String,bool> keywords = ...

static bool IsKeyword1(String id)
{ return keywords.ContainsKey(id); }
static bool IsKeyword2(String id)
{ return Array.BinarySearch(keywordarray, id) >= 0; }
```

**Example 197** Using Sets as Keys in a Dictionary

The standard algorithm for turning a nondeterministic finite automaton (NFA) into a deterministic finite automaton (DFA) creates composite automaton states that are sets of integers. It is preferable to replace such composite states by simple integers. This method takes as argument a collection of composite states and returns a renamer, which maps a composite state name (a Set<int>) to a simple state name (an int).

```
static IDictionary<Set<int>, int> MkRenamer(ICollection<Set<int>> states) {
  IDictionary<Set<int>, int> renamer = new Dictionary<Set<int>, int>();
  int count = 0;
  foreach (Set<int> k in states)
    renamer.Add(k, count++);
  return renamer;
}
```

## 24.10   The Queue<T> Class

An instance of class System.Collections.Generic.Queue<T> is a *queue*, in which elements can be added at the end and removed from the front. This is useful for implementing worklist algorithms and breadth-first graph traversal. The queue is stored in an underlying array that is automatically extended as needed. Class Queue<T> implements ICollection<T> and has the following additional members:

- Constructor Queue() creates a new empty queue.
- Constructor Queue(int capacity) creates a new empty queue with the given initial capacity.
- Constructor Queue(IEnumerable<T> enm) creates a new queue, enqueueing the elements produced by enm.
- T Dequeue() returns and removes the element at the head of the queue. Throws InvalidOperationException if the queue is empty.
- void Enqueue(T x) adds element x at the end of the queue.
- T Peek() returns the element at the head of the queue without removing it. Throws InvalidOperationException if the queue is empty.
- T[] ToArray() returns a new array containing the elements of the queue.
- void TrimToSize() trims the underlying array to the actual number of elements in the queue.

## 24.11   The Stack<T> Class

An instance of class System.Collections.Generic.Stack<T> is a *stack*, in which elements can be added and removed only at one end: the "stack top". This is useful for implementing worklist algorithms and depth-first graph traversal. The stack is stored in an underlying array that is automatically extended as needed. Class Stack<T> implements ICollection<T> and has the following additional members:

- Constructor Stack() creates a new empty stack.
- Constructor Stack(int capacity) creates a new empty stack with the given initial capacity.
- Constructor Stack(IEnumerable<T> enm) creates a new stack, pushing the elements produced by enm.
- T Peek() returns the element at the stack top without removing it. Throws InvalidOperationException if the stack is empty.
- T Pop() returns and removes the element at the top of the stack. Throws InvalidOperationException if the stack is empty.
- void Push(T x) adds element x at the top of the stack.
- T[] ToArray() returns a new array containing the stack elements; the stack top is in position 0.
- void TrimToSize() trims the underlying array to the actual number of elements in the stack.

**Example 198** Using a Queue in a Worklist Algorithm

Some algorithms use a *worklist*, here represented by a queue, containing subproblems still to be solved. For instance, given a set ss of sets, one can compute its intersection closure: the least set tt such that ss is a subset of tt and such that for any two sets s and t in tt, their intersection s ∩ t is also in tt. For instance, if ss is {{2,3},{1,3},{1,2}}, then tt is {{2,3},{1,3},{1,2},{3},{2},{1},{}}.

The set tt may be computed by putting all elements of ss in a worklist, then repeatedly selecting an element s from the worklist, adding it to tt, and for every set t already in tt, adding the intersection of s and t to the worklist if not already in tt. When the worklist is empty, tt is intersection-closed. Sets are represented using class Set<T> from example 192.

```
static Set<Set<T>> IntersectionClose<T>(Set<Set<T>> ss) {
  Queue<Set<T>> worklist = new Queue<Set<T>>(ss);
  Set<Set<T>> tt = new Set<Set<T>>();
  while (worklist.Count != 0) {
    Set<T> s = worklist.Dequeue();
    foreach (Set<T> t in tt) {
      Set<T> ts = t.Intersection(s);
      if (!tt.Contains(ts))
        worklist.Enqueue(ts);
    }
    tt.Add(s);
  }
  return tt;
}
```

**Example 199** Graph Traversal Using a Queue or Stack

A Node<T> is a node in a directed graph with a label of type T; a node has an array of neighbors. The call root.VisitBreadthFirst() prints the labels of all nodes reachable from node root in breadth-first order: nodes closer to the root are printed before those farther from the root. The keys in dictionary visited are the nodes already visited or in the worklist; they could be represented also by Set<Node<T>> from example 192. Making the worklist a Stack instead of Queue would give depth-first traversal.

```
public void VisitBreadthFirst() {
  Dictionary<Node<T>,bool> visited = new Dictionary<Node<T>,bool>();
  Queue<Node<T>> worklist = new Queue<Node<T>>();
  visited.Add(this, false);
  worklist.Enqueue(this);
  while (worklist.Count != 0) {
    Node<T> node = worklist.Dequeue();
    Console.Write("{0} ", node.label);
    foreach (Node<T> neighbour in node.Neighbours)
      if (!visited.ContainsKey(neighbour)) {
        visited.Add(neighbour, false);
        worklist.Enqueue(neighbour);
      }
  }
}
```

# 25 Namespaces

A program may be divided into *namespaces*. A type name t declared inside a namespace N may be used unqualified, simply as t, within the namespace. Outside the namespace, references to t must be prefixed by the namespace, as in N.t, or must follow the clause using N.

Namespace declarations may be nested, giving rise to composite namespace names such as N1.N2. A *namespace-declaration* can appear only at top-level in a compilation unit or inside a namespace declaration, cannot have access modifiers, and has this form, where declarations can appear in any order:

```
namespace N {
    class-declarations
    struct-declarations
    interface-declarations
    enum-type-declarations
    delegate-type-declarations
    namespace-declarations
}
```

The namespace identifier N may be composite, as in N1.N2. A namespace may consist of several separate and possibly mutually dependent declarations. Top-level declarations (of classes, struct types, interfaces, enum types, or delegate types) not within an explicit namespace declaration belong to the default anonymous namespace.

## 25.1 The using Directive

A using directive can open a namespace, or introduce an alias for a namespace, or introduce an alias for a type (useful for abbreviating constructed types; see section 23.9). A using directive must appear before any member of a compilation unit or a namespace declaration. A using directive has one of these forms:

```
using N;
using M = N;
using T = t;
```

The first form opens namespace N; the second form means that any namespace type member N.T can be referred to as M.T which is useful if N has form N1.····.Nn; the third form means that the type t may be referred to as T, where T is a type name and t is any type, possibly of form N.t1 or possibly constructed.

A using directive does not affect other using directives in the same namespace, so the order of using directives does not matter. Thus the declaration using N1.N2 opens the namespace N1.N2, but using N1; using N2 does not. Even after using N1, one must refer to N1.N2.C by its fully qualified name, not by N2.C. It is a compile-time error for two using directives to import the same name.

A local declaration (of a class, struct, interface, delegate type or enum type) may hide a declaration of the same name imported from another namespace by a using directive.

Microsoft's .Net Framework class library, which is used with C#, is divided into many namespaces. Namespace System contains classes such as Object, Math, Random and String, struct types such as Int32, and enum types such as DayOfWeek. Namespace System.Text contains classes such as StringBuilder. After opening the namespace with using System.Text one may use the unqualified name StringBuilder instead of the fully qualified name System.Text.StringBuilder.

**Example 200** Using Standard Namespaces from .Net Framework Class Library
These are the `using` directives belonging to example 206:

```
using System;
using System.Collections;            // IEnumerable, Queue
using System.Diagnostics;            // Debug
using System.IO;                     // TextReader, TextWriter
using System.Text;                   // StringBuilder
using System.Text.RegularExpressions;  // Regex
```

**Example 201** Declaring Namespaces
The namespace N1 contains a declaration of class C11 and struct S13. Namespace N1.N2 contains a declaration of classes C121 and C122. All are accessible in this compilation unit; the `internal` modifier restricts access only outside the compilation unit. Note the mutual dependence between N1 and N3.

```
namespace N1 {
  public class C11 { N3.C31 c31; }      // N1 depends on N3
  namespace N2 {
    public class C121 { }
  }
}
class C1 { }                           // Default accessibility: internal
namespace N1 {
  public struct S13 { }
}
namespace N1.N2 {
  internal class C122 { }
}
namespace N3 {
  class C31 { N1.C11 c11; }             // N3 depends on N1
}
```

**Example 202** Using Namespaces
This example uses the namespaces N1 and N1.N2 declared in example 201 above. If that example file is compiled to a library (`.dll`) and this example is compiled with reference to that library (see section 1.1), then C1 and N1.N2.C122, which are `internal` to that library, are not accessible in this example:

```
using N1;
using N1.N2;                    // using N2;  would not suffice here
class MyTest {
  public static void Main(String[] args) {
    C11 c11;
    C121 c121;
    // C1 c1;                   // Inaccessible: internal to above example
    S13 c13;
    // C122 c122;               // Inaccessible: internal to above example
} }
```

# 26  Partial Type Declarations (C# 2.0)

The declaration of a class or interface or struct type may consist of one or more parts, in one or more source files. All parts of such a type declaration must be compiled together. Members declared in different parts can refer to each other as if they were declared in an ordinary class, interface or struct type.

This is useful when different parts of a declaration are created in different ways. For instance, one part may consist of code generated by a program generation tool, and another part may consist of customization code written by a programmer. By separating the two, the generated code can be re-generated without destroying the customization code. Also, it may be useful to separate code with different purposes: one part may contain application code, and another part may contain code written for testing purposes only.

A class or struct type declared in several parts may have member classes, member interfaces and member struct types that are themselves declared in several parts of the enclosing type. Apart from these cases, each member (field, constructor, method, property, indexer, operator, event, delegate type, or enum type) must be completely contained in one part.

A partial type declaration must have the prefix `partial` before `class` or `interface` or `struct`:

> *class-modifiers* `partial class` C *class-base-clause*
>    *class-body*
> *interface-modifiers* `partial interface` I *base-interfaces*
>    `{ ... }`
> *struct-modifiers* `partial struct` S *struct-interfaces*
>    *struct-body*

The following rules apply to partial type declarations:

- All parts of a type declaration must be declared in the same namespace.

- A modifier (`new`, `sealed`, `abstract`, `public`, ...) on one part of a partial type declaration applies to the entire resulting type. The modifiers must be non-conflicting: a class declaration cannot have one part that is `sealed` and another part that is `abstract`.

- All parts of a partial type declaration that have access modifiers must have the same access modifiers (`public`, `protected`, `internal`, `private`). If no part has any access modifier, the resulting type has default access: `internal` for top-level types, `private` for nested types. The absence of an access modifier on a part does not imply default access.

- All parts of a class declaration that specify a base class must specify the same base class. This is the base class of the resulting type, if any base class was specified; otherwise it is Object.

- The base interfaces of a part must be implemented by the entire resulting type, not by that part in isolation. Different parts may list different base interfaces. The list of base interfaces of the resulting type is the union, without duplicates, of the base interfaces of the parts.

- If a generic type (section 23) is declared in parts, then all parts must have the same type parameters. All parts that have parameter constraints (section 23.4) must have the same constraints, in some order; these are the parameter constraints of the resulting generic type.

- An attribute (section 28) on a part applies to the entire resulting type, not only to that part. The list of attributes of the resulting type is the concatenation, in some order and possibly with duplicates, of the attributes of the parts.

**Example 203** Partial Type Declarations, Part One

This example contains a partial declaration of interface I and a partial declaration of class C, which in turn contains a partial declaration of struct S. The remainder of the partial type declarations is given in example 204. The two example files must be compiled at the same time, as in

```
csc Example203.cs Example204.cs
```

This creates an executable `Example203.exe` which contains the entry point `Main`. No single part of the declaration of class C is a valid declaration on its own: each part of C uses members declared in the other part; and similarly for struct type S.

All parts of the declaration of S have the same access modifier (`public`). Although only one part of class C has the `sealed` modifier and one part has the `public` modifier, the modifiers apply also to the other parts, and the resulting type C is a sealed public class. Similarly, although only one part of class C says that it implements interface I, all parts of C contribute to implementing I.

```
partial interface I {
  void M2(C.S n);
}
sealed partial class C : I {
  public void M1(S n) {
    if (n.x > 0)
      M2(n.Decr());
  }
  public partial struct S {
    public S(int x) { this.x = x; }
  }
  public static void Main() {
    C c = new C();
    c.M1(new S(5));
  }
}
```

**Example 204** Partial Type Declarations, Part Two (continued from example 203

```
partial interface I {
  void M1(C.S n);
}
public partial class C {
  public partial struct S {
    public int x;
    public S Decr() { x--; return this; }
  }

  public void M2(S n) {
    Console.WriteLine("n.x={0} ", n.x);
    M1(n);
  }
}
```

# 27 Assertions and the `Debug.Assert` Method

The class System.Diagnostics.Debug defines several overloaded versions of an `Assert` method:

```
static void Assert(bool chk)
static void Assert(bool chk, String msg)
```

Under ordinary execution of a program, a call `Assert`(*expression*) to `Assert` has no effect at all; the argument expression is not even evaluated. However, assertions in a compilation unit may be enabled by compiling it with option `/d:DEBUG`, using one of these command lines (see section 1.1):

```
csc /d:DEBUG Prog.cs
mcs -define:DEBUG Prog.cs
```

To selectively enable assertions in part of a compilation unit, one may insert the pre-processing directive `#define DEBUG` before that part, and the pre-processing directive `#undef DEBUG` after it.

When assertions are enabled, then a call to `Assert` will evaluate the arguments. If the result of the first expression is true, program execution continues normally. If the result is false, then the assertion fails. This means that a dialog box will appear, or a message will be logged (by a TraceListener), or the CLR debugger will be started; in any case, a message about the error will be given. The message will include the result of the string expression, if present. This simplifies trouble-shooting in a malfunctioning program.

An assertion failure should signal the failure of a fundamental assumption in the program.

An `Assert` call can serve two purposes: to document the programmer's assumption about the state at a certain point in the program, and to check at run-time that that assumption holds (provided the program has been compiled with assertions enabled, as shown above).

One may put an `Assert` call after a particularly complicated piece of code, to check that it has achieved what it was supposed to; see example 205.

In a class that has a data representation invariant, one may assert the invariant at the end of every method in the class; see example 206.

One should not use `Assert` calls to check the validity of user input or the arguments of public methods or constructors, because the check will be performed only if assertions are enabled at compile-time. Instead, use ordinary `if` statements and throw an exception in case of error.

**Example 205** Using `Assert` to Specify and Check the Result of an Algorithm

The integer square root of $x \geq 0$ is an integer $y$ such that $y^2 \leq x$ and $(y+1)^2 > x$. The precondition $x \geq 0$ is always checked, using an `if` statement. The postcondition on $y$ is specified by a call to `Assert`, and is checked if assertions are enabled at run-time — which is reassuring, given that the algorithm's correctness is none too obvious. The assertion uses casts to `long` to avoid arithmetic overflow.

```
static int Sqrt(int x) {  // Algorithm by Borgerding, Hsieh, Ulery
  if (x < 0)
    throw new ArgumentOutOfRangeException("Sqrt: negative argument");
  int temp, y = 0, b = 0x8000, bshft = 15, v = x;;
  do {
    if (v >= (temp = (y<<1)+b << bshft--))
      { y += b; v -= temp; }
  } while ((b >>= 1) > 0);
  Debug.Assert((long)y * y <= x && (long)(y+1)*(y+1) > x);
  return y;
}
```

**Example 206** Using `Assert` to Specify and Check Invariants

A word list is a sequence of words to be formatted as a line of text. Its `length` is the minimum number of characters needed to format the words and the inter-word spaces, that is, the lengths of the words plus the number of words minus one. Those methods that change the word list use `Assert` to specify the invariant on `length`, and check it if assertions were enabled at compile-time.

```
class WordList {
  private Queue<String> strings = new Queue<String>();
  private int length = -1;    // Invariant: equals word lengths plus inter-word spaces
  public int Length { get { return length; } }
  public void AddLast(String s) {
    strings.Enqueue(s);
    length += 1 + s.Length;
    Debug.Assert(length == computeLength() + strings.Count - 1);
  }
  public String RemoveFirst() {
    String res = strings.Dequeue();
    length -= 1 + res.Length;
    Debug.Assert(length == computeLength() + strings.Count - 1);
    return res;
  }
  private int computeLength() { ... }  // For checking the invariant only
}
```

An algorithm for formatting a sequence of words into a text with a straight right-hand margin should produce a line `res` of a specified length `lineWidth`, unless there is only one word on the line or the line is the last one. This requirement can be expressed and checked using a call to `Assert` (see the example file for details of the formatting algorithm itself):

```
Debug.Assert(res.Length==lineWidth || wordCount==1 || !moreWords);
```

# 28 Attributes

Attributes are used to attach meta-data to a *target*, where a target may be an assembly, class, constructor, delegate type, enum type, event, field, interface, method, module, parameter, property, return value, or struct type. An attribute is attached to its target by writing an attribute constructor call in square brackets [...] before the target declaration.

The type of an attribute argument can be any simple type except decimal, or Object or String or a public enum type or System.Type or a single-dimensional array of one of these types. Each argument expression must be compile-time constant, or a System.Type object, or a one-dimensional array of expressions that satisfy these requirements.

## 28.1 Some Predefined Attributes

The .Net Framework class library has hundreds of predefined attributes; here are some examples:

| Attribute Name | Targets | Meaning |
|---|---|---|
| Flags | Enum type | Print enum value combinations symbolically |
| Serializable | Class | Instances can be serialized and deserialized |
| NonSerialized | Field | Field is omitted when class is serialized |
| AttributeUsage | Class | Permissible targets for this attribute class |
| Diagnostics.Conditional | Method | Determine when (diagnostic) method should be called |
| Obsolete | All | Inform users that target should not be used |
| MTAThread | Method | COM threading model is multi-threaded apartment (MTA) |
| STAThread | Method | COM threading model is single-threaded apartment (STA) |

The Flags attribute is illustrated by example 69; the Serializable and NonSerialized attributes by example 207; and the AttributeUsage attribute by example 208.

## 28.2 Declaring and Using Custom Attributes

A custom attribute is declared as a subclass of class System.Attribute, and its name should have the form XAttribute, although it suffices to use the name X when using the attribute. The constructor of a custom attribute can take as arguments only simple types, enum types, and strings. To specify what targets the custom attribute can be attached to, use an AttributeUsage attribute.

If an attribute class has a public read-write instance property P, then it has a *named parameter* P. This named parameter may be set in the attribute by using an assignment of the form P = e where e is an attribute parameter expression. For instance, AttributeUsage has a named parameter AllowMultiple.

The custom attributes of a target can be accessed using the reflection mechanisms of C#. An example is given in the full source code of example 208, available at the book homepage.

The custom attributes are usually created anew at run-time for every such access: the body of the attribute constructor and the properties implementing named parameters are executed for each access.

**Example 207** Using the Serialization Attribute
The classes SC and SO have the Serializable attribute and therefore can be serialized and deserialized; field s of class SO has the NonSerialized attribute and therefore is not serialized and deserialized along with the other fields of the class. This example uses the namespaces System.Runtime.Serialization and either System.Runtime.Serialization.Soap or System.Runtime.Serialization.Binary.

```
[Serializable()]
class SC {
  public int ci;
}
[Serializable()]
class SO {
  public int i;
  public SC c;
  [NonSerialized()] public String s;
  public SO(int i, SC c) { this.i = i; this.c = c; s = i.ToString(); }
}
...
IFormatter fmtr = new SoapFormatter();    // Or: new BinaryFormatter();
// Serialize objects o1 and o2 and c to file "objects":
SC c = new SC();
SO o1 = new SO(1, c), o2 = new SO(2, c);
Stream strm = File.Open("objects", FileMode.Create);
fmtr.Serialize(strm, o1); fmtr.Serialize(strm, o2);
// Deserialize o1 and o2 from file; the sharing of c is lost:
Stream strm = File.Open("objects", FileMode.Open);
SO o1i = (SO)(fmtr.Deserialize(strm)), o2i = (SO)(fmtr.Deserialize(strm));
```

**Example 208** Declaring and Using a Custom Attribute
The AuthorAttribute is a custom attribute holding an author name and a month (of enum type Month from example 134). Its legal targets are classes and methods, and it may be used multiple times at each target.

```
[AttributeUsage(AttributeTargets.Class | AttributeTargets.Method, AllowMultiple = true)]
class AuthorAttribute : Attribute {
  public readonly String name;
  public readonly Month mm;
  public AuthorAttribute(String name, Month mm) { ... }
  public override String ToString() { ... }
}
class TestAttributes {
  [Author("Donald", Month.May)]
  public void MyMethod1() { }

  [Author("Andrzej", Month.Jul)]
  [Author("Andreas", Month.Mar)]
  public void MyMethod2() { }
}
```

# 29   Main Differences Between C# and Java

C# resembles the Java programming language, but has a number of additional features, listed below. The features marked (J1.5) are found also in Java version 1.5.

- The names of all members must be distinct: a method and a field cannot have the same name.
- Rectangular C-style multidimensional arrays as well as Java-style arrays of arrays; see section 9.2.
- Non-virtual as well as virtual instance methods; see section 10.7.
- Properties: `get`- and `set`-method calls that look like field access and assignment; see section 10.13.
- Indexers: `get`- and `set`-method calls that look like array indexing; see section 10.14.
- Most operators can be overloaded as in C++; see section 10.15.
- User-definable implicit and explicit conversions to and from user-defined types; see section 10.16.
- Call-by-reference parameter passing for methods as in Pascal, Ada, and C++; see section 12.15.2.
- Parameter arrays to define functions with a variable number of parameters; see section 10.7. (J1.5)
- C# 2.0: A `yield` statement for convenient definition of enumerators (iterators); see section 13.12.
- A `foreach` statement for convenient use of enumerators; see section 13.6.2. (J1.5)
- User-definable value types, most notably structs (section 14). A value of value type is stored on the evaluation stack or inline in an object or array or another struct, unlike objects, which are stored as separate entities in the heap. See sections 5.1, 14, and 16.
- C# 2.0: Nullable types; uniform handling of "absent" values, also for value types. See section 18.
- Implicit boxing of value types, including simple types such as integers; see section 5.3.3. This saves the syntactic clutter of wrapping, cast, and value extraction, but does not avoid the associated run-time cost. (J1.5)
- Enum types: a way of introducing named integer constants as in C and C++; see section 16. (J1.5)
- Delegates: methods as values, also known as closures; see section 17.
- C# 2.0: Anonymous methods: expressions that evaluate to nameless delegates; see section 12.20.
- C# 2.0: Generic types and methods; see section 23. (J1.5). Unlike in Java 1.5, type parameters can be instantiated with simple types, not just reference types. This avoids the run-time overhead of boxing and unboxing, and also permits exact run-time type tests and type-safe array assignment.
- Unlike Java packages, namespaces have no source file organization conventions; see section 25.
- Attributes for attaching meta-data to classes, members, parameters and so on; see section 28. (J1.5)
- The possibility to use unsafe code, pointers, and so on. This is discouraged in general programming.
- Unlike Java, a class declared inside another class or struct is always a static member class. There are no inner classes (non-static member classes), nor local or anonymous classes (inside methods).
- Unlike Java, there is no way to declare or limit what exceptions can be thrown by a method.
- Unlike Java, there is no way to declare that a local variable or parameter is read-only.
- C# has conditional compilation directives such as `#define` and `#if` (not described in this book).

**Example 209** Some C# Features Not Found in Java

The class LinkedList below declares a constructor with a parameter array, a property, an indexer, an iterator for the list's elements, an explicit conversion, an overloaded operator (+) and a method that takes a delegate as argument:

```
public class LinkedList : IEnumerable {
  private Node first, last;      // Invariant: first==null if and only if last==null
  private class Node { ... }              // Static member class
  public LinkedList() { first = last = null; size = 0; }
  public LinkedList(params Object[] arr) : this() { ... }
  public int Count { get { ... } }          // Property with get accessor
  public Object this[int index] {           // Indexer with get and set acc.
    get { return get(index).item; }
    set { get(index).item = value; }
  }
  private Node get(int n) { ... }
  public bool Add(Object item) { ... }
  public IEnumerator GetEnumerator() {       // Iterator, used by foreach
    for (Node curr=first; curr!=null; curr=curr.next)
      yield return curr.item;
  }
  // Explicit conversion
  public static explicit operator LinkedList(Object[] arr) { return new LinkedList(arr); }
  // Overloaded operator
  public static LinkedList operator +(LinkedList xs1, LinkedList xs2) { ... }
  public void Apply(Fun f) {                 // Taking delegate argument
    foreach (Object x in this)
      f(x);
  }
}
public delegate void Fun(object x);
```

Using the above class: implicit boxing (1) and unboxing (4), a property and an indexer (2 and 3), the foreach statement (4), an explicit conversion (5), an overloaded operator (6), and delegate creation (7):

```
static void Main(String[] args) {
  LinkedList xs = new LinkedList();
  for (int i=0; i<5; i++)
    xs.Add(i);                                      // (1)
  Console.WriteLine(xs.Count + " " + xs[2]);        // (2)
  xs[2] = 102;                                       // (3)
  foreach (int k in xs)                              // (4)
    Console.WriteLine(k);
  LinkedList ys = (LinkedList)(new Object[] {7, 9, 13});   // (5)
  LinkedList zs = xs + ys;                           // (6)
  zs.Apply(new Fun(Print));                          // (7)
}
static void Print(object x) { Console.Write(x + " "); }
```

# 30   References

- The definitive reference to the C# programming language (version 1) is *C# Language Specification*, adopted as Ecma Standard ECMA-334 in December 2001. The second edition of the standard is from December 2002. Download from <http://www.ecma-international.org/publications/>

- The C# version 2.0 extensions (generics, iterators, anonymous methods, partial types, and so on) are likely to be adopted into the Ecma standard also.

- Anders Hejlsberg, Scott Wiltamuth and Peter Golde: *The C# Programming Language*, Addison-Wesley November 2003, contains a version of the C# Language Specification, including a description of most C# 2.0 features.

- The Microsoft .Net Framework Software Development Kit (SDK) for Microsoft Windows, including a C# compiler and run-time system, is available from <http://www.microsoft.com/net/>

- The Mono implementation of C# and run-time system is available for Microsoft Windows, Linux, MacOS X, Solaris and other platforms from <http://www.go-mono.com/>

- The Microsoft .Net Framework class reference documentation is included with the .Net Framework SDK and is also available online at <http://msdn.microsoft.com/library/>

- The design and implementation of generics in C# and .Net is described in Don Syme and Andrew Kennedy: Design and Implementation of Generics for the .NET Common Language Runtime. In *Programming Language Design and Implementation (PLDI)*, Snowbird, Utah, 2001. Download from <http://research.microsoft.com/~dsyme/papers/generics.pdf>

- The Unicode character encoding (<http://www.unicode.org/>) corresponds to part of the Universal Character Set (UCS), which is international standard ISO 10646-1:2000. The UTF-8 is a variable-length encoding of UCS, in which 7-bit ASCII characters are encoded as themselves. It is described in Annex R of the above-mentioned ISO standard.

- Floating-point arithmetics is described in the ANSI/IEEE Standard for Binary Floating-Point Arithmetic (IEEE Std 754-1985).

- Advice on writing high-performance C# programs for the .Net platform can be found in Gregor Noriskin: *Writing High-Performance Managed Applications: A Primer*, June 2003; and in Jan Gray: *Writing Faster Managed Code: Know What Things Cost*, June 2003. Both are available from the MSDN Developer Library <http://msdn.microsoft.com/library/>.

# Index